Adam Clayton Powell and the Supreme Court

Adam Clayton Powell and the Supreme Court

Kent M. Weeks

DUNELLEN

New York

© 1971 by the Dunellen Publishing Company, Inc.
145 East 52nd Street
New York, New York 10022

International Standard Book Number 0-8424-0022-2.

Library of Congress Catalogue Card Number 70-132982.

Printed in the United States of America.

Contents

Acknowledgments

In the preparation of this book I have received encouragement
and assistance from many sources. A few deserve special comment. I am particularly grateful to the attorneys involved in the
Powell litigation. Peter Sobol, of the law firm of Cravath,
Swaine, and Moore, and Powell's attorneys, Frank Reeves,
Arthur Kinoy, and William Kunstler, kindly supplied court
briefs and other materials, as well as their insight, wit, and comments. George Meader and the American Civil Liberties Union
also provided briefs. Powell's administrative assistant, Odell

Clark, offered political commentary. I was able to peruse the
transcript of the oral argument before the Supreme Court in the
quiet reading rooms of the Supreme Court Library. Two reference sources were particularly valuable; the weekly coverage of
events in Congress by the *Congressional Quarterly* and the daily
chronicle of political events in the *New York Times.* The College of Wooster provided financial assistance for the hiring of
a student assistant for two summers and for the typing of this
manuscript by Jo Ann Yoder, who was ever capable and ever
willing.

I am exceedingly grateful to a respected student, Lee Rainey,
who joined me in this endeavor for two summers, during which
he assumed much of the responsibility for gathering material and

for the initial drafting of the early chapters of this book. His creativity, ideas, and steady efforts were invaluable. Another student, John Edward Lucas, joined me in researching some of the material for the final chapters during the third summer's work on the manuscript. His willingness and competent workmanship reaffirmed my belief that undergraduate students can be colleagues in an academic venture. To my students, who used two earlier drafts of part of the book as the Powell case unfolded, I am grateful for insightful comments. My wife, Karen, lent enthusiasm throughout. As critic, editor, questioner, commentator, and constant source of encouragement, she was an essential and loving partner in this enterprise.

The author takes full responsibility for any errors of interpretation in the analysis of what was surely one of the most complex cases to reach the Supreme Court in this century. Finally, I would thank Adam Clayton Powell who, with his perserverance and style, provided the subject matter for this study.

1   His Own Worst Enemy

On March 1, 1967, the House of Representatives voted to reject a committee recommendation imposing censure and other punishment on Adam Clayton Powell, Jr., and voted instead to exclude him from membership in the House. The incident was significant for its rarity alone; no member-elect had been excluded since Victor Berger suffered that fate in 1919, and the alternative punishment rejected by the House was utterly without precedent. The most significant aspect of the incident, however, was that Representative-elect Powell chose to challenge the action in federal court, eventually securing the first judicial interpretation of a hitherto unexplored section of the Constitution.

Adam Clayton Powell, Jr., was many things to many people. To his parishioners and constituents he was one of them who had fought his way into the white power structure, and through his conspicuous exploits they could enjoy vicariously the rich living his high office brought him. To white liberals, he was a valuable but erratic ally, a man who could push controversial and far-reaching legislation through Congress when he put his mind to it but who so often seemed totally uninterested in exercising his talents. And to many, Powell was an upstart, a crook, even a "Commie" (in the sense that that term is used to describe many American liberals). To these people, his black skin was only another source of offense.

This man who was to provoke so much controversy was born on November 29, 1908, in New Haven, Connecticut, the son of a Negro minister. The Powells moved to New York when young Adam was less than a year old, so that his father might take a post as pastor of the Abyssinian Baptist Church, in the center of Harlem. The church and the vast ghetto in which it is located were to become central factors in Adam Clayton Powell's public life.

Powell received an extensive education, graduating from Colgate University in 1930. He received an M.A. from Columbia in 1932 and a Doctor of Divinity degree from Shaw University in North Carolina in 1937 (which earned him the title "Doc" among some of his congressional associates.) Ordained in 1931, he succeeded his father as pastor of the Abyssinian Baptist Church in 1937, by which time he had already established a reputation as a political and social activist through his leadership of various Negro boycott movements, strikes, and protest demonstrations. In 1936, he began writing a column for the weekly *Amsterdam News*, Harlem's most influential Negro newspaper, which in later years became first a champion of Congressman Powell and then his vigorous critic.

During the war Powell served in the Manhattan Civilian Defense and as a member of the Consumer Division of the Office of Price Administration. The war years also witnessed Powell's entry into politics. He sought and won election to the New York City Council in 1941 as an independent representing Harlem, becoming thereby the first Negro to sit on the council. During his single term, he was an outspoken and early advocate of "black power" and "black pride."

Powell did not seek reelection to the city council. Instead, in 1944 he ran for Congress in Harlem's 22nd District, at that time in a state of acute political disorder. Working from his centers of strength, the Abyssinian Baptist Church and the

People's Voice, a Harlem weekly of which he was coeditor, he wrested the Tammany endorsement, and with it the Democratic nomination, from his opponent, a Tammany leader in one of the Harlem districts, while winning the Republican nomination at the same time. That November he was elected unanimously as the common candidate of the Democratic, Republican, and American Labor parties.

Once elected to Congress, Powell built a personal organization in Harlem based on his church, which has over 10,000 members, and his personal political club, the Alfred Isaacs Democratic Club. He did not become a part of the regular New York Democratic organization until 1959.

As a national political figure, a characterization to which Powell gained title as much by his outspoken opinions as by his position as second-senior of the small group of Negroes in Congress, Powell was anything but consistent and not at all restrained. From time to time he vigorously denounced New York leaders, including Mayor Robert Wagner and Carmine De Sapio. In 1952 he threatened to bolt the Democratic Party when Senator Sparkman of Alabama was nominated for the vice-presidency, but he failed to carry out the threat. In 1956 he claimed President Eisenhower loved "the flag, mother and Jim Crow,"[1] but in October he announced he would support Eisenhower for reelection and called on Negroes to repudiate Stevenson. Three years later he suggested he might bolt the party again if Lyndon Johnson were the 1960 nominee. In 1960 he announced he might bolt if John F. Kennedy were the nominee, preferring, he stated, Lyndon Johnson for the presidency. He carried out neither threat.

As a junior congressman, Powell was likewise outspoken. He was enraged by the evidences of segregation persisting in the District of Columbia and advocated its termination, as well as an end to segregation in the armed forces, establishment of a permanent fair employment practices commission, and legislation outlawing the poll tax and discrimination in interstate travel. Powell also originated the famous "Powell Amendment," a civil rights rider to a bill for federal grant-in-aid programs, which provided that federal funds should be withheld from any state that did not comply with the decisions of the Supreme Court. Liberals were put in an awkward position; they did not want to vote against the amendment and thereby appear to be supporting segregated schools. By introducing the amendment Powell forfeited the support of Southerners. His insistence on adding this amendment to the bill led to the defeat of the proposed federal program of grants to aid local school construction in 1956.

Powell's attendance record during his early years in Congress was very poor. On occasion he had the lowest record of attendance for roll-call votes of any member in the House, ranging down to responses on only 30 percent of the roll calls during the 82nd Congress. Instead of attending Congress, Powell spent his free time, which was considerable, in travel, entertainment, and night life. Through his conduct, Powell gained for himself a reputation among his colleagues for demagogy and unreliability, and Powell's congressional conduct coupled with his 1956 party bolt, did not endear him to the congressional leadership. He was denied a large office in the Cannon Building and a subcommittee chairmanship on the Education and Labor Committee, although his seniority entitled him to both; he did, however, become a subcommittee chairman on the less prestigious Interior Committee.

In 1961, Powell became chairman of the House Education and Labor Committee, a post that he was to use for both good and evil, apparently as the spirit moved him. Powell's ascension to this post was not, however, without opposition. Dissatisfied with various parts of Powell's record, Southerners and AFL-CIO President George Meany opposed giving Powell the chairmanship. However, Powell had the support of Speaker Sam Rayburn and took over the post at the beginning of the 87th Congress.

It became apparent in the ensuing years that this marked a turning point in Powell's career. During his tenure as chairman, he voted in 54 percent of the roll calls, still much below the average for House Democrats but a definite improvement nonetheless. At the same time, he demonstrated that he could employ the tact and diplomacy necessary for successful bill-managing, when he chose to do so. Powell handled major New Frontier and Great Society bills with such effectiveness that he received the thanks and congratulations of President Johnson on March 18, 1965.

But Powell's actions as chairman were not wholly satisfactory to all the committee members. Toward the end of the 89th Congress, they had formulated three major grievances against the chairman: he had used his position to kill or delay legislation; he had misused committee funds; and he had "capriciously" fired staff members. The dissidents decided to carry out a revision of the committee rules to curb the power of the controversial chairman. Leading the movement were Frank Thompson (D-N. J.) and Edith Green (D-Ore.), two senior committee members, but they picked as their spokesman a second-term congressman from Florida with a good pro-civil rights record, Sam Gibbons. Gibbons and Powell had once worked closely together, but during 1966 they had drifted apart, partly because of policy differences and partly because Gibbons had been pressing for an examination of Powell's financial affairs.

The rule changes were adopted by the committee on September 22, 1966. Eighteen Democrats and nine Republicans supported the changes, which decreased Powell's procedural weapons, useful for delaying bills, and his control over committee staff, and also required the approval of a yearly committee budget and a monthly accounting of funds spent. Ohio Republican William Ayres opposed the rule changes, and Powell and California Democrats Augustus F. Hawkins and Philip Burton did not vote.

There is no indication that Powell was greatly disturbed by

this development. After the vote he told newsmen, perhaps sarcastically, that in his opinion the new rules were "a very significant step forward," and that he hoped other committees would "adopt rules such as mine." About Gibbons he had a stronger statement. He charged on September 15, after the move to change the rules became known, that Gibbons was a "racist" and that he had sunk to a "new low in political irresponsibility and a new high in racial hysteria."[2]

Such a charge from Powell was nothing new; it represented his standard counter to such attacks. In 1963 he had replied to a criticism Senator John J. Williams had made of his costly European junket the year before by stating, "I say unequivocally that the Williams attack on me was motivated by racial prejudice because I am a Negro."[3] For Gibbons, however, Powell's statement was the last straw. He asked the House Administration Committee to look into Powell's congressional accounts.

Powell had had some difficulties with the Internal Revenue Service in the 1950's over alleged income tax evasion, and he had been indicted by a grand jury. Edward Bennett Williams, Powell's attorney, suggested, however, that the grand jury had handed down an indictment only after pressures were brought to bear by certain segments of the press. Williams claimed that "without the external pressures and without the passion aroused in the grand jurors, Adam Powell would never have been indicted and would never have been forced into a long, expensive, and politically damaging trial."[4] When the evidence was submitted to a jury, the vote was 10-2 for acquittal, and the government eventually dropped the charge. There were additional charges of tax fraud, and the government still claimed that he owed money. Finally, in 1966 Powell settled with the government for $27,833.17 in taxes and penalties, and in return the government withdrew additional charges pending against him and certain of his former employees.

Sticky as his income tax troubles had been at times,

however, they could not approximate the difficulties into which Powell next plunged himself. One day in February 1960, Representative Powell charged in a speech on the floor of Congress that one of his constituents, Mrs. Esther James, was a "bag woman" (graft collector for corrupt police) in Harlem. The charge apparently attracted little attention. But on March 6, Powell appeared on "Between the Lines," a New York television show, as a last-minute substitute for then Senator Hubert Humphrey, whose plane was grounded in Washington. During the course of the interview-type show, Powell repeated his charge. That precipitated one of the most complicated legal battles of all times. The title of an article in the *New York Times* suggests the complexity of the litigation: "Powell Case, in 6½ Years, Has Involved 80 Judges, 10 Courts, 4 Juries, 15 Lawyers and Congress."[5]

Mrs. James, an elderly Negro widow, brought a defamation suit against Powell, the television station, and the sponsor through her lawyer, Raymond Rubin. The station and sponsor settled for a total of $1,500, but Mrs. James pressed the suit against Powell, demanding $1 million in damages. The case came to trial on March 29, 1963, before a jury. During the trial Powell twice offered to settle, first for $10,000 and, when that was rejected, for $10,000 and a formal apology. That, too, was turned down, since attorney Rubin anticipated a favorable verdict. His expectations were gratified. The jury awarded Mrs. James $11,500 compensatory damages and $200,000 punitive damages. At least a part of the jury's decision was based on the fact that Powell was not present during the trial.

The case, however, was just beginning. Powell fought hard to avoid payment, and his numerous lawyers were ingenious in the appeals, motions, and countermotions they instituted. Raymond Rubin fought back tenaciously, though without complete success. The judgment, eventually reduced to $11,500 compensatory and $35,000 punitive damages, plus costs, became final on January 18, 1965, when the U. S.

Supreme Court denied certiorari,[6] although the Powell lawyers urged that the case raised important constitutional questions under the congressional immunities clause.

In Powell's battle against the courts, he did not stick to strictly legal weapons. On several instances he refused to appear when ordered, claiming congressional immunity, even though in some cases the House was not in session. Powell's legal problems were further complicated when Mrs. James instigated actions in New York and Puerto Rico, charging Powell had illegally transferred property to avoid paying the judgment. These suits eventually resulted in a judgment of $575,000 plus costs on December 14, 1965. Powell appealed, and the judgment was reduced, in a verdict of June 14, 1966, to $155,785.76, consisting of $33,250.76 unpaid on the earlier libel judgment, legal costs of $22,535, and punitive damages of $100,000.[7] While Powell appealed, the unpaid judgment collected 6 percent interest, and by the end of 1966 it was estimated to amount to some $164,000.

Far more harmful to Powell were to be his citations for contempt of court, which he incurred for disobeying various court orders and the arrest orders that stemmed from them. The first arrest order, granted May 8, 1964, by Justice Thomas C. Chimera of the Supreme Court of New York County, arose from a civil contempt order issued when Powell failed to appear in court despite his written promise to do so. In granting the order, Justice Chimera stated, "Moreover, the conduct of defendant in this matter, in my judgment, has been so flagrantly contemptuous of the authority and dignity of this court as to promote a tragic disrespect for the judicial process as a whole. . . ."[8]

Two years later, Mr. Justice Saypol commented as follows on motions to order Powell to pay the judgments against him and to punish him for contempt:

> The judgment debtor [Powell] is actually in default here, as is his established, uniform course . . . he is his own worst enemy. . . .

Considering the disdainful and demeaning and despising attitude of this judgment debtor toward the authority and dignity of the court ... there is no doubt nor would there be any hesitancy to adjudge the alleged misconduct to be criminal. ... The most that can be said for this debtor's misbehavior is that it reflects his own peculiar brand of civil disobedience.[9]

However, Justice Saypol did not grant the contempt order because of the technical defects.

On October 3, 1966, Justice Frank issued a second civil contempt order, with the order that Powell appear in court, stating:

The hearing was unique in that it evoked the corporeal presence of the judgment debtor for the first time in the course of the protracted proceedings in both this action and the companion libel litigation. This marked departure from his hitherto elusiveness was not, unfortunately, accompanied by a similar departure from his policy of ignoring, evading or abusing legal procedures in a campaign of relentless defiance designed to frustrate and impede the judgment creditor [Mrs. James] in the lawful collection of her judgments. ... It was merely another play in the seemingly endless series of maneuvers and dilatory tactics by which the judgment debtor manifests his distaste and disrespect for our legal processes. ...[10]

The Justice denied a motion to begin criminal contempt proceedings, since a similar motion was pending in another court, noting that to do so would "accomplish little beyond that of providing the judgment debtor with a new base for protracted procedural and appellate maneuvers and thereby further delay and frustrate the judgment creditor in the collection of her judgments. ..."[11] When Powell subsequently failed to appear as ordered, an arrest order was issued on October 14.

A third civil contempt order was issued on October 25, 1966, likewise for failure to appear. When Powell again failed to appear as directed by the order, an arrest order was issued on December 14.

None of the three civil contempt orders were appealed as such by Powell's lawyers. Since the arrest orders could not be served on Sunday, Powell continued to return to New York three Sundays a month to preach at his church. This came to a sudden end on November 28, 1966.

After a hearing on the defects in the legal papers, Judge Saypol had ordered a jury trial on matters relating to the motion to issue an order for criminal contempt. When the trial was completed, on November 17, 1966, Justice Matthew Levy found Powell guilty of criminal contempt in two instances of disobedience to court orders. In his opinion he acknowledged Powell's personal success:

> It is, however, not an easy task to arrive at a conclusion as to the punishment for criminal contempt of court to be meted out to a minister, a Congressman, a leader of men, a man, indeed, of many natural gifts, and he should be a man in relationship to the law that one would look up to, to respect.

And he again expressed concern about the deleterious impact Powell's behavior could have on the judicial system.

> The proof is overwhelming that the defendant has flamboyantly flaunted his willful flouting of the lawful mandates of the court to such an extent, indeed, that I was compelled to add to that record, in my recent opinion in this matter, the comment of the "attendant deleterious and corroding impact upon the judicial system as a whole and its serious consequential effect upon the general maintenance of law and order in our community." What the defendant presumes to do with impunity cannot go unpunished. Else the average person may rightly assume that he may do the same, and feel that when not permitted by the courts thus to act, there is discrimination against the less powerful persons, who rely, and justly rely, upon the courts for the due and impartial administration of justice.[12]

Justice Levy fined Powell $500 and sentenced him to 30 days in jail.

When the congressman did not surrender on November 23,

as ordered, Justice Arthur Markewich issued an order on November 28 for his arrest. Unlike the previous orders, however, the order could be executed on any day of the week, including Sunday. Powell's lawyers promptly appealed, and meanwhile Powell stayed out of New York State.[13]

Thus matters stood at the end of November 1966. Congressman Powell, chairman of the Education and Labor Committee, 89th Congress, representative-elect for the 90th Congress, was unable to enter his home state without being taken into custody on one or more outstanding arrest orders. Nor did he find Washington, D. C., where the House Administration Committee's Special Subcommittee on Contracts was preparing to hold hearings relating to their investigation of his activities as chairman, any too congenial. Hence, Powell spent December on his favorite retreat, Bimini Island in the Bahamas. There he basked in the sun and divided his time between Captain Brown's Bar and Hotel and the End of the World Bar. But while Powell relaxed, things were afoot in Washington, things that augured ill for the controversial Representative.

2 Political and Legal Scaffolding

The action of the House in voting to exclude Powell from membership was in response to his well-publicized wrong-doings and represented one of the rather infrequent occasions on which the House has undertaken to discipline an errant member. The House was forced to take action in the Powell case by the unusual publicity the representative's actions received. This unusually extensive coverage was produced in part by the timing of the incident, for morality in Congress had been much in the news because of two earlier cases, those involving the former secretary to the Senate majority, Robert G. Baker, and Senator Thomas J. Dodd (D-Conn.)

Baker allegedly had used his position to secure contracts for firms in which he was financially interested, had taken for his own use campaign contributions intended for members of the Senate, and had evaded the payment of income taxes. He was eventually convicted on seven counts on January 29, 1967. As a result of a Senate investigation of Baker's activity, the Senate established in 1964 the six-member bipartisan Select Committee on Standards and Conduct.

Thus, when the Senate was faced with the Dodd case in 1966, a rudimentary ethics procedure had been established. Dodd, who was charged with misuse of political contributions, double-billing of travel expenses, and improper use of his influence, was eventually censured on the first charge by the Senate on June 23, 1967.

The House, however, had not established an ethics procedure by the time the Powell case broke, although it had set up the Select Committee on Standards and Conduct on October 19, 1966. This committee was charged only with drafting a code of conduct, and the 89th Congress expired before it could make any progress.

In the absence of a well-defined ethics procedure, the House was forced to fall back on the vague procedures outlined in its precedents. These were regarded by the House as deriving from two constitutional grants of power: Article I, Sec. 5, cl. 1, "Each House shall be the Judge of the Elections, Returns and Qualifications of its own Members. . . ."; and Article I, Sec. 5, cl. 2, "Each House may determine the Rules of its Proceedings, punish its Members for disorderly Behavior, and, with the Concurrence of two thirds, expel a Member."

With the authority granted by clause 2, the expulsion clause, both houses of Congress have from time to time imposed as punishments for various offenses censure or expulsion (the denial of a seat to a member already sworn in). With the exception of the unusual circumstances surrounding the Civil War, expulsion has been seldom used. Only one Senator, William Blount, has suffered an expulsion unconnected with the Civil War. This occurred in 1797 on charges of treason. Twenty-two Senators were expelled for disloyal acts during the Civil War period. The three expulsions in the history of the House occurred under the same circumstances. Censure had been imposed 15 times by the House and seven times by the Senate in the period prior to 1966. The sole instance of other punishment occurred when Senators Tillman and McLaurin of South Carolina were suspended for fighting in the Senate Chamber in 1902. It should be noted that there are apparently no limits on the power to censure. However, the power of a house to expel a member for an offense committed prior to his election has been vigorously challenged.

The power derived from clause 1, the "judge qualifications" clause, is more difficult to analyze. The Constitution expressly establishes three qualifications (age, citizenship, and inhabitancy) and suggests the existence of others. (Art. I, sec. 3, disqualifies persons convicted on impeachment, for example.)[1] The power of a house to deny a seat to a member-elect lacking one of these expressed (or standing) qualifications by a majority vote prior to his taking the oath is unquestioned. This action, known as exclusion, has been taken many times.

It has been asserted by many Congressmen, however, that each house possesses the power to exclude a member-elect for a reason not expressed in the Constitution. This aspect of the power seems first to have been asserted by opponents of Philip Barton Key in 1808. They sought to disqualify Key on the grounds that he had served in the British Army during the revolution and thereafter had drawn a British pension. The move was unsuccessful. The power was again asserted in 1844 by those opposing the seating of Senator-elect John M. Niles, who was rumored to be mentally ill. He was seated after a committee heard medical testimony regarding his soundness. In 1858 exclusion was suggested by some members as a means of punishing a representative-elect for misconduct in a previous Congress. The suggestion arose in regard to Orsamus Matteson, who had resigned from the 34th Congress to escape a motion to expel him. It was proposed that he be excluded from the 35th Congress, but following a divided committee report denying the power to exclude, the motion was tabled. Exclusion was first imposed during Reconstruction, notably in the cases of various members-elect from Kentucky and Tennessee.

Several important precedents occurred after the Civil War. In 1870, B. F. Whittemore was excluded following his victory in a special election. Whittemore had previously held the seat but resigned to escape expulsion for selling appointments to the Military Academy, thus causing the special election. In 1900, Brigham Roberts, a representative-elect from Utah, was excluded for practicing polygamy, in violation of U. S. statutes, although a minority of the investigating committee vigorously challenged the power of exclusion. The precedent was repudiated by the Senate in the seating of Senator-elect Reed Smoot in 1907, despite similar charges. The last exclusion to occur was that of Victor Berger in 1919, although exclusion was proposed on three later occasions in the Senate. Berger was excluded following his conviction for violation of sedition laws.

Thus, although ample precedents to support such an action existed at the time of Powell's exclusion, the actions had always been challenged by a minority who denied the existence of a power to exclude for reasons other than failure to meet the three expressed qualifications of age, citizenship, and inhabitancy.

No challenges to the congressional actions of exclusion had ever been brought into court, and such a challenge would have to surmount two hurdles. One was the "speech and debate" clause of the Constitution, Art. I., Sec. 6, cl. 1, which provided "[The Senators, and Representatives] . . . shall in all cases, except Treason, Felony and Breach of Peace, be privileged from arrest during their attendance at the Session of their Respective House, and in going to and returning from the same; and for any Speech or Debate in either House, they shall not be questioned in any other Place." This clause was believed by many lawyers and congressmen to bar a suit against the Congress or its members to challenge an exclusion.

The second hurdle was the "political questions" doctrine, which derived from a series of Supreme Court opinions reaching as far back as *Marbury* v. *Madison* in 1803. This doctrine was given its most detailed exposition to date in the case of *Baker* v. *Carr* (1962). The Court's opinion, written by Justice Brennan, had stated:

Prominent on the surface of any case held to involve a political question is found a textually demonstrable constitutional commitment of the issue to a coordinate political department; or a lack of judicially discoverable and manageable standards for resolving it; or the impossibility of deciding without an initial policy determination of a kind clearly for nonjudicial discretion; or the impossibility of a court's undertaking independent resolution without expressing lack of the respect due coordinate branches of government; or an unusual need for unquestioning adherence to a political decision already made; or the potentiality of embarrassment from multifarious pronouncements by various departments on one question.[2]

A case found to contain any one of these criteria was regarded as nonjusticiable, that is, it would not be decided by a federal court, for to decide the case would be to violate the function of separation of powers. By refusing to decide such cases, the federal courts acknowledged that certain decisions were best left to coordinate branches of the federal government. However, the "political question" doctrine could be used as a "magical formula which has the practical result of relieving a Court of the necessity of thinking further about a particular problem. It is a device for transferring the responsibility for decision of questions to another branch of the government; and it may sometimes operate to leave a problem in mid-air so that no branch decides it."[3] Many congressmen and lawyers believed a challenge to an exclusion would contain one or more of these criteria, especially that positing a "textually demonstrable constitutional commitment" to the legislature, given the existence of the "judge qualification" clause.

Persons holding this view tended to ignore two facts, however. Brennan had also noted in the *Baker* opinion: "Deciding whether a matter has in any measure been committed by the Constitution to another branch of government, or whether the action of that branch exceeds whatever authority has been committed, is itself a delicate exercise in constitutional interpretation, and is a responsibility of this Court as ultimate interpreter of the Constitution."[4]

17

There was also a tendency to overlook what the *Baker* decision stood for. Although it had merely held that a federal court could consider the constitutionality of a state system of apportionment, *Baker* was really the beginning of a far-reaching series of cases in which the Supreme Court undertook to breathe life into representative government by assuring exact equality in representation and the right to have one's vote count in the policy process. Chief Justice Warren, for example, stated only five weeks after Powell appealed to the Supreme Court that *Baker* v. *Carr* was the most important decision made during his tenure on the court "Because I think a great many . . . other problems would have been solved long ago if everyone had the right to vote and his vote counted the same as anybody else's."[5] Thus the Supreme Court, to which a case challenging an exclusion could eventually go, could reasonably be supposed to have a special interest in the rights of the excluded member-elect and particularly in the rights of his constituents to be represented.

It was in this legal and institutional framework that the Powell episode arose. Before it was over, a new chapter had been written in our constitutional history.

3 The Fall of Chairman Powell

On November 30, 1966, an obscure California Democrat, Representative Lionel Van Deerlin, who had earlier in the month won election to his third term, issued an important announcement at his Washington office. He declared in a prepared statement, which appeared in the *New York Times* the following day:

> At a time when great criticism is being directed at young people for lax morals and unethical practices, it is more than ever the responsibility of Congress to set an example for moral and ethical conduct. If on January 10 Congressman Powell is still subject to a court order committing him to jail at any time he enters his home state, no tradition of Congress would be hallowed enough to justify seating him.

Consequently, Van Deerlin said, he would object to the seating of Powell in the 90th Congress. His announcement was timed so that Powell might have an opportunity to purge himself of contempt, and to give other congressmen a chance to consider what action to take, Van Deerlin concluded.

Van Deerlin emphasized that he was acting alone and had not sought help from other groups in the House. He reasoned that his attempt would nevertheless succeed if the issue was brought to a clearcut roll-call vote, although he envisioned a move by the House leadership to attempt to refer the matter to an investigatory committee.

Van Deerlin's move was motivated by the various arrest orders outstanding. On December 8 he made this clear by announcing that he would drop his plans to ask Powell to step aside if the New York congressman cleared himself of the charges so that he could freely return to New York.

Neither Van Deerlin's efforts, nor the House Administration Committee investigation, greatly disturbed the vacationing congressman. When interviewed on Bimini, Powell said, "I'm not going to fight them. If they don't want the best chairman in the House, okay, let'em get another candidate." He added, "I couldn't care less. It doesn't interest me."[1] But his passive attitude did not last long. Intending to oppose any attempt to oust him from Congress, he began searching for a way to move freely in New York.

On December 11, Van Deerlin's efforts received prestigious support. New York Democrat Emanuel Celler, chairman of the Committee on the Judiciary, declared that Powell had "flouted the law" and been "a bone in the throat of Congress." "I will support a motion to have Powell stand aside and not take his seat while a committee appointed by Congress can examine his wrongs and excesses," said Celler. "However, it would be too drastic to expel him from Congress."[2] "Anyway," he went on, "we'd expel him and his constituents would re-elect him and we'd expel him and they'd re-elect him and it would go on and on."[3]

Van Deerlin meanwhile was gathering information on Powell's court troubles. After conferring with New York District Attorney Frank S. Hogan, he stated that he had learned that there was no chance that Powell could purge himself of criminal contempt by the opening of Congress. Subsequently, Van Deerlin decided on a plan similar to that endorsed by Rep. Celler and said that he would, if recognized, introduce a resolution to have Powell investigated by a nine-man committee appointed by the speaker of the House.

During the investigation, which Van Deerlin estimated would last at least six months, Powell would enjoy all the privileges of a member except the right to vote.

Three months before the beginning of the 90th Congress, on October 5, 1966, the Committee on House Administration (which had a general supervisory power over House expenditures), designated the Special Subcommittee on Contracts to conduct an investigation of "alleged irregularities in expenditures from the contingent fund of the House and in the employment of clerks for Members and committees." There is no indication in the records that the subcommittee intended to delve into committees other than the Committee on Education and Labor, nor any member other than its chairman. For the purposes of the investigation, the subcommittee, which originally consisted of chairman Wayne L. Hays (D-Ohio), Joe D. Waggonner, Jr. (D-La.), and William L. Dickinson (R-Ala.), was enlarged by the appointment of Paul C. Jones (D-Mo.), Lucien N. Nedzi (D-Mich.), and Samuel L. Devine (R-Ohio).

The investigation was begun on September 26, 1966, even before the appointment of the subcommittee. General Accounting Office auditors reviewed payroll, travel, communications, and miscellaneous expenses, and indicated that a detailed review of travel expenses and of the clerk-hire status of Powell's wife, who was on his office payroll, would be of importance.

On December 9, subcommittee chairman Hays sent Powell a letter informing him that the subcommittee was looking into matters relating to the activities of the House Committee on Education and Labor and requesting that Powell appear before the subcommittee.[4] Powell, who was still on Bimini, sent a reply in which he protested certain improprieties committed by the subcommittee's investigators. Reports had reached him, Powell said, that his "staff members have been pilloried, asked personally embarrassing questions concerning matters which have no relation to the investigation. . . ."

"Several staff members have been asked intimate questions and details concerning my personal life," he protested. "This represents an unconscionable abuse of my right to be free from an invasion of privacy, a right which I am confident you value as tenderly as I do." He stated his belief that he and his committee had been singled out in the investigation and noted that the "conspiratorial tarnishment" of his name would be fought. The whole proceedings were "a sorry commentary on the sense of fair play the Congress is supposed to extend to all of its colleagues."

"In the interest of fair play," Powell requested that the following conditions be established for his appearance before the Hays subcommittee:

(1) The investigation include a comparative analysis of the travel vouchers of staff members of other full Committees and Subcommittees, including your own. I am prepared to provide immediate additional investigators and secretarial staff to assist your staff.

(2) The investigation include a comparable analysis of the travel undertaken by all other Committee and Subcommittee Chairmen.

(3) That I be permitted to read into the record the following articles and series of articles:

a. The *Life Magazine* article of June 6, 1960, by Walter Pincus and Don Oberdorfer, "How Congressmen Live High off the Public."

b. The *Congressional Quarterly* article of March 4, 1966, on Congressional foreign travel: "Nearly Half of Congress Takes U. S. Paid Trips."

c. The series of articles by Vance Trimble on Congressional payrolls beginning January 5, 1959, through December 1, 1959.

(4) That my accompanying counsel be permitted the privilege of cross examination of certain Congressmen whose travel and activities relate directly to the Education and Labor Committee. I shall submit the list of names to you privately for your prior approval.

5. That no staff members of the Education and Labor Committee be required to testify before your Subcommittee until conditions # 1 and # 2 have been fulfilled.

The subcommittee rejected Powell's conditions, and he did not appear. Nor was the committee able to question Corinne Huff, a secretary on Powell's staff, and Cleomine B. Lewis, a committee secretary, both of whom were subpoenaed but failed to appear.

The committee also failed to secure the attendance of Mrs. Adam Clayton Powell, nee Y. Marjorie Flores, who was employed by Mr. Powell's office at a yearly salary of $20,578 but resided in Puerto Rico. The committee investigators had determined in late September that her salary checks were being sent to Powell's congressional office (and had been since 1961). Photostatic copies of them were obtained from the Treasury Department, and they were shown to Mrs. Powell at her home in Puerto Rico on October 5 by two Secret Service agents. She examined the checks, which were endorsed "Y. Marjorie Flores—Adam C. Powell," and in most cases bore the notation "For Deposit Only To The Account of Hon. Adam C. Powell." Mrs. Powell told the agents that she had neither made nor authorized the endorsements and had never given her husband authority to negotiate the checks. She added that she had not seen her husband for over a year.[5]

The agents then interviewed Mrs. Powell's lawyer, Gonzalo Betancourt, who was at that time discussing support payments with Mr. Powell's lawyer. After conferring with Mrs. Powell, Mr. Betancourt announced that she would take no legal action one way or another in the matter of the checks. However, by a letter of November 22, Mrs. Powell asked the House Disbursing Office to send her salary checks to Puerto Rico.[6]

These peculiar facts naturally led the special subcommittee to desire to question Mrs. Powell further. Accordingly, a subpoena was made out and delivered to her on December 15, 1966, by a deputy U. S. Marshall. It directed her to appear in Washington on December 19, 1966, at 10:30 A. M.[7] Instead of honoring the subpoena she sent a telegram on December 19 to Chairman Hays, which he received in the early afternoon. It read simply: "Unable to testify public hearing." The following day a letter was received from Mrs. Powell, dated December 19 and addressed to Wayne Hays, in which she indicated her willingness to testify at a future date, after she had had time to arrange for travel with her four-year-old son. Immediately Mrs. Powell was sent a cablegram indicating that paid round-trip airline tickets had been arranged for her and her son and that the subcommittee would also reimburse her travel expenses; if she wished to arrange care for her son in San Juan, reasonable care costs would be reimbursed.

The Administrative Committee's chief clerk, Julian Langston, also tried to telephone Mrs. Powell, but was informed that she had no number listed and could not be reached. He also called the U. S. marshall in Puerto Rico and asked him to urge Mrs. Powell to honor the subpoena. None of the messages reached her, her house was closed, and her whereabouts were unknown.

On December 28 two telegrams were received from Mrs. Powell's attorneys. The first indicated that they had heard through the press of hearings set for December 29, but that they had no other information. The second indicated that the U. S. marshall had informed them that one ticket was available for Mrs. Powell for December 29. It was impossible for her to make arrangements to travel, they said, but Mrs. Powell was willing to cooperate at a future date.

There was another exchange of telegrams in which the committee requested her presence on December 30 and her attorneys informed the committee she could not appear before January 5, because she did not want to bring her son and needed time to arrange for his care. The subcommittee replied: "This committee has given Mrs. Powell ample and final notice of its interest in her appearance. She remains under subpoena. Mrs. Powell is expected to appear... December 30. ..." With that the furious flow of correspondence came to an end. Mrs. Powell never appeared.

Ten other subpoenaed committee staff members did appear to testify at the hearings held on December 19, 20, 21, and 30. Their testimony, coupled with the analysis prepared by the staff of GAO auditors under Robert Gray, made it apparent that there had been numerous irregularities in the handling of Committee travel funds, as well as various other abuses.

The subcommittee therefore submitted to the full committee on January 3, 1967, the following conclusions:[8]

Conclusions

1. Testimony indicates that Representative Powell used an assumed name on many airline flights purchased with Committee credit cards. . . .
2. Testimony indicates that Corinne A. Huff, a staff employee of the Committee on Education and Labor, prior to June 30, 1966 (on July 1, 1966, Miss Huff was transferred to Representative Powell's clerk-hire payroll), made many trips under an assumed name on many airline flights purchased with Committee credit cards. . . .
3. Representative Powell placed on the staff of the Committee . . . one Sylvia J. Givens, who had been hired for the express purpose of doing domestic work for Representative Powell when he traveled, as well as for performing clerical work in his Committee offices.
4. After the initiation of this investigation, Representative Powell paid to Eastern Air Lines the cost of travel of himself, Miss Huff, Miss Givens, and Mr. and Mrs. Stone, which had been purchased with Committee airline credit cards for transportation to Miami en route to Bimini, British West Indies, except that Representative Powell did not pay the cost of a return trip for Sylvia J. Givens. . . .

* * *

6. Representative Powell favored at least one member of his staff with personal vacation trips, the transportation of which was procured through the use of airline credit cards of the Committee. . . .
7. Persons having no official connection with the Congress have been provided with transportation by Representative Powell and the travel purchased by air travel credit cards of the Committee. . . .

8. The failure of a number of staff employees of the Committee ... to submit vouchers for transportation expenses or subsistence on many trips performed by them, allegedly upon official business, raised a serious question before this special subcommittee as to whether such travel was actually on official business or was for purely personal reasons. . . .

* * *

11. The record of the hearings raises a strong presumption that Y. Marjorie Flores (Mrs. Adam C. Powell) is receiving compensation, as a clerk for Representative Powell, in the sum of $20,578 per year in violation of Public Law 89-90, 89th Congress, in that she is not performing the services for which she is compensated in the offices of Representative Powell in the District of Columbia or in the state or the district which he represents, as required by said statute.

* * *

The subcommittee filed eight recommendations based on these findings. Six detailed tighter controls over the spending of House funds. The final two directly concerned Powell:[9]

7. The subcommittee recommends that the Committee on House Administration direct the Clerk of the House of Representatives to forthwith terminate salary payments to Y. Marjorie Flores. . . .
8. The subcommittee recommends that the report and record of these hearings be made available to each Member of the Congress and that the Committee on House Administration forward the report and record to such agencies and departments of the Federal Government as it shall deem appropriate.

The full House Administration Committee met January 3 to consider these recommendations. All eight were adopted,with only one objection, that of Augustus F. Hawkins (D-Cal.). He reportedly felt that to remove Mrs. Powell from the payroll could be interpreted as racial discrimination, because other House members might also have employees similarly in violation of the law.[10] The committee turned down a motion by Representative William L. Dickinson (R-Ala.) that the committee file specific requests for action against Powell with the Justice Department.

Except for Emanuel Celler's statement on December 11, neither Van Deerlin's nor the special subcommittee's efforts attracted much attention in early December. But when bits of the facts discovered by the Hays subcommittee began to leak out and appear in the press after the hearings began December 19, the tempo of the controversy rose rapidly. Editorials across the nation began to call for varying degrees of punishment for Powell, sentiments which were echoed in the ever-mounting stream of letters from the public that piled up in congressmen's offices. House Minority Leader Gerald R. Ford made the only Republican comment on the Powell affair to be issued before Congress convened. Referring to the Hays investigation, he said, "When all this evidence comes to the House January 10, there is a distinct possibility that Mr. Powell might not be seated."[11]

The first expression of support for Powell seems to have been uttered on December 24. On that date A. Philip Randolph, president of the Brotherhood of Sleeping Car Porters, and other Negro leaders announced plans for a Ministers' and Laymen's Assembly which would meet in Washington January 8 to protest the Hays investigation and Van Deerlin's proposal. "We feel he has committed no crime," Randolph said of Powell. "There may be some mistakes in judgment. . . . This does not mean that we believe in everything Mr. Powell has said or done. We are concerned about basic issues, the right of a member to take his seat after he has been elected."[12]

A massive rally in support of Powell was held in Harlem on December 29. In attendance were numerous Harlem and national Negro leaders. Their anger had been further aroused by the suggestion, rapidly gaining popularity, that Powell be deprived of his chairmanship as punishment. The usually mild A. Philip Randolph led off the meeting by characterizing the attempt to discipline Powell as "racism masquerading behind a screen of Congressional piety and self-righteousness." Other speakers, among them Livingston Wingate, a Powell associate expanded on this theme: "It's not America against Adam Clayton Powell, oh, no. It's America against the black people. They're not after Adam, they're after his black power."[13] The meeting resolved to organize as many busloads of Negroes as possible for the rally in Washington on January 8. Subsequently a formal organization, the Pilgrimage to Preserve Powell's Chairmanship, was set up to gather participants for the rally.

The Congress of Racial Equality issued a statement that said in part, "The backlash has now come to the halls of Congress and the effect directed at Powell is, in effect, a warning to all black people in America that 'You be good darkies or else.' "[14] A somewhat more moderate statement issued by the NAACP at its annual meeting on January 3 urged that no action be taken against Powell in the absence of an established code of congressional ethics.

While statements in support of Powell continued to flow from Negro, church, and civil liberties groups, the conviction grew among House liberals that the most effective way to deal with Powell would be to deprive him of his seniority, his chairmanship, or both, in the Democratic caucus. Reps. James G. O'Hara (D-Mich.) and Frank Thompson, Jr. (D-N. J.), gradually emerged as the leaders of this effort.

This new development had no effect on Van Deerlin's plans. He confirmed on January 4 that he would present his motion to have Powell step aside, regardless of what action was taken by the caucus on January 9, and announced he would oppose any plan more lenient than his proposal for an investigating committee. He indicated that his plans had already received "amazing" support from his colleagues. The same day he sent a short letter outlining his course of action to all his fellow Representatives. This was followed a few days later by a four-page analysis of the exclusion of Brigham H. Roberts in 1900 for practicing polygamy in violation of federal law and a summary of Powell's problems with the New York courts, including quotations from judicial opinions admonishing Powell.[15]

On January 5, Powell issued through his Washington office his first major statement on the efforts to have him step aside or to deprive him of his chairmanship.[16] He had been "deeply moved by the unexpected outpouring of support" from Negroes and Negro organizations, he said. "Their combined voices raised in my behalf has made it clear to me that the fight to retain my chairmanship—and this is really the only issue in this struggle—must be militantly pressed," he said. "This we owe to coming generations of black children who will one day decide the future of this country."

The statement, entitled "Fifteen Facts," made a number of allegations and stated a number of facts about the "undercover conspiracy" to take away his chairmanship. Powell said that because his case was still in litigation in the appellate courts of New York, he had not exhausted all the remedies available to him; hence he was "not a 'fugitive from justice' which has been so loosely and irresponsibly bandied about in editorials." Moreover, the New York courts had summarily abrogated his privilege as congressman to be immune from arrest while Congress was in session. He had committed no crime, he said:

> I have not tarnished the name of the House through any violation of Federal laws, particularly the U.S. Civil Code governing conflicts of interest for Congressmen. Nor have I misused my position to obtain Federal contracts for corporations represented by me or by my law firm. Nor have I bilked the United States government out of $1,000,000 by selling it inferior merchandise which affects the conduct of the war in Viet Nam.

The voters in his district had been aware of the circumstances in his personal life when they cast their votes for him—he had received 74.1 percent of the vote. He contended that the effort against him in the House and in the press was motivated by the desire to deprive "one of America's most powerful Negro politicians of his power." In support of his contention that race was an issue in this effort, he noted that only six members of the House were Negroes; of the 20 House committee chairmanships, only two were held by Negroes; and that there were more Negroes employed by his committee than by any other in the House or Senate. "The move to unseat me or to have me step aside is also a move to fire 12 well-paid Negro staff members." He said also that Frank Thompson, one of the leaders in the move to unseat him, had led the fight on behalf of the Mississippi House delegation which was challenged twice during the 89th Congress. He concluded from these and other facts, he said, that "a political conspiracy of enormous dimensions involving certain influential members of the press and I deeply regret, a number of my colleagues in Congress, has not only been mounted against Adam Clayton Powell, but against black political leadership, black people and black progress."

House Speaker John W. McCormack (D-Mass.) had an inconclusive conference with Van Deerlin on January 5 and met with a number of members of the Democratic Study Group, an independent group of House liberals. They were told that McCormack would not support a move to discipline Powell in any way, not even as a compromise to forestall more drastic action on the floor.

McCormack's position confused the House liberals. The executive committee of the Democratic Study Group declared its neutrality in the Powell matter on January 6. This was indicative of the division rampant in that body. Although DSG chairman Frank Thompson was the leader of the drive to take away Powell's chairmanship, in the hopes of heading off efforts to deny him his seat, Thompson could not rally the DSG membership in support of his efforts.

On January 9, Powell's supporters tried another tactic. Ninety-two of his constituents filed a suit seeking an injunction staying the New York courts from ordering

Powell's arrest while Congress was in session. They contended that the arrest order violated their civil rights by denying them "a reasonable opportunity to confer with and make their views known to their elected Representative."[17]

Monday, January 9, also was the day on which the Democratic caucus met, and it was in the caucus that Powell received his first bitter dose of punishment. The caucus was attended by Powell, who had returned from Bimini the day before. In marked contrast with his usual behavior, Powell was quiet, even contrite during the caucus, and did not charge, as he had in his January 5 statement, that he was being attacked because he was a Negro.

The caucus action on Powell began when Rep. Morris K. Udall (D-Ariz.) offered the following resolution:

> Be it resolved. That the Democratic caucus hereby instructs its Committee on Committees to designate as chairman of the Education and Labor Committee for the 90th Congress, the gentleman from Kentucky, Mr. Perkins.

Udall, a DSG member and a strong advocate of civil rights legislation, had been chosen to manage the resolution in the hopes of blunting Powell's charges of racism. The Arizonian argued that his proposal might prevent further punitive action when the House convened the next day, and made it clear that his action was in response to the findings of the Hays subcommittee. Powell replied that the new rules adopted by his committee and those recommended by the House Administration Committee had put an end to his use of public funds for his private travels.

A substitute resolution was then introduced by Rep. Abraham J. Multer (D-N. Y). It provided that Powell should step aside temporarily as chairman while a special committee investigated his personal and official conduct. This compromise had been drawn up by Speaker McCormack, who had abandoned his previous stand. His attempt to support sanctions to dilute the anti-Powell forces came too late. He was unable to muster the necessary support and the substitute was defeated by a standing vote of 88-122, with 37 Democrats not voting. McCormack had misguaged the growing congressional sentiment against Powell.

Then Udall's original resolution designating Perkins as chairman of the Education and Labor Committee was adopted on a voice vote. Powell later estimated this latter vote had been 3 to 1 in favor of the resolution. Thus did Powell lose his chairmanship.

Powell was greatly shaken. His speech was slow and hesitant, and his voice broke as he talked to reporters. He was obviously confused and shocked. "I don't expect to get it back," he said of his chairmanship. "It was a lynching—Northern style." He said, "Many of the great liberals of the North voted against me, including some members of my own Committee." Powell repeated his claim of January 5 that other members had committed more serious offenses.[18]

Powell then went to his office, where a large group of his supporters was gathered. Their expressions of sympathy and confidence revived a little of the old flamboyant Powell. "Are you going to quit politics?" a newsman asked him. "Are you going to quit breathing?" Powell replied. He then spoke briefly to his supporters, quoting from ancient Sanskrit writings about living life to the fullest. "Keep the faith, baby," he told them, "spread it gently and walk together, children."[19]

4 The Public, the Congress, and the Scofflaw

Noon on Tuesday, January 10, 1967, was the time established by law for the meeting of the first session of the 90th Congress. Pursuant to this requirement 434 representatives-elect assembled in the Hall of the House. Not even the pall cast over the meeting by the death of the much-liked Representative-elect John Fogarty a few hours before could completely blot out the prevailing atmosphere of joviality.

Outside on the Capitol steps, a group of about a thousand Powell supporters were assembled. Although it was illegal to gather there, Capitol police had been instructed to let them remain. Powell's friends were far from jovial. Their noisy vigil lasted all afternoon and was punctuated by several shouting matches and scuffles, a fist fight, and about 10 draft-card burnings.

Inside, amid lengthy speeches, the House elected John McCormack speaker. Finally, at about 1:30, the speaker was ready to swear in the members-elect. He called on the members to rise, but was interrupted by Van Deerlin, who was seeking recognition.[1] When recognized, Van Deerlin announced, "Mr. Speaker, upon my responsibility as a Member-elect of the 90th Congress, I object to the oath being administered at this time to the gentleman from New York [Powell]. I base this upon facts and statements which I consider reliable. I intend at the proper time to offer a resolution providing that the question of eligibility of Mr. Powell to a seat in this House be referred to a special committee. . . ."

McCormack broke in. "Does the gentleman demand that the gentleman from New York step aside?" Van Deerlin replied in the affirmative. The speaker replied, "The gentleman has performed his duties and has taken the action he desires to take under the rule. The gentleman from New York will be requested to be seated during the further proceedings."

An objection was also raised to the seating of freshman Benjamin B. Blackburn (R-Ga.). The speaker then administered the oath to the remaining members-elect. He next recognized Rep. Udall. Udall, in an atmosphere now heavily charged with tension, offered H. Res. 1:

> Resolved, that the Speaker is hereby authorized and directed to administer the oath of office to the gentleman from New York, Mr. Adam Clayton Powell.
> Resolved, that the question of the final right of Adam Clayton Powell to a seat in the ninetieth Congress be referred to a Select Committee, composed of seven members, to be appointed by the Speaker, and said committee shall have the power to send for persons and papers and examine witnesses on oath in relation to the subject matter of this resolution; and said committee shall be required to report its conclusions and recommendations to the House within sixty days from the date the members are appointed.

H. Res. 1 had been conceived by the House Democratic leadership during the days immediately before Congress met, in an attempt to appease the mounting anger against Powell while still seating him, at least for a while. Once again it was the liberals who initiated moderate action against Powell to head off the more serious action being demanded by other Congressmen in response to constituent pressure. Udall had been picked to manage the resolution because of his well-established position as a supporter of civil rights legislation. Under the rules of the House, the resolution would be debated for one hour, with Udall in control of the time. At the end of the hour (or sooner, if Udall chose), a vote would be taken on ordering the previous question. A motion for the previous question is a debate-limiting device which, when carried, results in terminating debate and forcing a vote on the subject at hand. Under House rules, the motion requires a majority vote. If the previous question passed, a vote would be taken on the resolution itself. If the previous question failed, the floor would be open for amendments or substitutes to the resolution.

Before beginning debate, Majority Leader Carl Albert (D-Okla.) asked that, by unanimous consent, Powell be allowed to speak during the debate. Rep. Dickinson (R-Ala.) started to object, but was quieted by Republican colleagues. Udall then commenced his opening speech.

> Mr. Speaker, let me make it clear that I share the feelings of most of my colleagues, the feelings of my outrage that many of you have expressed. . . . I have supported and still support measures to strengthen our proceedings for dealing with questions of ethics. I am keenly aware of the strong public feelings that this matter has aroused. I also have had some telegrams, telephone calls, and threats from both sides of this question.

Udall summarized the charges against Powell and the actions taken by the Democratic caucus the day before. He then explained the main issue facing the House.

> Mr. Speaker, let me put into sharp focus today the clear distinction between the resolution I offer and the resolution I am advised may be presented by the minority side.
> Mr. Powell appears before us today with a certificate of election, which is just as good as yours or mine. He was elected by a 3-to-1 majority. His people said that they wanted him to be their Congressman, and I presume they will send him back, if we expel him, with a 10-to-1 majority.

I propose to seat him, but I propose to seat him conditionally until a fair judicial inquiry can be held. . . .

This inquiry would be composed of the top lawyers in this House, and they would report back in 60 days' time, and we would then decide after the hearing what should be done.

The Republican resolution, on the other hand, from what I have been told, would probably move that he be barred from the House, and then given a trial.

I suggest that the fair and reasonable thing to do, and that which American tradition requires, is that we follow my resolution.

* * *

Let us make a clear distinction between Adam Powell, Member of Congress from the 18th District, and Adam Powell, chairman of a powerful committee. The abuses with which he has been charged stem almost entirely from the fact that he had the power of the chairman, not the power of Adam Powell, an individual Congressman—but that he had the power of a chairman. These are the charges and these are the responsibilities that he has been charged with abusing.

Let me make it clear that the mighty has fallen, the ax has come down, the story of Adam Powell, free-wheeling chairman, is ended; that house has tumbled down, and nothing we do will change it. . . .

We may be asked—and we probably will be—to do more today.

* * *

How much more do we want to do? How much more should [we] do? Are we going to kick a man when he is down? Are we going to go beyond that without a trial and deny him a seat in the House?

* * *

Adam Powell has never really had a chance to sit down and state his case to a group of his peers who hold the power to recommend what happens to him as a Member of the House. Maybe he will decline. Maybe he cannot prove a case. But he has never had a chance to state a case.

* * *

Mr. Speaker, I say that this is about fair play to the people Adam Powell represents. There are 450,000 people—American citizens—in Manhattan who are represented by this man. They have said they want him to be their Congressman. You might not have made that choice and I might not have made it. But they want him. They elected him 3 to 1 and have elected him 11 times. These people are among the poorest people and the most troubled people in this country. They are living under more difficulties and more problems than perhaps any people anywhere. If there is any constituency that needs a Congressman in this body and in these times, this is that constituency. They have said that they want him as their spokesman. I am prepared to let him sit and vote for them until we can have a full and fair hearing and a trial.

* * *

The question is not really, should he be seated. The question is—should he have a hearing before we decide whether he is going to be seated.

This other question, this question of racism, is not involved. This question of a double standard is not involved. But get this straight—cold practical fact is—rightly or wrongly—that 20 million of our fellow citizens are going to always feel that it was involved if we act hastily today.

* * *

Mr. Hanna (D-Calif.) then posed a significant parliamentary inquiry. "If I understand the rules of the House correctly," he said, "to expel a Member from this body would require a two-thirds vote. As I understand the gentleman's resolution, however, the question upon the final seating of Mr. Powell would require only a majority vote. Am I correct in that statement?"

The speaker replied, without explanation, that this statement was correct; only a majority would be required. Udall, however, did not feel comfortable with the speaker's ruling. "I am not one that is against majority rule very often, but something as drastic as this—I would be a little happier if we did it by a two-thirds vote. If someone proposed to take my seat in Congress away from me I would want two-thirds of my colleagues to do it," he said.

Rep. Hays then took the floor. He commented briefly on the findings of his subcommittee and announced his support for the Udall resolution. He was followed by Minority Leader Gerald Ford. Citing Article I, Sec. 5, of the Constitution,

Ford explained that "the issue, as I see it, is exclusively the question of the qualifications of one of our numbers elected November 8 to sit as a Member of the House of Representatives."

Ford then outlined the substitute resolution the Republicans would offer if the opportunity arose. Drafted in response to a nearly unanimous vote in the Republican caucus the day before, the Republican proposal also called for a select committee appointed by the Speaker, to consist of five Democrats and four Republicans. The committee would be required to report to the House within five weeks of its appointment. In the meantime Powell would be required to stand aside, although he would receive the usual pay and allowances. Stressing that Powell's qualifications to sit had never been reviewed by the House, Ford urged:

> What we must do today in the determination of the qualifications of Mr. Powell is to establish a committee, a blue-ribbon committee, that will investigate all of the allegations that have been made heretofore and report within the period of five weeks. . . . .
>
> In my humble judgment we probably ought to establish, as quickly as possible—and tomorrow is not too soon—an overall Select Committee such as was approved in the dying days of the 89th Congress in order that all charges or allegations that have been made in the past or which might be made in the future, can be considered concerning any one of us who now serves in the House of Representatives.

With the two alternatives clearly posed, debate became more general. Udall yielded portions of his hour, a few minutes at a time, to a variety of representatives. One of the first was Van Deerlin.

> Mr. Speaker, the gentleman from Arizona asks what is wrong with seating the gentleman from New York today, and bringing back a committee report as to his fitness to serve some time in the future.
>
> The only thing that I see wrong with this is that, except in

contests involving the outcome of an election, there is no precedent in the entire history of the United States in which the House of Representatives has expelled a Member, once seated, for matters having to do with his conduct in a previous Congress, or with matters not concerning his status as a Member of Congress.

I believe if you wish to decide the fitness of the gentleman from New York to serve in this Congress that we had better decide today to exclude him from being seated until a committee brings back its report. . . .

Certain diversions have been made in the argument that is before us today, and among these is that the gentleman from New York has somehow or other not had his day in court.

This may be technically true, but I would point out that there are nearly a dozen judges in the State of New York who will tell you where the fault lies.

The immunity which we in Congress enjoy stems . . . from article I, section 6 of the Constitution. . . .

* * *

If article I, section 6, is to be so twisted as to provide a protective cover—if election to the House of Representatives is to carry a license for scofflaws—if this Chamber is to provide a haven for fugitives—then, before the bar of public opinion, I say "God help the Congress of the United States."

* * *

Van Deerlin thus raised a question, the answer to which was not at all clear. Could the House, even by a two-thirds vote, expel a member or a member-elect for conduct committed prior to the current Congress?

Mr. CORMAN (D-Calif.). The decision which we must make on this resolution to seat the gentleman from New York [Mr. Powell] goes to a narrow and simple question—his qualifications. The issue of fitness must necessarily be delayed to another day and raises different questions. Those of us who vote for the seating of the gentleman conclude merely that he is over 25 years of age, a citizen of the United States, and an inhabitant of the State of New York. To imply, as has been done by the minority leader, that the right of the gentleman to be seated raises the rather nebulous question of "his effect on the image of the House," goes clearly beyond our jurisdiction today and shows little regard for the Constitution of the United States.

Mr. MULTER (D-N. Y.). One of the first rules of construction is that you must take into account the order in which the various items appear in the legislation or, in this case, the Constitution. In the Constitution the first reference to the qualification of Members refers, not to fitness, but to qualifications, and they are citizenship, age, and not residency, but inhabitancy in the State. None of those items is in question with reference to the gentleman we are talking about today. . . . He has been duly elected. There can be no question of his qualifications as referred to in the Constitution. That has not been raised in or outside the Congress. . . .

After the qualifications are set forth in the U. S. Constitution, we then find the statement which the minority leader has referred to accurately. It states that we are the judges of the election, returns and qualifications of our colleagues.

That means the qualifications set forth in that document, our Constitution. We can neither add to nor detract from them. Once the voters of a congressional district have chosen their Representative, his fitness to serve is determined beyond question by us, his colleagues, providing only that he meets the three qualifications set forth.

A still later provision of that same Constitution gives us the right to punish Members for their misbehavior. Note, however, it is only a Member that may be punished and not a Member-elect.

There is grave doubt whether the 90th Congress may punish a Member for what he did as a Member of the 89th Congress.

Certainly, however, we have no right to punish one who is not a Member of this Congress.

The right to punish may include expulsion. It does not include exclusion.

* * *

Mr. STRATTON (D-N. Y.). I believe the basic issue in the Powell case is a matter of residence, which is one of the Constitutional qualifications for membership in the House. If a Representative-elect chooses to remain outside of his state rather than comply with the duly constituted orders of the courts of his own state, then I believe there is a very real question of whether he is in fact still a resident of the state which he purports to represent, as the Constitution says he must be. The Constitution says he must be an inhabitant of his state at the time when he is elected.

* * *

Mr. GOODELL (R-N. Y.). There are no precedents—no precedents—for seating a Member and putting him in limbo pending investigation. There are only three cases of expulsion in this House where qualification is the issue as distinct from election. . . .

* * *

Mr. UDALL. The very next order of business, after we dispose of this matter, is going to be a resolution offered by a Democrat, our leader, Carl Albert, to seat a Republican Congressman from Georgia when we have not had the first semblance of an investigation, and when there is a serious and genuine question whether he really won the election.

* * *

Mr. GOODELL. The gentleman is well aware that there is a long line of decisions on election cases where there is a certificate by the secretary of state on election. This is entirely different in the precedents and in the rules of the House from the question of qualifications of a Member.
Mr. UDALL. Mr. Powell's certificate is just as good, just as valid, has just as big a seal and as many ribbons on it as the certificate of the gentleman from Georgia.
Mr. GOODELL. There is not a single precedent in the annals of the House for seating a man whose qualifications have been questioned under these circumstances before his trial.

* * *

Mr. HAWKINS (D-Calif.). Mr. Speaker, I rise in opposition to any action being taken against the gentleman from New York [Mr. Powell] , which applies only to him and not to other Members of this body. While my position differs both from the Udall resolution and its alternative to deprive Mr. Powell of his seat now, the Udall resolution is at least the lesser of the two evils and we have no other choice for a vote at this time.

* * *

I strongly advocate high ethical standards and the most comprehensive rules to judge all Members. I further support modification of the worn-out seniority system that has permitted chairmen to operate without strict scrutiny; but I cannot in good conscience punish any man without a fair trial and with unequal justice.

* * *

Mr. WRIGHT (D-Tex.). A committee chairmanship is a privilege,

41

and not a right. It is a gift of this House. It is ours to bestow or withhold.

By withholding it in this case, we have clearly established the precedent that the House of Representatives will not tolerate the misuse of public funds. . . .

* * *

Membership in the House is not given by us. It is given by the citizens of each congressional district. It is a gift we cannot bestow. We should act in extreme prudence and painstaking fairness whenever we presume to take it away.

* * *

When we divest a duly elected Member of his right to sit and vote in this Chamber, we disenfranchise the people of an entire congressional district. We rob them of their voice and of their vote. They are the ones who are punished, and these people do not stand before us today accused of any particular malfeasance.

With most of his hour gone, Udall yielded the floor to Powell.

My beloved colleagues with whom I have served for 24 [sic] years: I know this is an agonizing moment for all of you. I know if you could vote on a secret ballot, your vote would be different from what you have proclaimed publicly, because you know I have been here 24 years, and he who is without sin should cast the first stone. There is no one here who does not have a skeleton in his closet. I know, and I know them by name.

Now Mr. Speaker, I will talk first about residence. When a man pays his income tax in New York State, and when he pays the new city tax now imposed upon us by our former beloved colleague, Mayor Lindsay, and when he appears in New York and preaches—and it has been in the papers regularly—then he is a resident. The law does not say how long you have to stay. I have been preaching in the Abyssinian Baptist Church up until a couple of months ago every Sunday without fail.

The next thing they talk about is criminal contempt. The dean of the House [Rep. Celler] knows more about this than any lawyer here, and he says that New York is a gray area. I am in criminal contempt but not on a felony, and that is what our constitution of the House says—a felony. I am not in criminal contempt on a felony.

Next, you are prejudicing my case. There is nothing wrong with a man appealing his case, is there? I would fight for the right of anyone here to appeal his case. The appellate division right now—and the gentleman from New York [Mr. Goodell] was with the Department of Justice and knows—the appellate division right now is handing down decisions. Also the case has been moved into the Federal court and ultimately will go to the U. S. Supreme Court. What I am fighting for is not for me but for you. I am fighting for the right of a Congressman to say what he says in this well when he leaves here and this has never been judged or adjudicated. The makers of public opinion can print what we say, but we are not allowed to do so. That is the sole issue. That cost me thousand of dollars in legal fees, as you can well imagine.

You talk about my qualifications. There has been no bill of particulars. Someone can rise two years from now and use the same phrase, "qualifications" on any of you without a bill of particulars, and you would not be seated.

Gentlemen, my conscience is clean. My case is in God's hands. All I hope is that you have a good sleep tonight.

During the hour-long debate a number of questions were raised repeatedly; the questions were to have continued significance throughout the long Powell controversy. Can the House refuse to seat (exclude) members-elect for failure to meet qualifications other than the specifically enumerated ones of age, inhabitancy, and citizenship, or are there others that can be judged by the House? Can the House expel a member-elect, or is expulsion (which requires a two-thirds vote, in contrast with a simple majority for exclusion), confined solely to members who have been seated? Can the House expel a member for conduct committed prior to the opening of Congress, or is expulsion confined to acts committed during the Congress in which expulsion is undertaken?

Udall then moved the previous question. Since by that time it was clear that Powell would be investigated, the vote on the previous question had become the crucial vote of the day, as it would decide whether Powell would be seated prior to the investigation or not. If the previous question passed, the

Udall resolution would be almost assured of adoption, although many members did not find it completely satisfactory. The defeat of the previous question, however, would be followed by the submission of the Republican amendment.

Normally, a question of House organization would be a party matter, and a Democratic majority of 246 to 186 would assure passage of the previous question. But it had already become apparent that the Powell matter was no ordinary issue, and the Democrats were exhibiting differences of opinion. Van Deerlin had made known in December his support for a procedure like that proposed by the Republicans, and his colleagues in the Democratic Study Group were reported to be deeply divided on the Powell question. The always uncertain control which the leadership was able to exercise over the Southern Democrats was also a cause for concern. The unity of the Democratic Party was definitely in doubt as the voting began.

When the roll call was complete, the previous question had been defeated 126-305. All 186 Republicans had voted nay. They had been joined by 119 Democrats. The Northern Democrats had split 113-41 in favor of the previous question, but their Southern colleagues voted 13-78 against. A major revolt had occurred in the Democratic ranks, and the Southern Democrat-Republican coalition, having recouped its strength in the 1966 elections, had demonstrated that it was once again a power to be reckoned with.

The Speaker then recognized Minority Leader Ford. He presented the Republican amendment, which eliminated all of the text of the Udall resolution and replaced it with the following wording:

> Resolved, that the question of the right of Adam Clayton Powell to be sworn in as a Representative from the State of New York in the Ninetieth Congress, as well as his final right to a seat therein as such Representative, be referred to a special committee of nine Members of the House to be appointed by the Speaker, four of

whom shall be Members of the minority party appointed after consultation with the minority leader. Until such committee shall report upon and the House shall decide such question and the right, the said Adam Clayton Powell shall not be sworn in or permitted to occupy a seat in this House.

[The next paragraph authorized the committee to hold hearings and issue subpoenas.]

Until such question and right have been decided, the said Adam Clayton Powell shall be entitled to all pay, allowances, and emoluments authorized for Members of the House.

The committee shall report to the House within five weeks after the members of the committee are appointed the results of its investigation and study, together with such recommendations as it deems advisable. Any such report which is made when the House is not in session shall be filed with the Clerk of the House.

Ford was given control of an hour, as Udall had been, and a few preliminary comments were made by several members. Ford then yielded time to Rep. Conte (R-Mass.). Conte announced that he had an amendment to Ford's amendment to establish a Select Committee "not only to investigate the charges against Mr. Powell of New York, but to investigate any other charges or any other transgressions by any other Member of Congress. . . ." Ford informed him that in his opinion the amendment was not germane. Conte's proposal also drew a rejoinder by Hays, who declared that the House Administration Committee was ready and able to investigate any charges brought before it. Conte's amendment was not introduced. Ford also gave his opinion, in response to an inquiry by Rep. Holifield (D-Calif.), that a majority vote would be needed to seat Powell at the end of the five-week period. Debate continued briefly until Ford yielded to Udall, who wished to explain his position in the coming votes. He said:

Of course, I am opposed to the adoption of the substitute for the original resolution, but the question will then come on whether we adopt the Udall resolution as modified by the substitute. On that question I shall vote "aye."

I do so for this reason. A motion to seat the gentleman from New York [Mr. Powell] has been offered. It is obvious that the motion to seat him will not pass. . . . If nothing happened, if the resolution were to be beaten, nothing is done. The gentleman from New York [Mr. Powell] would be excluded, the case would be over, and he would be gone.

* * *

This particular episode demonstrates why a mere glance at a congressman's vote may not yield an accurate understanding of his position on the issue. Udall confronted the unhappy choice of voting for a resolution of which he did not approve, or of voting against the resolution and seeing Powell excluded.

Ford then moved the previous question, which passed by a voice vote. A voice vote also led to the adoption of the amendment. On a roll-call vote the amended resolution was adopted 363 to 65. All 186 Republicans voted yea, as did 89 Northern Democrats and 88 Southerners. The small anti-investigation, immediate-seating protest vote was cast by 63 Northern Democrats and two Southern Democrats. The House then voted to seat Blackburn pending the outcome of an investigation of his election by the House Administration Committee, and then proceeded to complete its other organizational business.

It was generally acknowledged that the lopsided votes were due to the tremendous public pressure brought to bear on the Congressmen in the mail from their constituents, compounded by the failure of the professional civil rights lobby to bring any countervailing pressure into play. In a story in the *Washington Post* of January 9, one Midwestern congressman described the situation before the opening of Congress as follows:

Maybe it's part backlash. Adam may have become the symbol of whatever it is people don't like about "black power." Whatever it is, some of us are getting more mail on this issue than on Vietnam. You're in a position now of either voting against him or being held up as a man who voted to subsidize the high life of a fugitive from justice. It could cost a man his seat.

Representative-elect Powell reacted bitterly to the proceedings. He spoke to his supporters outside the Capitol at about 4 P. M., as soon as the outcome of the voting had beome apparent, and urged them to withhold city, state, and federal income taxes for ăt least five weeks or until he was again seated in Congress. Powell maintained that to do otherwise would be to accept taxation without representation.

The controversial ex-chairman did not refrain from comment on his colleagues. "Today marks, in my opinion, the end of·the United States of America as the land of the free and the home of the brave," he said. Pointing to the Capitol with his cigar, Powell announced, "This building houses the biggest bunch of elected hypocrites in the world."[2]

5   Sifting the Evidence

Embittered and worried by the actions of the Democratic caucus and the House, Powell announced on January 11 that he would attempt to settle with the New York courts and pay a portion of the $164,000 judgment against him. And about a week later he named a coterie of eight lawyers to assist him in his fight for his seat: Mrs. Jean Camper Cahn, formerly with the OEO and at that time in practice in Washington; Robert Carter of New York, general counsel for the NAACP; Hubert T. Delany, also of New York, an assistant U. S. district attorney and former domestic relations judge; Arthur Kinoy of New York, a Rutgers law professor; William M. Kunstler of New York, a member of the board of directors of the ACLU; Frank D. Reeves and Herbert O. Reid, both of Washington, from the Howard University Law School; and Henry R. Williams, past president of the Harlem Bar Association, then in practice in New York. Significantly, seven of the eight lawyers had participated in the case of *Bond* v. *Floyd*, concluded some two months before, in which the Supreme Court ordered the Georgia legislature to seat a Negro representative they had excluded for statements opposing the Vietnam war.

Meanwhile Mr. Powell's supporters were busily condemning the House action and planning efforts on his behalf.

Floyd McKissick of CORE and Stokely Carmichael of SNCC vowed political retribution for Congressmen who had voted against seating Powell. Carmichael extended his threat to President Johnson as well.

On January 11, a meeting of the Leadership Conference on Civil Rights (a coordinating organization for 112 Negro, labor, religious, and civic groups) provided an opportunity for a broad cross section of the civil rights movement to take a position on the House action. Despite the urgings of the CORE and SNCC representatives, the conference apparently did not consider the matter of great importance, since few of the representatives had instructions relating to the Powell affair from their organizations. The conference passed a mild resolution urging Congress "to adopt a code of ethics for all its Members, to democratize its rules of procedure and to set standards for all committee chairmen."[1]

A much more militant course of action was proposed by a spokesman for A. Philip Randolph. This consisted of a call for a Negro summit conference to plan strategy in the wake of Powell's temporary exclusion. The announcement, reported in the *New York Times* on January 13, listed five topics of consideration: 1. The blacklisting of Congressmen of both parties from Northern industrial centers with large Negro populations who were "directly or indirectly" responsible for the defeat of the resolution to seat Powell. 2. The "ending of the Negroes' political dependence on the good graces of the Democratic and Republican parties." 3. Planning the defeat of certain congressmen. One name mentioned was that of Emanuel Celler, who, it was charged, had not exerted sufficient effort to save Powell. 4. These efforts were to be complemented by planning intensified Negro voter registration in the Northern urban industrial areas. 5. And finally, a campaign was to be organized to restore Powell to his chairmanship and seat.

On the same day the executive committee of the United Council of Harlem Organizations proposed a one-day national work stoppage by Negroes and sympathetic whites. A few days later, the congregation of the Abyssinian Baptist Church approved regular prayer meetings in support of Powell and the opening of an office at the church on a 24-hour-a-day basis to coordinate efforts in support of the representative-elect.

Yet another plan was announced January 16 by Floyd McKissick of CORE. He called for a new "political apparatus" (which he denied would be a third political party) designed to produce a stronger Negro bloc vote in 1968 than had ever existed before.

Powell's backers also took to the courts in their efforts to aid him. On January 18 a group of 92 constituents refiled a suit to enjoin the sheriff of New York County from executing Justice Markewich's arrest order of November 28. The suit, which had originally been filed January 9, had been thrown out for defects in the papers. Meanwhile a group called Harlem Citizens for Community Action brought suit in the federal district court to enjoin the President from seeking a tax surcharge while the 18th District was without representation.

The same day also witnessed a retreat from a previous position. When it was announced that Emanuel Celler would head the Select Committee established pursuant to H. Res. 1, A. Philip Randolph was quick to deny previous announcements that Negro groups would seek Celler's defeat in the next election, describing Celler as a staunch champion of civil rights.

Powell also suffered a direct legal setback on January 18 when Supreme Court Justice John M. Harlan denied Powell's petition to prevent the enforcement of the arrest order of November 28.

While the Powell supporters had been laying their plans, House Speaker McCormack had been struggling to put together a roster for the Select Committee. This had not been an easy task, as many members were reluctant to serve on the special group. The membership was finally determined and announced to the House on January 19. The distinctly blue-ribbon membership included the following: Emanuel Celler, Chairman, Democrat of New York. Born in Brooklyn in 1888, Celler graduated from Columbia in 1910 and from Columbia Law School in 1912. He was admitted to the bar in 1912 and practiced law until elected to the 68th Congress in 1922. Reelected to every following Congress, he was dean of the House and most senior Democrat during the 90th Congress. As chairman of the Judiciary Committee he was floor manager for the 1964, 1965, and 1966 civil rights bills. He voted for the previous question (which was the crucial vote) on the Udall resolution (which would have seated Powell prior to the investigation) and for the amended resolution (which denied Powell a seat pending investigation) on January 10.

James C. Corman, Democrat of California. Born in Galena, Kansas, in 1920, he graduated from UCLA in 1942 and the University of Southern California Law School in 1948. He was admitted to the bar in 1949 and was in private practice until 1957. Corman served on the Los Angeles City Council from 1957 until his election to the 87th Congress in 1960. He was 145th in seniority during the 90th Congress and served on the Committee of the Judiciary and the Select Committee on Small Business. He supported the 1966 civil rights bill and voted for the previous question on the Udall resolution, and for the amended resolution.

Claude D. Pepper, Democrat of Florida. Born in Dudleyville, Alabama, in 1900, Pepper taught school for a year before attending the University of Alabama. He graduated in 1921 and received an LL.B. from Harvard Law School in 1924. Pepper was an instructor in law at the University of Arkansas in 1924-25 before taking up private practice. He served in the Florida House in 1929-30, on the State Board of Public Welfare in 1931-32, and on the State Board of Law Examiners in 1933-34. Pepper was in the U. S. Senate from

1937 to 1951 but was defeated for renomination in 1950 and 1958. Elected to the House in 1962, Pepper was the 179th-ranked Democrat in the 90th Congress and a member of the Rules Committee. He voted for the 1966 civil rights bill, for the previous question on the Udall resolution, and for the amended resolution.

John Conyers, Jr., Democrat of Michigan. Conyers, the lone Negro on the Select Committee, was born in Detroit in 1929. He graduated from Wayne State in 1957 and from Wayne State Law School in 1958. Thereafter he engaged in the practice of law and was a member of the Executive Board of the Detroit NAACP and of the Advisory Board to the Michigan ACLU. He was first elected to the 89th Congress. The 198th Democrat in seniority, he served on the Judiciary Committee in the 90th Congress. Conyers voted for the 1966 civil rights bill, for the previous question on the Udall resolution, and against the amended resolution.

Andrew Jacobs, Jr., Democrat of Indiana. Jacobs was born in Indianapolis in 1932, graduated from Indiana University in 1955, and received an LL.B. from that school in 1958. Thereafter he was engaged in private practice. Jacobs served in the Indiana House of Representatives in 1959-60 and first won election to Congress in 1964. During the 90th Congress he ranked 211th among the Democrats and served on the Committees on the Judiciary and the District of Columbia. He voted for the 1966 civil rights bill, for the previous question on the Udall resolution, and for the amended resolution.

Arch A. Moore, ranking minority member, Republican of West Virginia. Born in Moundsville, West Virginia, in 1923, Moore received his A.B. (1948) and LL.B. (1951) from West Virginia University. He was admitted to the bar in 1951. Moore served in the State House of Delegates from 1953 to 1955 and won election to Congress in 1956. During the 90th Congress he ranked 48th among the Republicans and served on the Judiciary Committee, the Select Committee on Small

Business, and the Joint Committee on Immigration and National Policy. He voted against the 1966 civil rights bill, against the previous question on the Udall resolution, and for the amended resolution.

Charles M. Teague, Republican of California. Teague was born in Santa Paula, California, in 1909. He graduated from Stanford University in 1931 and Stanford Law School in 1934. He was admitted to the bar in 1934 and thereafter engaged in private practice. First elected to the 84th Congress in 1955, he was the 41st-ranked Republican at the start of the 90th Congress (actually senior to Moore) and served on the Agriculture and Veterans' Affairs Committees. He opposed the 1966 civil rights bill and voted against the previous question on the Udall resolution and for the amended resolution.

Clark MacGregor, Republican of Minnesota. Born in Minneapolis in 1922, MacGregor received an A.B. from Dartmouth in 1944 and an LL.B. from the University of Minnesota in 1948. A trial lawyer from 1948 to 1960, he was first elected to Congress in 1960. During the 90th Congress he was the 77th-ranked Republican and served on the Judiciary Committee. MacGregor voted for the 1966 civil rights bill, against the previous question on the Udall resolution, and for the amended resolution.

Vernon W. Thompson, Republican of Wisconsin. Thompson was born in Richland Center, Wisconsin, in 1905. After graduating from the University of Wisconsin in 1927, he taught school for two years and received a law degree from the University of Wisconsin in 1932. He was assistant district attorney of Richland County for two years, Richland Center city attorney for six years, and three-term mayor of that town. Thompson was in the Wisconsin State Assembly from 1935 to 1949, serving as floor leader for three terms and as speaker for three terms. He also served on the Advisory Commission on Rules, Pleading, Practice, and Procedure to the Wisconsin Supreme Court, as secretary of the State

Legislative Council, and as a member of the Wisconsin Judicial Council before becoming state attorney general in 1951. Thompson held that post until his election as governor in 1956. He was governor in 1957-58 and then engaged in private law practice until elected to the 88th Congress. The 87th Republican in seniority in the 90th Congress, he was a member of the Committee on Foreign Affairs. Thompson voted for the 1966 civil rights bill, against the previous question on the Udall resolution, and for the amended resolution.

While the Select Committee was organizing a staff, a statement was made public which was the first joint declaration specifically on the Powell matter to be made by a group of major Negro leaders since the House action of January 10. The statement, signed by Martin Luther King, Jr., A. Philip Randolph, Bayard Rustin, Roy Wilkins, and Whitney Young, and reported in the *New York Times* of January 23, said in part:

> Within the civil rights movement there are differences of opinion with regard to the behavior and record of Congressman Powell. Without condoning all of Mr. Powell's actions, we believe that the civil rights movement is commonly agreed on two positions.
> Not only has Mr. Powell been denied due process . . . and what could be of greater concern to the civil rights movement? . . . but his Harlem constituents have been improperly deprived of representation in the House.

The statement went on to state that further action against Powell would be judged in the light of congressional action on a uniform code of ethics. Significantly, the statement made no charge of racism. However, the denial-of-due-process theme it raised was to assume major importance in the next few weeks. In addition to the policy statement, the Powell supporters also announced the postponement of the Randolph-sponsored summit conference announced on January 13. The reason given was that too many people had wanted to attend.

Once the Select Committee was organized, its first problem was to determine the scope of its investigative authority. This had been by no means made crystal-clear in H. Res. 1.[2] Early in the committee's existence it was urged by the Manhattan Democratic organization to investigate the facts of Powell's "bag woman" charges. The committee rejected this recommendation and formulated the matters into which it wished to inquire, as follows:

1. Mr. Powell's age, citizenship, and inhabitancy;
2. The status of legal proceedings to which Mr. Powell was a party in the State of New York and in the Commonwealth of Puerto Rico, with particular reference to the instances in which he has been held in contempt of court; and
3. Matters of Mr. Powell's alleged official misconduct since January 3, 1961.[3]

The committee also received an amicus brief transmitted by the American Civil Liberties Union on January 25.

Meanwhile, Powell was making good on his promise to settle his problems with the New York courts. On January 31, Jubilee Industries, Inc., paid $32,460 to Raymond Rubin, Mrs. James's attorney. This money was an advance on Powell's expected earnings for his record "Keep the Faith, Baby," which was being distributed by that company. Thus, after this payment Powell, according to Rubin's testimony to a Select Committee investigator, owed an additional $4,302.40, composed of the unpaid balance on the libel judgment and various court costs, plus an estimated $135,000 on the transfer-of-assets judgment. The four contempt citations and their respective arrest orders continued in force. This effort of Powell's seemed to hold out some hope of success. "If he can clear up his New York court troubles, we will have no alternative but to recommend he be seated," one committee member was quoted as saying in a *New York Times* report on February 1.

The Select Committee's hearing got under way with the sending of a letter from Chairman Celler to Powell on

February 1, 1967. The letter invited Powell to appear before the committee on February 8 and advised him that he would be asked about the matters the committee had determined to investigate. The letter concluded, "You are advised that you may be accompanied by counsel and that the hearings will be conducted in accordance with paragraph 26, rule XI of the Rules of the House of Representatives."[4] In return the committee was notified that Powell's eight lawyers would appear on his behalf. The committee counsel met with Powell's lawyers on February 3 and advised them that among the "alleged acts of official misconduct" to be investigated were the matters reported on by the Hays subcommittee in January.

Powell's lawyers filed a motion that the Select Committee recommend to the House that he be seated, having been duly elected and being possessed of "all the constitutional qualifications for membership" in the House. As proof of this they submitted numerous documents, including reports of the New York City and State election authorities, a photostat of Powell's birth certificate, transcripts of various court testimony concerning Powell's place of residence, New York State income tax returns for 1962, 1963, 1964, and 1965, and an estimated city income tax declaration for 1967. The Powell lawyers also submitted a memorandum in support of their motion. This brief set forth the basic arguments that Powell's lawyers would make through the course of their battle. The brief argued that Powell, possessing the three qualifications for membership prescribed by the Constitution, should receive the recommendation of the Select Committee for his immediate swearing-in and seating:[5]

Point One

The House of Representatives is required under the Constitution of the United States to seat a duly elected Congressman who meets all the constitutional qualifications set forth for membership in the House in Article I, Section 2, Clause 2: "No Person shall be a Representative who shall not have attained to the Age of twenty-five Years, and been seven Years a Citizen of the United States, and who shall not, when elected, be an Inhabitant of the State in which he shall be chosen."

A. This was the clear mandate of the Constitutional Convention.

1. The history of the proceedings at the Convention, during which the age, citizenship and inhabitancy qualifications were accepted, reveals the clear intention of the Enactors that the legislature was to have no power to alter or add to the constitutional qualifications. See Professor Charles Warren, *The Making of Our Constitution* (1928), at p. 420.

"Such action would seem to make it clear that the Convention did not intend to grant to a single branch of Congress, either to the House or to the Senate, the right to establish any qualifications for its members, other than those qualifications established by the Constitution itself, viz., age, citizenship, and residence. For certainly it did not intend that a single branch of Congress should possess a power which the Convention had expressly refused to vest in the whole Congress. As the Constitution, as then drafted, expressly set forth the qualifications of age, citizenship, and residence, and as the Convention refused to grant to Congress power to establish qualifications in general, the maxim *expressio unitus exclusion alterisu* [inclusion of some means the exclusion of others] would seem to apply. . . . The elimination of all power in Congress to fix qualifications clearly left the provisions of the Constitution itself as the sole source of qualifications."

2. This conclusion of the Convention that the Legislature may not refuse to seat a duly elected member who meets the Constitutional requirements, reflected the concern of the Founders that the vesting of any power in the legislature to modify or alter the strict constitutional qualifications was "improper and dangerous."

(i) See Farrand, *Records of the Federal Convention,* Vol. 2, p. 249.

"Mr. [Madison] was opposed to the Section [a proposal later defeated that each House have general power to fix qualifications] as vesting an improper & dangerous power in the Legislature. The qualifications of electors and elected were fundamental articles in a Republican Govt. and ought to be fixed by the Constitution. If the Legislature could regulate those of either, it can by degrees subvert the Constitution. A Republic may be converted into an aristocracy or oligarchy as well by limiting the number capable of being elected, as the number authorized to elect. In all cases where the representatives of the people will have a personal interest distinct from that of their Constituents, there was the same reason for being jealous of them, as there was for relying on them with full confidence, when they had a common interest. This was one of the former cases. . . . It was a power also, which might be made subservient to the views of one faction against another. Qualifications founded on artificial distinctions may be devised, by the stronger in order to keep out partizans of [a weaker] faction. . . . Mr. [Madison] observed that the British Parlimt. possessed the power of regulating the qualifications both of the electors, and the elected; and the abuse they had made of it was a lesson worthy of our attention. They had made the changes in both cases subservient to their own views, or to the views of political or religious parties."

(ii) The same concern led Alexander Hamilton to conclude in Number 68 of the Federalist Papers:

"The qualifications of the person who may choose or be chosen, as has been remarked on another occasion, are defined and fixed in the Constitution; and are unalterable by the Legislature."

3. All leading commentators agree that the intention of the Constitutional Convention was to establish a firm Constitutional mandate that the Legislature has no power to vary, alter or add to the constitutional qualifications and must seat as a member any duly elected representative who meets these qualifications.

* * *

Point Two

The most important and persuasive precedents of the House and Senate recognize this fundamental constitutional mandate.

The brief then analyzes six occasions—spanning almost a century and a half—on which the House or Senate considered the implications of the qualification clause and affirmed that the constitutional qualifications of age, citizenship, and inhabitancy were the sole qualifications for membership. Quoted approvingly in the brief is a House Judiciary Committee report in the cases of Ames and Brooks in the 42nd Congress (1872):

... The answer seems to us an obvious one that the Constitution has given to the House of Representatives no constitutional power over such considerations of "justice and sound policy" as a qualification in representation. On the contrary, the Constitution has given this power to another and higher tribunal, to wit, the constituency of the Member. Every intendment of our form of government would seem to point to that. This is a government of the people, which assumes that they are the best judges of the social, intellectual, and moral qualifications of their Representatives, whom they are to choose, not anybody else to choose for them; and we, therefore, find in the people's Constitution and frame of government they have, in the very first article and second section, determined that "The House of Representatives shall be composed of Members chosen every second year by the people of the States," not by representatives chosen for them at the will and caprice of Members of Congress from other States according to the notions of the "necessities of self-preservation and self-purification" which might suggest themselves to the reason or the caprice of the Members from other States in any process of purgation or purification which two-thirds of the Members of either House may "deem necessary" to prevent bringing the "body into contempt and disgrace."

* * *

Point Three

The legislature has deviated from the constitutional mandate on rare occasions under intense partisan pressure and public hysteria. These isolated cases have been subsequently overruled or discarded by the House or Senate.

1. The case of Brigham Roberts in the 56th Congress, 1899, 1 Hinds, Section 474 involved a member-elect from Utah who was barred from his seat on the ground that he was a polygamist in accord with the Mormon faith and had been convicted of violating the federal Edmonds Act prohibiting polygamy. The House, responding to a wave of anti-Mormon feeling throughout the country, barred Roberts despite a strong minority report which reasserted the constitutional principles previously adhered to by the House. Only a few years later the Senate sharply repudiated the *Roberts* action, seating, in the case of Reed Smoot of Utah, in the 58th Congress, 1903, 1 Hinds, Sections 481-484, a Senator-

elect despite his adherence to the Mormon faith. The Senate forcefully reasserted the governing constitutional mandate that the sole question before the legislature is the presence of the constitutional qualifications.

* * *

2. Following the Civil War, in a group of cases, the House barred members-elect who had participated in the Rebellion. See the cases of the Kentucky Members in the 40th Congress, 1867. However, it was pointed out in subsequent Congresses that the Congress itself recognized that this action was unconstitutional under Article I, finding it necessary to adopt Section 3 of the Fourteenth Amendment to sanction barring of members-elect on this additional ground of loyalty to the Confederacy.

* * *

3. The case of Victor Berger in the 66th Congress, 58 Cong. Rec. (1919) involved the refusal to seat a Congressman-elect who had been found guilty in World War I of violation of the Espionage Act. The House took the position that Berger had in effect committed "treason" which foreclosed his right to hold office under the United States pursuant to the congressional constitutional power to fix the penalty for treason. The majority House report further justified the exclusion of Berger under Section 3 of the Fourteenth Amendment, barring from the office of Representative any one who has "given aid or comfort to the enemies" of the United States.

Point Four

Only this Term of Court the Supreme Court of the United States has forcefully reminded the Nation that a legislature may not exclude a duly elected Representative of the people on the basis of its own conception of public interest.

In *Bond* v. *Floyd*,– U. S. –, 87 S. Ct. 339, December 5, 1966, the Supreme Court, in a unanimous opinion written for the Court by the Chief Justice ordered seated in the Georgia legislature, a Representative-elect who possessed all the constitutional qualifications but had been barred by the legislature for reasons unrelated to these qualifications. In his dissenting opinion below, later upheld by the Court, Chief Judge Tuttle of the Fifth Circuit Court of Appeals, after examining carefully all the relevant

61

precedents of the United States House of Representatives and Senate, held that—

"Bond was found disqualified on account of conduct not enumerated in the Georgia Constitution as a basis of disqualification. This was beyond the power of the House of Representatives. It runs counter to the express provisions of the Georgia Constitution giving to the people the right to elect their representatives, and limiting the Legislature in its right to reject such elected members to those grounds which are expressly in Georgia's basic document."

The Supreme Court, in its opinion by the Chief Justice, ordered Bond seated in the Georgia House of Representatives, finding, in addition to Chief Judge Tuttle's conclusion, that the action of the Georgia House violated the First Amendment. In the course of the opinion, the Chief Justice, for the Court, took the occasion to remind the nation that the fundamental constitutional mandate of the Founding Convention was that a legislature had no power to refuse to seat a representative who meets the constitutional qualifications.

* * *

The first day of committee hearings was February 8. All the members of the committee were present. Also in attendance were Mr. Powell and seven of his eight lawyers. After inserting in the record the materials previously received, the chairman received from the Powell lawyers a second brief amplifying the arguments they had previously submitted. Celler then announced that the committee would take official notice of the published hearings and report of the Hays subcommittee, and that the committee had decided to allow counsel for the representative-elect to be heard for legal argument. He stated in addition that Powell would be permitted to make a statement to the committee after his interrogation.

The chairman then recognized Mr. Carter, one of Powell's counsel, for oral argument.[6]

Mr. CARTER. It is our view that Mr. Powell has submitted with the motion his evidence, a certified copy of his evidence of the election from the 18th Congressional District of New York and his possession of all the qualifications that are set forth for membership in the House of Representatives, that are set out in article 1, section 2, clause 2, of the Constitution of the United States.

* * *

These, in our judgment, Mr. Chairman and members of the committee, are the sole and exclusive qualifications prescribed by the Constitution, and they control this inquiry and disposition of this case.

* * *

Mr. Carter then summarized the various arguments made in the briefs.

Chairman CELLER. The Committee will take under advisement your motion, and the arguments made thereunder.
Mr. KINOY. Mr. Chairman, I have a few important procedural and jurisdictional motions to make on behalf of the Member-elect. I ask the Chair's permission to make those motions since they go to the heart of the proceeding.
Chairman CELLER. It will be perfectly all right. Will you be very brief?

* * *

Mr. KINOY. Thank you, Mr. Chairman. On behalf of the Member-elect, we make the following motions: First, the Member-elect, Adam Clayton Powell, Jr., respectfully moves this committee to limit its inquiry pursuant to Article I, section 2, clause 2 of the Constitution of the United States to the three sole qualifications set forth therein for membership in the House. . . .
Chairman CELLER. The Chair indicated already it would take that motion under advisement. That is a repetition of what your colleague has indicated.

In the course of three more motions, Kinoy moved that the Select Committee terminate further proceedings and report that Powell be sworn as member of Congress because (1) the committee proceedings were null and void in that they were beyond the scope of inquiry constitutionally permissible, (2) the committee failed to give Powell reasonable notice of any charges against him, and (3) the committee failed to accord him any of the attributes of an adversary proceeding, as required by the Constitution. Finally, Kinoy moved that Powell be afforded:

> ... all of the rights and protections guaranteed by the Constitution of the United States and the rules and precedents to a Member-elect whose right to a seat in the House of Representatives is contested, including but not limited to the following: 1. Fair notice as to the charges now pending against him, including a statement of charges and a bill of particulars by any accuser. 2. The right to confront his accuser, and in particular attend in person and by counsel all sessions of this committee at which testimony or evidence is taken, and to participate therein with full rights of cross-examination. 3. The right fully in every respect to open and public hearings in every respect in the proceedings before the Select Committee. 4. The right to have this committee issue its process to summon witnesses whom he may use in his defense. 5. The right to a transcript of every hearing.

All the motions were taken under advisement. Chairman Celler then asked Mr. Powell to stand and take the oath prior to testifying.

> Mr. CONYERS. Mr. Chairman, are we going to act on the motions that have been made?
> Chairman CELLER. We will take them under advisement.
> Mr. REEVES. Mr. Chairman, may I be heard on the point that is being raised by Congressman Conyers? We are in the position as counsel for Congressman Powell. . . .
> Chairman CELLER. No. Mr. Powell will stand and be prepared to take the oath. Will you rise, please. . . .
> Mr. REEVES. Mr. Chairman, may I ask the question. . . .
> Chairman CELLER. I am sorry. Mr. Powell has been asked to take the oath. We have been very patient in listening to the dilatory motions. We will take them under advisement.
> Mr. REEVES. Mr. Chairman, I appeal to the Committee. . . .
> Chairman CELLER. The Chair will not recognize the gentleman. Mr. Powell, will you please rise?
> Mr. CONYERS. Mr. Chairman, as a member of this committee I must ask an inquiry in good faith. Are we to understand that

these motions that have been made, as to which disposition has been stayed, that we are now going to proceed to hear the Member-elect and then subsequently rule on motions which go to the heart of the procedure before us?

Chairman CELLER. Yes, sir. We are going to hear the testimony, and we will rule on the motions subsequently. That is not unusual. It has been done very frequently.

Mr. CONYERS. May I ask, Mr. Chairman, that the committee recess, at least briefly, on a personal point of this one member who has some serious concern that I would like to share with my distinguished chairman, if I may.

Chairman CELLER. I would like to accede to the gentleman's request. The gentleman must remember that we have a limited time within which we must act. It will not meet our problem to pass upon these motions. They in due course will be considered fully, naturally, and I say that, fully maturely, by this committee. Therefore I now ask Mr. Powell to rise and be prepared to take the oath.

A request by the Powell counsel for a recess was likewise denied. Powell declined to take the oath until the motions were ruled upon, but William Geoghegan, chief committee counsel, began questioning him anyway. After several routine questions, Powell was asked if he was pastor of the Abyssinian Baptist Church. At this point he declined to testify further. His lawyers indicated he would not do so until the motions received a favorable ruling. Consequently, Celler announced a 30-minute recess (which lasted about an hour), during which the committee met in executive session.

When the hearing reconvened, Chairman Celler announced that all the motions were denied. He qualified this, however, by stating:

This is not an adversary proceeding. The committee is going to make every effort that a fair hearing will be afforded, and prior to this date has decided to give the Member-elect rights beyond those afforded an ordinary witness under the House rules.

The committee has put the Member-elect on notice of the matters into which it will inquire by its notice of the scope of inquiry and its invitation to appear, as well as by conferences with, and a letter from its chief counsel to the counsel for the Member-elect.

Prior to this hearing the committee decided that it would allow the Member-elect the right to an open and public hearing, and the right to a transcript of every hearing at which testimony is adduced.

The committee has decided to summon any witnesses having substantial relevant testimony to the inquiry upon the written request of the Member-elect or his counsel.

The Member-elect certainly has the right to attend all hearings at which testimony is adduced and to have counsel present at those hearings.

Thus, with the important exception of the right to cross-examine witnesses giving testimony to the committee, the procedural guarantees sought by Powell's attorneys were granted.[7] It appears that while the committee did not give a bill of particulars, it did make a reasonable effort to give notice of the scope of the investigation in its letter to Powell of February 1 and its conference with Powell's lawyers two days later. Understandably the committee did not accede to the motion to limit inquiry to the three qualifications of Article I, Sec. 2, Cl. 2.

Powell's attorneys then announced they were willing to proceed under protest. The Representative-elect took the oath and testified in response to questions that he had been born in 1908 in New Haven, that he was a minister at the Abyssinian Baptist Church, and that he paid New York taxes. He also stated that he had last been in New York in November 1966, but could not remember if he had spent the night there. He further testified that during 1966 he had frequently been in New York on Sundays and occasionally on Mondays, but he could not recall any specific date on which he spent the night in his apartment. On the advice of counsel, he declined to name other places where he had spent his time during the previous two years. He likewise declined to testify concerning the New York arrest orders, whether he intended to return to New York while they were pending, and in regard to the matters raised by the Hays report, as well as sundry other questions. Faced with this impasse, Chairman Celler advised him:

> Now in the light of your refusal to testify to these questions, the committee has no alternative but to draw whatever inferences reasonably flow from this public record.
> Without the benefit of your testimony the Committee will have to draw upon other sources for information it deems relevant, competent, and material to the enumerated issues under investigation.
> Under these circumstances, Mr. Powell, I urge you, as chairman, and personally, to reconsider your refusal. We will be glad to declare a short recess, should you wish to consult your advisers on this score.

But the counsel for Powell persisted in their objections that the committee could not ask questions not related to age, citizenship, and inhabitancy. The counsel did submit a large quantity of additional documentation, including all the items submitted earlier as well as a statement from the Chase Manhattan Bank, Powell's New York voter registration cards, a telegram from the commissioner of the New York City Board of Elections, Powell's New York driver's license, the *Congressional Directory* of the 89th Congress, 2nd Session, the Congressional pictorial directory for 1967, 43 checks with which Powell paid his apartment rent and utility bills in New York, and Powell's application for an absentee ballot in 1966.

Following the submission of the documents, the chairman recognized Mrs. Cahn.

> Mrs. CAHN. Mr. Chairman, before you close these proceedings, it is my understanding from the letter that Mr. Geoghegan read, and my conferences with him, that Mr. Powell would have the chance to make a statement at the end of his testimony. We request at this time that he be given the opportunity to make that statement.

Chairman CELLER. That he will not be permitted to do now. I made this statement:

> The committee wishes to inform Representative-elect that he will be afforded the opportunity to make a statement to the Committee at the close of his interrogation on all matters contained in the letter of invitation to him to testify.

I would suggest that you bide your time and renew your application subsequently.

Mr. REEVES. Do I understand, Mr. Chairman, that you are withdrawing the privilege to make the statement at the close of his interrogation?

Chairman CELLER. I didn't withdraw. I said I suggest the application be made subsequently. The request to make the statement now is denied.

With that the hearing adjourned. While it had been meeting, the House had approved by a voice vote, with no real debate, a budget of not more than $25,000 for the committee.

Also on February 8, the House Republican Policy Committee urged that the House establish a 12-member bipartisan committee to govern ethics in the House. And a step was actually taken in this direction when the House Administration Committee announced at the opening of the day's floor session that it was expanding its three-man subcommittee on contracts to seven members and empowering it to oversee the ethics of representatives under the name of the Subcommittee on Ethics and Contracts.

The day after the committee's first hearings, it was reported that Powell's lawyers were already preparing his case for appeal to the Supreme Court. Such reports were to persist throughout the month. Another important announcement was made on February 12. Whitney Young announced that the Negro summit council had been called off because many people did not wish to participate in such a conference while the Select Committee was deliberating.

On February 10 Chief Counsel Geoghegan sent Powell a letter informing him of a second hearing to be held February 14. He reminded him that he could request the summoning of witnesses and invited him to testify at the coming hearing. He further stated that Powell would be permitted to make a statement at that time. Geoghegan also asked if Powell would refuse to give any testimony about his legal troubles and his alleged official misconduct in reference to, first, the seating phase of the committee's inquiry and, second, the phase dealing with possible punishment or expulsion. Geoghegan also sent a copy of the letter to Mrs. Cahn and advised her that the committee had subpoenaed Corinne Huff and Mrs. Powell.

On February 11, the new House Education and Labor Committee chairman, Carl D. Perkins of Kentucky, announced a reorganization of the committee staff. Twelve Powell aides (six of them Negroes) were not rehired, among them special assistant to the chairman C. Sumner Stone. Nine of those fired appealed to the committee majority, on the grounds that they had been given insufficient notice, but they succeeded only in having their pay extended through February 15, despite criticism of their firing by the NAACP. The committee members defended the reorganization as a move to boost the efficiency of the staff. One committee member said of the ex-Powell aides, "I never saw some of those people."

The most ambitious effort in Powell's behalf up to that time, a 24-hour general strike centered in Detroit, took place on February 13. The effort was endorsed by the Detroit CORE chapter and the city NAACP president, but was opposed by other NAACP officials and Negro labor leaders. There was some disagreement on the success of the effort. Schools and businesses reported that class and job attendance was normal, but the strike leaders claimed the protest was a success.

The committee met again for hearings on February 14 as planned, but the representative-elect was not present.[8] The seven lawyers who had attended the previous hearing were present, and they indicated that Powell did "not plan to attend the hearing in its present posture." Mr. Carter also read a statement in reply to the Geoghegan letter of Febraury 10. He stated:

* * *

The short of our position is that H. R. No. 1 authorizes inquiry solely and exclusively into Congressman Powell's qualifications for membership in the House. If we are in error in that regard, then we take the flat position that the House could not, pursuant to H.R. No. 1, or indeed pursuant to any resolution, authorize any committee to make the kind of simultaneous inquiry which this committee proposes to undertake. Before the power to punish a "member," pursuant to Article I, Section 5, Clause 2 can be invoked, the determination of membership must have been concluded on the basis of qualifications for membership as set forth in Article I, Section 2, Clause 2 of the Constitution.

* * *

Accordingly, we are of the opinion that any questions except those relevant to the constitutional qualifications of Member-Elect Powell are outside the jurisdiction of this committee, and we have so advised the Member-Elect.

Moreover, it is our considered opinion that this Select Committee cannot legally and constitutionally pursue these two objectives simultaneously.

Powell's lawyers subsequently submitted a full brief in support of this statement. In addition to covering the arguments developed in earlier briefs, it emphasized precedents in which the member under investigation was accorded various rights of an adversary hearing.[9] It was not altogether clear why Powell did not appear at the February 14 hearing, particularly since he had sought, unsuccessfully, to make a statement at the previous hearing and the committee had indicated that he would be allowed to make a statement at the second hearing. One suggestion offered later was that Powell decided not to testify after the committee ruled that he did not have the right to cross-examine.[10] Another was the reason noted in the above statement, which was to be the repeated argument of Powell's attorneys that any inquiry into matters beyond the constitutional qualifications was outside the jurisdiction of the committee.

The committee then called as a witness one of their assistant counsel, Ronald Goldfarb, who had been assigned to untangle and report on Powell's legal problems in New York and Puerto Rico. He recited the status of the various actions and introduced into the record numerous court orders and opinions. It is indicative of the tangled nature of the numerous motions and countermotions that in several instances learned counsel had to admit his uncertainty on details, conceding once that he was "somewhat baffled."

The next witness was Dean Franklin, owner and pilot of Chalk Airlines, a small firm which provided air service between Miami and Bimini. Mr. Franklin produced various passenger lists containing the names of Powell and certain committee staff members, which were received into the record. He also indicated that Chalk Airlines had carried to Bimini various items of freight for Powell's yacht. Some of the bills for this service were sent to Powell himself, the rest to a company called Huff Enterprises, Ltd., at 2161 Rayburn Bldg., Washington (Powell's congressional office). Mr. Franklin testified that the bills were all paid by Huff Enterprises.

Next the committee called Robert D. Gray, a General Accounting Office auditor who had supervised the accounting work of the Hays committee and was doing the same for the Select Committee. He testified regarding the analysis under way by the auditing staff of air travel from Washington to Miami and Miami to Bimini.

The final witness to appear was Dennis Ford, submanager of the Barclays Bank establishment in New York. He had been subpoenaed in the hope of obtaining data on the operations of Huff Enterprises, Ltd., in the Bahamas, where Barclays also maintained branches. However, the bank's lawyer had advised that the committee had no power to subpoena records in the Bahamas; thus Mr. Ford brought no records. This course of action earned him a stern rebuke from the committee and imperative directions to produce the records desired. (There is, however, no indication in the committee publications that this was ever done.)

Chairman Celler then called as a witness Corinne Huff, but she was not present. Mr. Geoghegan announced that a subpoena had been delivered to her in the Bahamas on February 11, and with that the hearing adjourned.

After the hearing, Chairman Celler was asked about the apparent intention of the Powell lawyers to challenge the Select Committee procedure in court. Said Mr. Celler:

> That raises a very, very interesting question. The separation of powers might prohibit that. If the Supreme Court ever attempted to override the House in the language of the late Justice Felix Frankfurter, it should be entering a political thicket. Which view would prevail? Have they got more soldiers than we have?[11]

The Select Committee held its final hearings two days later, on February 16, 1967. Neither Powell nor any of his lawyers attended.[12]

The first witness was Mrs. Adam Clayton Powell, née Yvette Marjorie Flores. One of Mrs. Powell's counsel was Joseph Rauh, Jr., of the ADA; he had supported Powell early in his difficulties with Congress. She testified that she had been on Powell's congressional payroll for two years prior to their marriage in 1960, but that she had lived in Puerto Rico since 1961. She had, however, remained on Powell's clerk-hire payroll until December 1966. Originally, she stated, she had kept busy translating correspondence, but the amount of work sent her from Washington gradually dwindled to nothing by the summer of 1965. She had last seen and spoken with Mr. Powell in September 1965, but prior to that time had insisted he bring her back to Washington to work. The then-chairman had always refused.

Mrs. Powell's most startling revelation however was that since shortly after her marriage she had received only two monthly salary checks, those for November and December of

1966 which, in accordance with directions she had sent to the Clerk of the House, were sent to her in Puerto Rico. The checks issued by the Treasury for January 1965 through July 1966, which were introduced into the record, were all signed "Y. Marjorie Flores, Adam Clayton Powell." Mrs. Powell said the handwriting did "look familiar" to her. Most of the checks had been marked "For deposit only to the account of Hon. Adam C. Powell," and all had been deposited in the House Sergeant-at-Arms Bank, where Powell maintained an account. The checks ranged in amounts from $1,295.29 to $1,488.00. Mrs. Powell's salary as secretary to Representative Powell had been $20,578 a year prior to her removal from the payroll in early January 1967, following the Hays committee report. Mrs. Powell estimated that in 1965 and 1966 she had received support for herself and her son from Mr. Powell totaling about $8,700, mostly in large checks drawn on Powell's account with the Sergeant-at-Arms Bank. Mrs. Powell was then excused.

Chairman Celler then read into the record a letter from Adam Clayton Powell on official Committee on Education and Labor stationary. The letter, addressed "Dear Friend," was an advertisement for Powell's record, "Keep the Faith Baby!" Celler did not indicate how he had obtained the letter.

The final witness to be called was C. Sumner Stone. He testified about an official trip he had made to Bimini to consult with Powell on committee business and amplified on testimony he had given to the Hays subcommittee. The committee also made an effort to clear up some of the mystery surrounding the enigmatic Huff Enterprises. Stone testified that he was an incorporator of that company and owned one of the 17 outstanding shares. Congressman Moore informed Stone, to his surprise, that according to records the committee had found, Stone was not only not an incorporator but also owned five of the 17 shares. Further questioning revealed that Stone, who for a time had been vice-president of the company, knew nothing about Huff Enterprises' plans, activities, or assets, if any.

When Stone had completed his testimony, the hearing ended. The committee subsequently received for the record the final brief of Powell's lawyers and reports from the chief clerk of the Committee on House Administration and the assistant secretary of state dealing with foreign currency advanced to Powell for official foreign travel. The committee then began its deliberations.

The next day saw two new developments in Powell's New York court battle. His attorney paid $4,447 to Mrs. James, thereby satisfying the original libel judgment. This also vacated the original civil contempt order of May 8, 1964. On the same day, Justice Emilo Nunez denied a motion by Mrs. James to cite Powell for contempt of court a fifth and sixth time. The Justice called Powell a "lawless lawmaker," but said that to grant the motions would only provide Powell "with a new base for procedural and appellate maneuvers, delaying tactics, and to once again show his contempt for law and the courts. . . ."[13]

Powell also picked up additional declarations of support while the Select Committee deliberated. Both a high official of the National Council of Churches and the Presbytery of the New York Presbyterian Churches charged that Powell had been denied his constitutional rights.[14] And on February 22, James Meredith, civil rights hero, and 28 other Negro law students at Columbia University charged that racism had played a "key role" in Powell's treatment.

After the hearings, the committee members settled down to the difficult job of evaluating the evidence, briefs, and precedents. Gradually they came to the conclusion that they would have to recommend the seating of the representative-elect. As Rep. MacGregor put it, "The more we studied, the more we realized Powell should be seated."[15] The members also agreed that Powell merited some sort of punishment. The question of what punishment, however, threatened to divide the committee irreconcilably, a result not even the most adamant members wanted.

Conyers felt that a stiff censure would be sufficient, while Celler and Corman favored a harsher punishment. They were uncertain, however, about the proposal to dock Powell's pay. The Republicans on the committee urged still stiffer punishment. Most difficult of all to accommodate was the position taken by Representative Pepper. He was insistent that Powell should in some way be removed from Congress, but still was convinced that he had a right to be seated. Consequently he moved that Powell be seated and then expelled. When this was rejected, he urged (somewhat inconsistently) that Powell be excluded. This too was rejected. Pepper also joined with Conyers in opposing any form of punishment between the opposite positions the two held. This impasse persisted until February 22, with the deadline for submitting the report the next day.

Finally, the "moderates" agreed on a set of punishment provisions. Only Conyers and Pepper had to be won over. Conyers agreed after the addition of his special views, and finally Pepper was won over by a similar tactic.

The report, duly submitted on February 23, began by recounting the history of the controversy and the Select Committee.[16] The report then reviewed the facts relating to Powell's inhabitancy and concluded, "On the basis of these facts and under the applicable precedents . . . Mr. Powell meets the inhabitancy qualification of the Constitution."

The report then turned to a review of Powell's behavior. His relations with the New York courts were considered first and the conclusion was reached that his behavior ". . . clearly brings great disrespect on the House of Representatives." Next to be considered were Powell's actions as committee chairman. The report reviewed the evidence and conclusions of the Hays subcommittee and then made the following summary of the committee's own findings:

By analysis of immigration records and records of certain air taxi operators, this Committee has been able to establish that many airline flights to and from Miami by Mr. Powell, Miss Huff, and staff members, which flights were charged to the Education and Labor Committee, were in fact destined for or originated at Bimini in the Bahamas, and therefore, did not, in all likelihood, involve official committee business.

* * *

In view of the unusual volume of Miami travel the Committee made a detailed analysis of flights to and from Miami. Although this analysis was necessarily incomplete, it showed (a) that a substantial number of these flights were destined for or originated at Bimini; (b) that on a substantial number of the flights Mr. Powell or other committee staff members traveled under assumed names; and (c) that in several instances tickets paid for by the Education and Labor Committee clearly were used by a person not on the committee's staff and having no apparent connection with its official business.

* * *

In addition, the Select Committee ascertained from the Department of State that, as chairman . . . Mr. Powell received from the State Department in 1961, 1962, 1963, and 1964 reports as to the amount of expenditures of foreign exchange currency in U. S. funds he made while abroad during these years. . . . Mr. Powell filed with the Committee on House Administration reports listing substantially lower sums for these expenditures. . . .

The committee report then considered Powell's behavior as a member of the House. It stated:

The Committee concludes from the foregoing evidence that Mrs. Powell has not performed any official duties whatever since at least the summer of 1965 and has not performed any official duties in Washington or New York since 1961. Accordingly, Mr. Powell has improperly maintained Mrs. Powell on his clerk-hire payroll from August 14, 1964, when House Resolution 294 was adopted until December 1966, resulting in improper payments in the amount of $44,188.61.[17]

* * *

We conclude that Mr. Powell has not only failed to assist this Committee and the Hays subcommittee in their inquiries but also that he has, in his own words to the Hays subcommittee, "militantly fought" the efforts of both committees to ascertain the true facts concerning the charges against him.

The report then summarized the conclusions about the power to impose punishments that the committee had formed from the study of the precedents:

> The power of the House of Representatives upon majority vote to censure and to impose punishments other than expulsion is full and plenary and may be enforced by summary proceedings. This discretionary power to punish for disorderly behavior is vested by the Constitution in the House of Representatives, and its exercise is appropriate where a member has been guilty of misconduct relating to his official duties, noncooperation with committees of this House, or nonofficial acts of a kind likely to bring this House into disrepute.
>
> This Select Committee is of the opinion that the broad power of the House to censure and punish Members short of expulsion extends to acts occurring during a prior Congress. Whether such powers should be invoked in such circumstances is a matter committed to the absolute discretion and sole judgment of the House. . . .
>
> * * *
>
> Cases may readily be postulated where the action of a House in excluding or expelling a Member may directly impinge upon rights under other provisions of the Constitution. In such cases, the unavailability of judicial review may be less certain. Suppose, for example, that a Member was excluded or expelled because of his religion or race, contrary to the equal protection clause, or for making an unpopular speech protected by the first amendment. . . . The instant case, of course, does not involve such facts. But exclusion of the Member-elect on grounds other than age, citizenship, or inhabitancy could raise an equally serious constitutional issue. The Supreme Court has stated in *Baker* v. *Carr*, supra (369 U. S. at 211):
>
>> Deciding whether a matter has in any measure been committed by the Constitution to another branch of Government, or whether the action of that branch exceeds whatever authority

has been committed, is itself a delicate exercise in constitutional interpretation, and is a responsibility of this Court as ultimate interpreter of the Constitution.

The Committee believes however, that, in view of Mr. Powell's breach of the privileges of the House and of the trust reposed in him by the House, action by the House punishing the Member-elect by censure and fine after he is seated, is immune to judicial review.

Upon the basis of the facts reviewed and the committee's interpretation of the power to judge qualifications, the committee recommended that Powell be sworn in as a member of the 90th Congress. As punishment he was to be publicly censured, fined, and divested of his 22-year seniority. The report noted that Rep. Conyers believed Powell should not be punished beyond severe censure and that Rep. Pepper felt that Powell should not be a member of the House. The "whereas" clauses preceding the resolution took notice of the following: Powell possessed the three requisite qualifications for membership; his repeated "contumacious conduct" toward the courts in the State of New York had caused him to be judged in contempt of court; he had improperly maintained Mrs. Powell on his clerk-hire payroll; as committee chairman he had permitted improper expenditures of government funds for private purposes; and his refusal to cooperate with the Celler and Hays committees was "contemptuous" and "conduct unworthy of a Member." The resolution was worded as follows:

Now, therefore, be it resolved,

1. That the Speaker administer the oath of office to the said Adam Clayton Powell, Member-elect from the 18th district of the State of New York.

2. That upon taking the oath as a Member of the 90th Congress the said Adam Clayton Powell be brought to the bar of the House in the custody of the Sergeant-at-Arms of the House and be there publicly censured by the Speaker in the name of the House.

3. That Adam Clayton Powell, as punishment, pay to the Clerk

of the House to be disposed of by him according to law, $40,000. The Sergeant-at-Arms of the House is directed to deduct $1,000 per month from the salary otherwise due the said Adam Clayton Powell and pay the same to said Clerk, said deductions to continue while any salary is due the said Adam Clayton Powell as a Member of the House of Representatives until said $40,000 is fully paid. Said sums received by the Clerk shall offset to the extent thereof any liability of the said Adam Clayton Powell to the United States of America with respect to the matters referred to in the above paragraphs 3 and 4 of the preamble to this resolution.

4. That the seniority of the said Adam Clayton Powell in the House of Representatives commence as of the date he takes the oath as a Member of the 90th Congress.

5. That if the said Adam Clayton Powell does not present himself to take the oath of office on or before March 13, 1967, the seat of the 18th District of the State of New York shall be deemed vacant and the Speaker shall notify the Governor of the State of New York of the existing vacancy.[18]

Only Rep. Conyers filed additional views:

1. The question of the right of a Member-elect to be administered the oath and the responsibility of the House to punish its Members should be distinguished with great precision.

2. Any Member or Member-elect and his counsel should be afforded the right to cross-examine all witnesses brought before this committee or any other committee inquiring into the qualifications, punishment, final right of a Member to be seated, or other related questions.

3. In his appearance before this Select Committee, his declination to accept the invitation extended by the Hays subcommittee, and his conduct with reference to the litigation in the New York courts, Adam Clayton Powell, Member-elect, acted at all times upon advice of counsel. Therefore, it cannot accurately be held that his conduct impugned the dignity of Congress or was in disrespect of Congress.

4. A review of all cases of alleged misconduct brought before the House and Senate indicates that punishment has never exceeded censure. There is no precedent for the removal of accumulated seniority combined with a monetary assessment, as is proposed in the instant case.

Thus, the committee had concluded that while exclusion on grounds other than age, citizenship, or inhabitancy could raise a serious constitutional issue, punishment after the member-elect was seated was constitutionally permissible. And, it said, the facts of this case warranted punishment short of expulsion.

The report was not received kindly by the Negro community. A. Philip Randolph released a statement to the press on February 25 in which he characterized the recommendations as "outrageously and incredibly reprehensible and abominable for any free people to be afflicted with." Two days later Randolph and Cleveland Robinson, national president of the Negro American Labor Council, urged Powell not to take his seat on the terms proposed by the committee.

The immediate House reaction to the report and recommendations seemed to be generally favorable. The Democratic Study Group, the main liberal bloc in the House, announced it would provide no organized opposition. And some pro-exclusionists reasoned that Powell would resign or never take the oath, rather than accept censure. Thus adoption of the recommendations would cover the House so far as the Constitution was concerned and still get rid of Powell. All in all, leaders of both parties reasoned that there were enough votes to assure passage of the resolution. So confident (or as others suggested later, so out-of-touch) were they that they did not take a preliminary head count on the issue.

The filing of the report was followed by other efforts on the subject of ethics. At a meeting in Detroit, Conyers announced he would consult with the speaker of the House about disciplining other "errant" members of Congress. This, he said, would end charges that Powell's treatment was a result of racial bias. At a news conference on February 23, Rep. Pepper declared that if there had been a House committee on ethics or standards, "this able man [Powell] could have been saved from this tragedy and humiliation." And on the 27th, 43 GOP freshman congressmen signed a statement calling on Congress to establish immediately rules governing ethical conduct of members. This statement was accompanied by the introduction of numerous bills to establish a Committee on Standards and Conduct.

Through this whole period the cause of all the furor was strangely quiet. Powell called a news conference on Bimini on February 24, then canceled it on the advice of his lawyers. Henry Williams, one of Powell's lawyers, later quoted Powell as saying that his wife's testimony before the Select Committee was not true and that he had paid for her support. Williams said a letter from Mrs. Powell's lawyers proving the support payments were made was in Powell's Washington office.

On the 25th Powell told a crowd in Bimini that if he lost his congressional seat, he would run again and win. Powell must have been expecting the worst. He boasted to friends and reporters, "Even if I'm dead—as long as they keep me propped up—I will be elected." Powell made no further statements. His lawyers, fearing his quick tongue would cause further deterioration of their situation, advised him to be quiet for a while.

6 Therefore, Be It Resolved

March 1, 1967, was designated as the day on which the House would consider H. Res. 278. The resolution would be debated under the same sort of rule that was used on January 10, with Celler in control of the time. Thus, opponents of the measure would have to seek to defeat the previous question, as had been done on January 10.

Opponents of the measure were of two types. By far the less common and less organized were those who believed, on constitutional or political grounds, that the Select Committee's recommendations were too harsh. Rep. Conyers emerged unexpectedly as the spokesman of this group when he announced his intention to vote against the previous question. This announcement precipitated a brief quarrel with Moore, who claimed Conyers had reneged on a firm commitment to the Select Committee to support the previous question. Conyers replied that he regarded his proposed move as justified by the additional views he had filed with the committee report.

The second type of opposition came from those who felt the committee recommendations were inadequate or too lenient. Van Deerlin, Stratton (D-N. Y.), Gibbons, Long (D-Md.), and others of this group met on February 28 to consolidate the effort to exclude Powell.

The same day several of the group spoke on the floor. Their remarks made clear that their opposition to the seating of Powell centered on four main points. First, they interpreted the mood of the public as calling for the reestablishment of morality in government. The exclusion of Powell, they contended, would be a proper step in this direction. Second, they condemned the Select Committee's report and resolution as poorly conceived and drafted, noting some minor inconsistencies in wording. The proposed $40,000 fine was subjected to special criticism. Questions were raised as to its legality, and demands were made that the full amount misappropriated be recovered. Third, they regarded the determination of the Select Committee on the power to judge qualifications as totally untenable, and argued that to accept it would at once abdicate the constitutional powers and shirk the constitutional duty of the House. Finally, criticism was levied at the Select Committee for its failure to deal more fully with Powell's contempt citations, which some held raised questions as to his inhabitancy.

Thus, when the House met at noon the next day, it was obvious that the Select Committee's recommendations would not be accepted without a stiff fight and without efforts at amendment. Still, it was believed that H. Res. 278 would pass. The leadership of both parties endorsed the committee report, and it was known to have the support of many Democrats. Republicans, who had been told by their leadership to vote according to conscience, were believed to be about evenly divided between adoption of the report and exclusion, with no support for Conyer's position.

After disposing of a few minor matters, the House took up debate of H. Res. 278. By unanimous consent, an additional hour was yielded to Celler, who acted as manager of the resolution. He yielded half of the two hours to Moore, the ranking Republican on the Select Committee, with the proviso that it was to be used for debate only. Thus left in complete control of the offering of amendments and the moving of the previous question, Celler began his opening statement.[1]

Mr. Speaker, the nine men appointed by the Speaker of the House were weighted with the heaviest responsibility that can be placed on any group—to sit in judgment on their fellow man. . . .

* * *

There are those who believe we acted too leniently, others that we acted "to annihilate by humiliation," as one man put it. Some say in words of common parlance, "kick him out."

Mr. Speaker, to them I say read the precedents. Expulsion is the most drastic action. It had been rarely availed of, and then only during the Civil War for treason, the treason being spelled out of Members joining and fighting on the side of the Confederacy against the Union. Except for three instances of treason, resolutions of expulsion either failed to receive the necessary two-thirds vote, or lost, and a resolution of censure was substituted and approved.

Mr. Powell's wrongdoing does not rise to the heights of malevolence such as treason. Remember he was reelected by his constituents after and despite well-advertised shortcomings. That was an important factor in our deliberations. However, it was not controlling, because the House of Representatives can also pass judgment on conduct which is injurious to its processes, its dignity, and its official committees. Yet we could not permit his dalliance and defaults to go unwhipped without suitable sanctions and discipline. We had to face up to the necessity of meaningful punishment.

The penalties imposed satisfy a stern sense of justice.

You will note that we went beyond censure. Never before has a committee devised such punishment short of expulsion which went beyond censure. . . .

Exclusion or expulsion seemed deceptively simple. Yet neither could bring into play the punishments herein devised, keeping as well the recommendations of this committee within the boundaries of the Constitution and the precedents. Some may demand exclusion—ouster at the threshold by majority vote. The Constitution lays down three qualifications for one to enter Congress—age, inhabitancy, citizenship. Mr. Powell satisfies all three. The House cannot add to these qualifications. If so it could add, for example, a religious test or conceivably deny seats to a minority by mere majority vote.

85

Madison and Hamilton were aware of the danger of permitting the House to regulate qualifications. They therefore said the Constitution unalterably fixes and defines qualifications. Madison said that to allow the Congress such power would be improper and dangerous.

There is the charge of racism, which has been heard. That is as baseless as it is cruel. Baseless because we have within recent memory condemned and punished white Members. Cruel because it gives a false impression to the Negro, especially to the lowly Negro, that the black man is singled out for penalties. This is a canard that arouses hostile emotions and results in acts that only add fuel to the backlash.

* * *

Mr. MOORE (R-W. Va.). There is an abundance of beginning in the field of ethics in this report.

If Members lay it aside and torture their consciences that we have not done enough to punish the Member-elect from the State of New York, I would only take a moment to say that in their desire to mete out the maximum punishment, . . . if they desire to approach the problem of expulsion or exclusion, they could very well be on a collision course with courts of this land. Some would care not to have such a circumstance present itself.

* * *

It is my fond hope, Mr. Speaker, that the Members of this House will fully understand that truly this resolution is the annihilation of a Member of this House by total humiliation. In the event of its adoption the only thing that a Member-elect from the State of New York will have in this House is a key to an appropriate suite in some one of the several office buildings and that beyond that it will be up to him to regain the faith of the membership here.

* * *

Mr. LONG (D-Md.). Mr. Speaker, I urge my colleagues to vote down the previous question, so that I may be recognized later to offer an amendment to exclude Mr. Powell from the House of Representatives before he is sworn in.

* * *

If we have the moral obligation to exclude Mr. Powell, do we have the constitutional right?

The Constitution says that "No person shall be a Representative who shall not have attained the age of 25 years and been seven years a citizen of the United States, and who shall not, when elected, be an inhabitant of the State in which he shall be chosen."

In the language of mathematics, these are necessary but not sufficient conditions. They say a man must meet these conditions to be seated, but they do not say that he must be seated if he does meet them.

In four major cases, the House of Representatives did in fact decide that it could exclude a Member-elect for reasons other than the constitutionally-cited limitations.

No court has ever considered or reversed any of these decisions of the House.

Two strong doctrines, in fact, militate against such court consideration.

First is the doctrine of separation of powers; the Constitution provides that each House shall be the judge of the elections, returns and qualifications of its Members.

Second is the political questions doctrine. The courts will not handle questions inherently in the power of other coordinate branches at the same level of Government.

Mr. Powell's conduct as stated in the resolution has disqualified him for membership in the House of Representatives, and this Chamber has both the duty and the constitutional right to exclude him from taking a seat.

* * *

Mr. WATSON (R-S. C.). Mr. Speaker, much has been said here about "annihilation by humiliation." We cannot believe Powell can be humiliated. Is there a humiliating bone in the body of the man under discussion? Has he displayed any repentance or given any indication that he is regretful? Why, even at this moment, Mr. Speaker, as we are debating this agonizing and difficult issue, where all of us are on the spot, where is Adam Clayton Powell? As far as I know he is down in Bimini with a glass in one hand and a woman in the other. Can you think a man so calloused to his fate today [can] be humiliated? Certainly none could logically contend that.

The Members know what the courts of New York said about this man being repentant in the position he is in there. There is no indication of regret, and there is no trace of repentance or retribution on his part. Can we believe that we can humiliate him by bringing him down into this House and letting him receive a censure? To you and to me it would be important, but to him, he has already thumbed his nose at this House and told us we are a bunch of hypocrites. He has said, in effect, "I care nothing what you think about the situation. I am above the law. I am above the Congress."

* * *

Mr. STRATTON (D-N.Y.). There is still one important point which the select committee has failed to examine carefully, and that is the continued defiance of the gentleman from New York [Mr. Powell] in choosing to disregard the orders of the courts of New York State. In fact, this was the real issue that first brought his case before this body.

Mr. Speaker, let us not forget that his defiance of the courts was based upon his membership in this House. As a part of his defiance he has deliberately and intentionally for some months removed himself physically from the State of New York, so that he would not have to conform with the rulings and decrees of its courts. By thus removing himself, I believe, a very grave cloud has been raised over the question of his inhabitancy, one of the basic constitutional qualifications for membership in this House.

Now we are told that we should not act on this matter of inhabitancy because the nine men on the Supreme Court might make a different decision on it, and we are also told that perhaps the courts of New York State might make a different decision on inhabitancy. But, Mr. Speaker, the Constitution of the United States says clearly that we in this House shall be the judge of inhabitancy, and I believe that we have a responsibility to insist that until the gentleman from New York has removed this cloud over the matter of his inhabitancy, and has demonstrated that he can go back into the State and district which he seeks to represent—and he can go back only by purging himself of contempt of court in New York—we ought not to seat him in this House.

* * *

Mr. TEAGUE (R-Cal.). Mr. Speaker, several Members on both sides of the aisle have told me within the last few days that they are satisfied that the recommendations of the select committee are sound and should be adopted but they are afraid that they could not vote to do so. They said that their mail was 100 to 1 to "throw the rascal out" and that under this kind of pressure, it would be most difficult for them to vote to seat Adam Clayton Powell even with the severe punishment we have suggested.

Mr. CORMAN (D-Cal.). I urge each Member to consider carefully the words [of the Constitution] that control this case. The Constitution says that we are the sole judges of the qualifications of our Members, but the document specifies what these qualifications must be. They are age, citizenship, and inhabitancy. The word qualification was not haphazardly selected by the Founding Fathers. They did not mean fitness or acceptability, and we are not recommending that Adam Clayton Powell is found to be either of those two things. We do say that he is qualified to be Member of this House as that word "qualified" is given meaning by the Constitution. For those who question whether the House could survive under such strict interpretation, I would suggest to you that it has nicely for nearly 200 years, because the Founding Fathers and all of those who have lived under this Constitution since that time have accepted the fact that the people themselves are capable of self-government. They are capable of making the decision as to who is fit to be their Congressman. . . . our system is safe and secure because there is no appellate authority above the decision of the people themselves. The men who wrote the Constitution thought the system would work, history has proven that it does work, and we today have an opportunity for a vote of confidence of that system—a vote which regretably, must take place on a complex and unpleasant set of circumstances.

* * *

Mr. CURTIS (R-Mo.). It sounds very strange to me to hear from certain people who have long recognized the various implied powers that exist in the Constitution—and I am among those who do recognize implied powers—words that indicate that all of a sudden they are forgetting all about this theory and are moving toward strict constitutional construction.

Let me suggest that when the Constitution provided that the Congress had the right to expel, it certainly implied that it has the right to exclude. In fact, look at the fiction that is gone through by some who would seat Mr. Powell and then move to expel him almost immediately or to have him continue to step aside. The implication that the power to exclude exists in the power to expel is quite obvious.

I would add one caveat: The power to expel requires a two-thirds vote and therefore, any power that comes as an implication therefrom would also require a two-thirds vote. Indeed I think that this is proper.

Let me go on to try to lay at rest the arguments that if you will then open up the area of qualifications, you will then get into such things as religion and political beliefs and so forth. This is a red herring, because, of course, there are other sections of the Constitution that would forbid any such qualifications based on this, but we are not talking about this in this case.

* * *

Conyers was the next to speak. He began by declaring his conviction that the Select Committee had carried out its task without racial or partisan bias. Pepper he singled out for special praise. He then explained that all members of the committee had signed the report to emphasize their common agreement on the constitutional mandate that Powell be seated. Conyers went on to explain why he could not accept the committee's recommendations:

> The committee report, in its findings of fact and law, erroneously, I feel, found Member-elect Powell guilty of contumacious and contemptuous behavior in his conduct with reference to the litigation in the New York courts. In his refusal to accept the invitation extended by the Hays subcommittee and in his appearance before the Select Committee [at] all times he was acting on the advice of counsel, and very distinguished counsel at that. In fact, Mr. Powell was acting in accordance with precedents set by the last Member-elect whose right to be sworn in was challenged and referred to a special committee. Certainly, Mr. Powell's conduct in strictly following the precedents and legal counsel cannot be judged as contemptuous by this law-making and precedent-following body. It certainly should not be used as one of the bases for imposing severe punishment upon him. In fact, using against Mr. Powell his refusal to testify in a case brought against him, where he was advised by counsel that such testimony was not legally required, is clearly flying in the face of the fifth amendment guarantee that no man shall be required to testify against himself.

* * *

Though prior committees judging the right of a Member-elect to be sworn allowed the Member-elect to cross-examine witnesses against him, our committee, over my strong objections, unfortunately denied this usual right to the Member-elect. It was only after the Member-elect's procedural motions to gain something like a normal judicial procedure were overruled by majority vote of the committee that he decided not to testify beyond what he felt were the clear constitutional questions of his qualifications. All the other evidence against him by various witnesses was relied on without ever giving him a chance to cross-examine.

When we deny any Member, or Member-elect, the full right to cross-examine any and all witnesses, to be allowed the provisions of due process that are guaranteed in the Bill of Rights and in the 14th amendment to the Constitution—and I surely do not believe that was meant to exclude Members of Congress—I believe everybody has the right not to be deprived of life, liberty or property without due process of law.

* * *

There are no extraordinary circumstances in this case which require unusual punishment. Let me review what I consider to be the two relevant sets of precedents.

First. Five cases of censure in history of Congress involving monetary offenses. Censure has been imposed only five times in the history of the Congress for financial misconduct. Two of the Members were censured for offering bribes to influence other Members' votes on legislation. The three other Members had accepted bribes in return for making appointments to the military academies. In none of the five cases was punishment imposed beyond that of censure. In the entire history of the House no punishment beyond censure or expulsion has ever been imposed on a Member for any type of offense, financial or otherwise.

Second. Examples of financial misconduct by Members regarding misuse of funds in their capacities as Congressmen which were never punished nor even recognized by the House. No motion of censure regarding financial matters has been carried since 1873. No motion of censure, whatever the offense, has been passed or even offered since 1921. But I regretfully must point out that this is not because Members of Congress have not been found to be guilty of financial irregularities directly connected with their roles as Congressmen.

* * *

But there is something else about Adam Powell, the symbol of Negro America, a personal hero of mine, that makes this a tragedy that I cannot do other than make sure every Member on this floor is perfectly cognizant of before we, hopefully, vote for the previous question here today. The Congressman Adam Clayton Powell is a false caricature of the Powell to whom the churches, the synagogues, the labour unions and educational institutions— not just black Americans but all Americans—owe an unparallelled debt for the unexcelled legislation that has been passed in the House of Representatives under his leadership as the Chairman of the Committee on Education and Labor.

* * *

As Conyers indicated at the close of his speech, he had dropped his plan to oppose the previous question. No reason was given for this, but in all likelihood Conyers was alarmed by the strength of the pro-exclusionists who were also seeking to offer amendments.

Mr. GIBBONS (D-Fla.). I did not think I could let history be so perverted on this floor as it has been here. I think that every Member of this body should realize that on five occasions in this Chamber, right here, Members-elect have been excluded and never seated. I will give you their names and the States where they were from.

Mr. Roberts, who was a Member-elect from Utah; Mr. Berger, who was a Member-elect from Wisconsin; Mr. Brown and Mr. Young from Kentucky; and Mr. Whittemore from South Carolina.

Let us take the Whittemore case that occurred in the 1870's. Mr. Whittemore sold appointments to the Service Academies. He was investigated and censured. He resigned. He went home. He was reelected, and he came back up here. Do you know what the Congress did? They did not seat him in this Chamber. He was excluded.

* * *

Mr. HALL (R-Mo.). I submit to the Members that all the humiliation, all the pleas that have been brought, all the evidences of censure in this report toward this man who has referred to all of us as hypocrites, and who dared us to rest well on the night of January 10—and I never rested better in my life—indicate this man is uncensurable, unembarrassable, and irresponsible.

* * *

Mr. GROSS (R-Iowa). For altogether too many months the public was fed a steady diet of whitewash and coverup in the cases of

Walter Jenkins and Bobby Baker, among others. Ethical standards in Government seemed to be at their lowest point. There was the grave question of whether law enforcement officials had the courage and dedication to come to grips with this situation.

In recent weeks there seemed to be some improvement in the moral climate, due in part to the conviction of Bobby Baker and James Hoffa, and the refusal of the House on January 10 to seat Adam Clayton Powell.

The House of Representatives today can either help this moral climate or it can further destroy it.

Mr. Speaker, I have a reasonably strong stomach, but it will revolt at the aroma that will arise if today Adam Clayton Powell is offered a seat in this Chamber.

* * *

Mr. DEVINE (R-Ohio). Much emphasis has been placed on depriving a 22-year Member of his seniority. Of course, this has a great personal impact on the Member, but in 1965 the majority party stripped seniority from a highly respected Member with 20 years of service, John Bell Williams, and he did not steal a thing.

There is talk of humiliation, and to unseat would make a martyr of the man. Who are we kidding? Humility does not appear to be one of his virtues. In fact, the *New York Times* on the day before yesterday, with a Bimini dateline, quoted a reporter as saying, "You don't seem worried at all."

To which the subject of this discussion is reported to have responded: "Negro people have a policy of wearing the world like a loose garment—You will never understand, but it is fun to be colored."

* * *

Mr. WIGGINS (R-Cal.). The report of the Celler committee fully and accurately documents the "tragic disrespect for the judicial process" by Powell and his "monstrous defiance of the law." The members of that committee properly concluded that such conduct "clearly brings great disrespect on the House of Representatives." Can any other Member who disregards the Constitution and the unchallenged legal precedents interpreting it so as to cast a politically popular vote do other than bring further disrespect to this body?

* * *

Rep. Pepper then addressed the House. He recounted his efforts to have the committee recommend the removal of

Powell from the House. He emphasized that his reason for signing the committee report was that stated by Conyers; he wished to emphasize the necessity of seating a member-elect possessed of the three expressed qualifications. He was followed by Select Committee members MacGregor and Jacobs, who expressed the same views. MacGregor noted:

> Many of you in this Chamber have joined me in criticizing the Supreme Court for its broad constructions of the Constitution. We have called for strict interpretations, and will again. How anomalous it would be for those of us in this Chamber who have berated the Supreme Court for its broad constructions of the Constitution to now act on the question of Mr. Powell's exclusion under the broadest interpretation possible.

With time nearly gone, Minority Leader Gerald Ford took the floor.

> I do not admit that we do not have the authority to exclude the gentleman from New York. I believe we well may have that authority.
>
> * * *
>
> Unfortunately, during the course of this debate, statements have been made which would indicate, if not challenged, that this Congress has the power to exclude a Member-elect only if such Member-elect does not satisfy the three constitutional qualifications. I do not believe that the historical record or the precedents of this House support this conclusion.
>
> * * *

Moore and Celler then spoke briefly in summation, and the House moved to a vote on the previous question. When the tally was completed, the previous question had failed by a vote of 202 to 222. This narrow defeat was due both to a split in the leadership and to a revolt against it. Majority Leader Albert, Majority Whip Boggs, Minority Leader Ford, and Minority Whip Arends all voted for the previous question, but 12 of the 20 Democratic committee chairmen opposed it. Of the 240 voting Democrats, 131 opposed the previous question, including 28 Northern Democrats who usually could be counted on to follow the leadership. They were joined by 113 of the 184 voting Republicans. Of the Select Committee members, only Pepper voted nay.

Representative Curtis then rose and offered a substitute for the Select Committee's resolution. The text of the substitute had been handed to him by Republicans Moore and Ford during the roll call on the previous question. Moore and Ford had felt that it would be wise to present a substitute posing a clear-cut issue. That issue, they felt, should be exclusion. Thus, their substitute read:

> Resolved, that said Adam Clayton Powell, Member-elect from the 18th District of the State of New York, be and the same hereby is excluded from membership in the 90th Congress and that the Speaker shall notify the Governor of the State of New York of the existing vacancy.

Curtis was then recognized for one hour. He emphasized his view that the power of exclusion could be implied from the power of expulsion, and repeated that he felt exclusion would require a two-thirds vote. He was commenting on the grounds on which he felt the House could exclude a member-elect when interrupted by Mr. Burton (R-Cal.), who inquired about the requisites for due process.

> Mr. BURTON. Just to clarify the gentleman's position, as I understand it, the gentleman made allusions to certain conditions which, if found as a matter of fact by this body, would be the equivalent of that felonious conduct if similarly found under the judicial system.
>
> Mr. CURTIS. The gentleman is correct.
>
> Mr. BURTON. In other words, if those acts which constitute a felony when found by the judiciary—are found by the House—it should be a basis for exclusion? Is that the gentleman's opinion?
>
> Mr. CURTIS. Yes, that is very, very true.
>
> Mr. BURTON. Then may I ask the gentleman that in arriving at any such conclusion, can we assume the gentleman would insist

95

upon due process as we understand due process being followed in this body in establishing those facts that would form the basis for such a finding?

Mr. CURTIS. The gentleman is now talking about something that is very close to my heart, and it is also in the recommendations of [the] Joint Committee on Organization where we have pointed out that the Congress has been derelict for years in not creating a committee of ethics which will establish a code, clearly, and at the same time establish the machinery for enforcing that code.

* * *

I think the conduct of the proceedings by the [Select] committee was exemplary. And I believe the rights of the accused in this instance were fully protected. And I believe the manner in which this investigation was conducted was in accordance with the highest traditions of our judicial courts, or of any other fact-finding tribunal.

Mr. BURTON. I have one final question:

I think, given the mission of the committee, the gentleman's statement is correct, but I think if the committee were an explicit fact-finding commission, as concerning conduct that would be tantamount to a felony, I am sure that the gentleman would agree with me that anyone so charged should be given a bill of particulars, his counsel should have the right to cross-examine his accusers, and he should have the power to call in witnesses of his own selection.

I am also sure the gentleman would agree with me that the very essential aspect of due process was not present in the Select Committee's deliberations because it was not part of their primary mission.

Mr. CURTIS. Let me say to the gentleman that he has stated what I hope we will establish. But let me say beyond that, that I do not think it is necessary for the Congress to do what he describes because we are not considering endangering the life and limb of any individual as one would be in a criminal court. We are talking about a precious privilege to serve in the Congress. This is not a right—it is a privilege. . . . I still would hope that we would establish these kinds of procedures, but I do not think it is necessary here.

* * *

Mr. CELLER. Despite a laudable record of faithful obedience to the constitutional mandate, the Congress has in rare instances of extreme political tension wavered from its usual adherence to constitutional principle and precedent. These deviations occurred in three categories of cases reflecting anti-Mormon—case of Brigham Roberts—anti-Confederate—cases of Kentucky members—and antiradical—case of Victor Berger—feeling. I urge the repudiation of such precedents which reflect the prejudices of prior eras.

Modern congressional practice of strict adherence to constitutional qualifications is required in the instant case. This House should not resurrect a long discredited view of the Constitution and follow precedent bespeaking furor instead of fairness.

* * *

Mr. ICHORD (D-Mo.). Assuming that the amendment is adopted and the resolution is adopted, the resolution states that the gentleman from the 18th District of New York is hereby excluded from the 90th Congress. My question is: Would this also preclude the gentleman . . . from filing for the vacancy that will be declared if the resolution is adopted?

Mr. CURTIS. In my judgment it would, but on the other hand, this would be the result of another jurisdiction, in effect, and we might, if they did proceed that way, be faced with this problem again. But I think the way this is worded, it should be interpreted in that fashion.

* * *

Mr. EDMONDSON (D-Okla.). I would like to ask the gentleman if in his view the unanimous committee findings . . . as to the wrongful misappropriation of public funds in amounts in the committee report totaling up to over $46,000—if these findings are in his view a basic and fundamental requirement to the action that is being taken here today?

Mr. CURTIS. Yes, indeed, they are.

* * *

Mr. HOLLAND (D-Pa.). I can agree neither with those who assert that the entire thing stems from racial considerations, nor with the fervid assertions of those who state that there are no racial overtones whatever involved.

* * *

We have been told that "if the gentleman from New York were white, he would have been punished long since." Like who, Mr. Speaker? Is Adam Clayton Powell the only sinner in this House? Does the House have such a long and complex list of precedents of censuring and demoting and fining Members who do not meet its high moral standards? I can think of a few cases in recent years where Members of this House were guilty of far greater moral and even criminal offenses than the gentleman from New York is even charged with, and yet I cannot remember that the House took action. We left punishment for these offenses to the voters of these Members' districts.

There is some reason, surely, that the Powell case alone has given rise to such drastic punishment. I find it impossible to shake the conviction that a large part of the intense public campaign against Mr. Powell stems from the fact of his race. Some of this stems directly from the view entertained in many quarters of this country that the Negro enjoys the rights of full citizenship only on a tentative basis—that if a Negro offends community sensibilities in any way, he and all other Negroes should be made to suffer for it. . . .

Adam Powell is being judged, not for his sins alone. He is being punished for the statements of Stokley Carmichael and the bad poetry of Cassius Clay and the sins of every other Negro in the country, just exactly as every law-abiding decent Negro citizen finds the pattern of discrimination against him "justified" by the argument that some Negroes break the law.

No, Mr. Speaker, I cannot accept the notion that Adam Powell is being punished by color-blind justice. I, too, have read the mail that has been cited as "evidence of deep public concern." Let me quote some of the mail that I received for the records: "Shame on you and Congressman   . You are both nigger lovers. We will remember you at the polls next election."

That postcard was, of course, anonymous. I received, naturally, some letters opposed to Mr. Powell which avoided using racial slurs, and a few which did not even seem to be motivated by racial ill will. But the mail I have received on this subject left no doubt in my mind that it was largely motivated by the notion that a Negro Congressman ought to be more circumspect, more humble, and more "grateful" than his white colleagues need to be. I submit, Mr. Speaker, that whatever may be the motives of individual Members in this case, the effort to exclude the gentleman from New York, could not have succeeded, and might not even have been attempted, had Adam C. Powell done everything he is accused of doing, but had he been—to coin a phrase—"less colorful." And I think, Mr. Speaker, that we all know that to be true.

And I believe, too, Mr. Speaker, that there would not have been the intense newspaper and other public pressure—which dates back to the very day Mr. Powell assumed the chairmanship of the Education and Labor Committee—had he not been so vigorous and so successful a fighter for long-needed economic, social, educational and labor legislation. This, too, while not cited in the Select Committee's report and while never mentioned in the editorials that demand Adam Clayton Powell's scalp—this, too, I say, is part of the "case against" Adam Clayton Powell.

* * *

Mr. GUBSER (R-Cal.). Had we passed the committee's recommendations, Adam Clayton Powell would have been seated and he would have been punished. Furthermore, he would still be liable to expulsion.

If the Curtis amendment is adopted, a legal cloud will be cast over our action. I, personally, would favor seating him and then doing the thing which is clearly [prescribed] by the Constitution and is subject to no doubt whatsoever. We should seat him and then expel him.

I shall vote against the previous question on the Curtis amendment simply because I believe future and perfecting amendments should be allowed. But if the previous question is ordered, then I will be placed on the horns of an impossible dilemma.

Mr. Speaker, I want to expel Adam Clayton Powell, by seating him first, but that will not be my choice when the Curtis amendment is before us. I will be forced to vote for exclusion, about which I have great constitutional doubts, or to vote for no punishment at all. Given this raw and isolated issue, the only alternative I can follow is to vote for the Curtis amendment. I shall do so, Mr. Speaker, with great reservation.

* * *

With the hour for debate nearly gone, Curtis moved the previous question on the amendment and on the resolution. The previous question passed on a standing vote, 151 to 66, and was confirmed 263 to 161 on a roll call. Before the vote could be taken on the Curtis substitute, however, the antiexclusion forces made one final effort to save their rapidly deteriorating position.

Mr. BURTON. Mr. Speaker, I raise a point of order.

The SPEAKER. The gentleman will state his point of order.

Mr. BURTON. In view of the fact that this resolution, among other things, states that the Member from New York is ineligible to serve in the other body [Senate], and therefore clearly beyond our power to so vote; and in addition to that fact it anticipates election results in the 18th District of New York, a matter upon which we cannot judge at this time, I raise the point of order that the resolution is an improper one for the House to consider, and that it clearly exceeds our authority.

The SPEAKER. The Chair will observe to the gentleman that if the point of order would be in order it would have been at a previous stage in the proceedings, and that the gentleman's point of order comes too late.

Burton raised this point because the language of the Curtis amendment, "excluded from membership in the 90th Congress," could be interpreted to mean that Powell was to be excluded from both the House and the Senate during the entire 90th Congress and that the resolution could bar Powell from membership even if he should be reelected from the 18th District in a special election. There had been relatively little chance that Rep. Burton's effort would have succeeded, even if the speaker had ruled the resolution out of order, for the later roll calls indicated that the pro-exclusionists could probably have mustered sufficient votes to overturn the speaker's ruling.

There was now nothing left for the antiexclusionists to try, and the House moved to the second key vote of the day, the roll call on the adoption of the Curtis amendment. It passed by a solid margin, 248 to 176. The Republicans gave the amendment most of its margin of victory, voting 125 to 59 in favor of the Curtis proposal. The Democrats were almost equally divided, 123 to 117, in favor of the amendment, but the breakdown of Northerns and Southerners was revealing. The Northern Democrats voted 40 to 110 against, the Southerners 83 to 7 for the amendment.

The final important vote, the roll call on the adoption of

the amended resolution, resulted in the exclusion of Powell by a heavy margin, 307 voting for exclusion, and 116 against. The size of the vote, well over two-thirds, was sufficient to satisfy both those who felt exclusion could be accomplished by a majority vote and those who, like Curtis, believed it required a two-thirds vote. (The speaker had ruled, when the matter was debated on January 10, that exclusion required only a majority vote.) The Republicans voted 173 to 11, the Northern Democrats 49 to 100, and the Southern Democrats 85 to 5, in favor of the resolution. This time the floor leadership voted aye, as did Select Committee members MacGregor, Moore, Pepper, and Thompson. The other members of the committee voted against the resolution. The House completed action on the Powell question by adopting the resolution's preamble on a voice vote. The entire proceedings, including debate and roll calls, had lasted some four and a half hours.

There appears to be no simple explanation for the rejection of the Select Committee's proposals and the exclusion of the Representative-elect. One Northern Democrat certainly overstated the facts when he charged, "At no time—neither on January 10 nor on March 1—did the leadership come up with any strategy to prevent this mess." The leadership was slow in gauging the continual increase of anti-Powell feeling, but they definitely had a strategy: punish Powell enough, first by taking away his chairmanship, if necessary by censure, to appease his accusers but still keep him in Congress. However, bipartisan agreement on the details of this strategy was often lacking, as illustrated by the Udall and Ford resolutions, and by the disagreement in the Select Committee on the amount of punishment necessary. When a compromise was finally reached, the leadership found on March 1 that they could not hold together the votes needed for their strategy.

This inability to deliver the votes was due to a "back-bench" revolt, which reinforced the Southern Democrat-convervative Republican coalition with such liberals as Van Deerlin. The failure of many members of both parties to follow their leadership was due in large measure to the intense pressure placed on them by constituents and the news media. But this situation was aggravated by the fact that Powell did not receive support from civil rights groups comparable in the strength with the attacks upon him by other segments of society. After the exclusion Roy Wilkins of the NAACP held Powell himself responsible: "The truth of the matter is that Powell never called on the civil rights movement. He never invited their help. . . . Only Adam's office knew of the tremendous volume of mail received by Congressmen against Powell. If we had known this, we could have done something."[2] Though numerous organizations announced support for Powell and many rallies were held in his support, concentrated pressure was not brought to bear on individual congressmen. Thus some representatives felt they could safely respond to the demands of their white constituents without fear of reprisals from Negro voters. And some congressmen shared the feeling of outrage expressed by their constituents; at a time when concern about congressional ethics had brought Congress into public ridicule, some members felt that they had to do something when confronted with a case in which wrongdoings were so openly and arrogantly flaunted. When the previous question on the committee's resolution failed, support for exclusion began to grow, as members were forced, like Rep. Gubser, to choose between their desire to discipline Powell and their qualms about the legality of the Curtis proposal.

Once the final vote had been taken, however, there was little doubt what the next act in the Powell drama would be. As Emanuel Celler remarked after the session, "If I were representing Adam Clayton Powell, I'd take the case to court right away. I think he's got a good case."[3]

7 Through a Political Thicket into Political Quicksand

While the House wrestled with the Powell question in Washington, the cause of all their problems was spending a pleasant afternoon at the End of the World Bar on Bimini. Sipping a concoction of Cutty Sark and milk provided by an obliging reporter, he bantered with newsmen. The once-powerful ex-chairman was outwardly little disturbed by his ouster, of which he learned from a radio news broadcast. "I'm feeling fine," he maintained. "Why should I be angry, with all these lovely friends I have on Bimini?" Would he run for reelection, someone asked. "That depends upon my good people in Harlem. I wouldn't deny my people. I'll do anything my people want me to do."

Top Negro leaders did not take the House action as calmly as did Powell. Martin Luther King charged that the exclusion was not only unconstitutional but also motivated by racism. Floyd McKissick of CORE called the House decision "a slap in the face of every black man in this country" that "clearly indicates . . . a great amount of racism exists. . . ."[1] Their sentiments were echoed by many others. And despite Powell's outward calm, he was not content to accept the House decision as final. His lawyers quickly put into motion a court battle aimed at reinstatement.

While Powell's lawyers were mapping their legal strategy,

the New York Court of Appeals announced on March 2 an opinion which must have been very heartening after the months of adversity. Powell himself broke into a broad smile when he heard of the court's "beautiful" ruling, as he called it. The New York court, by a 6-1 vote, reversed the judgment against Powell in the fraudulent-transfer-of assets suit. The judges disallowed the $100,000 in punitive charges because they felt Powell's conduct was not sufficiently "gross and wanton" to justify them. The case was then remanded to the Manhattan Supreme Court for a review of the remainder of the judgment under Puerto Rican law.

Upon receipt of the official notification that Powell's former seat was vacant, Governor Rockefeller of New York issued an order on March 6 setting April 11 as the date for a special election to fill the vacancy. The next day James Meredith announced that he would oppose Powell. Meredith, who described himself as an "independent Democrat," had decided to run as a Republican after consulting Republican leaders. A hero of the civil rights movement, and the first Negro to attend the University of Mississippi, Meredith was then a law student at Columbia. He was making the race, it was reported in the *New York Times*, because "the people deserve more than they're getting. Whatever influence Adam Clayton Powell once had, he doesn't have any more." That Powell would be the Democratic candidate was never in doubt, and he told newsmen on Bimini that he was certain he would be reelected. He dismissed Meredith as "the white man's candidate."

On March 8, Powell was visited by Floyd McKissick for a session of election strategy-planning. He was followed a few days later by Stokely Carmichael, who likewise pledged his support for Powell. At the same time a move was begun to qualify Powell as the nominee of the Congress Party in the special election. This effort, led by John Young, a former Powell aide, was designed to give the voters in the Harlem district a chance to support Powell without voting for a Democratic Party candidate.

The great surprise in the election campaign came on March 13. Shortly after midnight James Meredith issued the simple statement "I have decided not to run in the 18th Congressional District." The decision had obviously been made not long before the announcement, since the previous afternoon Meredith had declared that he was still firm in his intention to make the race. A news conference later in the day explained his sudden change of mind. He had been visited the night of the 12th by Floyd McKissick and Charles Evers, brother of the slain civil rights worker Medgar Evers. In a three-hour conference they pressed on Meredith the view that if he ran against Powell, it would be the end of his political career. It was their arguments that finally induced Meredith to quit the race.

On Bimini, Powell, accompanied by Negro entertainer and political activist Dick Gregory, praised Meredith's decision to withdraw. Then Powell announced that he intended to return to Harlem on Palm Sunday, March 19, to walk the streets and preach in his church despite the arrest order issued November 28. His statement was laced with references to Jesus and to a text from the Book of Jeremiah, which he had quoted frequently since his exclusion: "If a man falls, shall he not rise again?"

Almost as if it were answering Powell's announcement, on March 14 the Appellate Division of the New York Supreme Court issued an opinion upholding Judge Markewich's arrest order. The court maintained that before it ruled on the issue, Powell would have to return to New York and submit to arrest. When Powell heard of the court's decision, he reiterated that he would return, even though he would be liable to nine months in jail if arrested. In response, the city sheriff's office began making special arrangements for what would be their first Sunday arrest since the office was established in 1942.

When the sheriff's preparations became known, the reaction of Powell's Harlem constituents was angry. They planned a mass parade in his support on Palm Sunday and warned that any attempt to arrest Powell could lead to violence. Henry Williams, one of Powell's lawyers, backed them up by warning Sheriff John McCloskey that to arrest Powell on Sunday would constitute false arrest and criminal assault. He threatened to sue the sheriff if Powell were taken in custody.

In this emotion-charged atmosphere, the officials of the Abyssinian Baptist Church advised Powell that his arrest on Palm Sunday might provoke violence and urged him not to return. Motivated by a desire to avoid arrest, or to avoid violence, or both, Powell did not carry out his plans. Palm Sunday passed normally in Harlem.

In the midst of the excitement, the district political leaders met on the 15th to name their candidates officially. The Convervative Party, obviously with no expectation of victory, nominated Rev. Erwin F. Yearling, a Negro and Baptist minister who was a founder and director of the Negro Congress of Racial Pride. The Republicans, having lost their strongest candidate when Meredith left the race, had to content themselves with Mrs. Lucille Pickett Williams, a local Republican official and former beautician who was serving as secretary to the New York State Cosmetology Advisory Committee. In her first news conference she admitted she had no hope of beating Powell.

The leaders of the Democratic Party met in the basement of the Abyssinian Baptist Church and unanimously nominated their former congressman. No other names were proposed. A few days later, Powell's attorneys arranged for him to fly secretly to Miami. There he quickly signed the required form accepting the Democratic nomination. It was notarized at the airport by a Pan American employee and Powell returned immediately to Bimini. His lawyers took these unusual precautions because they feared he would be arrested if it were known in advance that he was returning to American soil. The newly formed Congress Party also nominated Powell, but he failed to file the acceptance of their nomination required by law.

Reverend Yearling, realizing that he had no hope of beating Powell, made one ingenious effort to bar Powell from the race. He filed suit March 20 to have Powell's name removed from the ballot on the grounds that H. Res. 278 barred the ex-congressman during the entire 90th Congress. The case was considered by Powell's old nemesis, Justice Arthur Markewich, who dismissed the suit on March 29. Justice Markewich characterized the House resolution as "inexpertly carpentered" and acknowledged that Powell had been excluded "for alleged unfitness measured by certain standards which are not completely defined." Said the Justice, "I don't think the resolution really states any more than, so to speak, that the other members of Congress don't desire [Powell's] company."[2] The suit was likewise dismissed on appeal.

Thereafter the campaign was practically dull. The candidates refrained from name-calling. Rallies and parades generally attracted few voters, and the Republican and Conservative campaigns were hampered by a lack of funds and popular support.

As it became more and more apparent that Powell would be reelected, a difference of opinion became evident on the question of the reaction of the House. Emanuel Celler believed that enough members had changed their minds on the issue to make it possible to seat Powell if he were reelected. But Gerald Ford expressed the opinion that the House was still firm on barring the ex-congressman. That the indignation about Powell was still strong was evidenced by the response to a letter drafted by Representatives Gross, Lennon, and Hall urging the Justice Department to expedite the consideration of the Select Committee report. It was signed by some 150 members.

Two final events highlighted the last dozen days of the campaign. On March 30 Powell, still on Bimini, announced the formation of an all-Negro "third force" to "elect the black man." Joining him in the announcement were a number of Negro officeholders and civil rights workers from all over the country, including Georgia State Representative Julian Bond and Floyd McKissick. And on April 1, the ADA national convention in Washington passed a resolution calling for the seating of Powell without punishment, on the grounds that the Congress had violated the Constitution and Powell's rights.

Over the weekend of March 4, Powell's battery of lawyers occupied themselves with mapping strategy for a legal battle to contest his exclusion, and on March 8, exactly a week after the House approved H. Res. 278, they filed a suit in the District Court for the District of Columbia. The suit was brought against Speaker John McCormack, Majority Leader Carl Albert, Minority Leader Gerald Ford, Emanuel Celler, Arch A. Moore, Jr. (and was later amended to include Thomas Curtis), House Clerk W. Pat Jennings, House Sergeant-at-Arms Zeake W. Johnson, Jr. and House Doorkeeper William "Fishbait" M. Miller.

Suing with Powell were 13 nonwhite constituents, all of whom had voted for him in the preceding election. The group included five women.

Filed by Powell's lawyers, the *Complaint for Declaratory Judgment, Injunctive Relief, and Mandamus* alleged in part:[3] House Resolution 278, excluding Powell from membership, was in violation of the section of the Constitution which set forth the exclusive qualifications for membership and that which provided that members of the House would be elected by the people of each state; and the action was a violation of the rights of the electors to elect a representative of their choice. The plaintiffs, being nonwhite citizens, were subjected to discrimination based upon race and color, forbidden by the 5th, 13th, and 15th Amendments and the female plaintiffs were deprived of rights guaranteed under the 19th Amendment. The resolution in effect constituted a bill of attainder and an ex post facto law, in violation of the Constitution.[4] The hearings before the Select Committee and the proceedings in the House, in which charges were made and punitive action taken, were undertaken without Powell's being accorded the elemental rights of due process, in violation of the 5th and 6th Amendments.

The complaint then requested the convening of a three-judge court to issue preliminary and permanent injunctions restraining the defendants from enforcing H. Res. 278. The complaint requested that mandamus be granted ordering the defendants to swear in Powell and to accord him the rights, privileges, and emoluments of a representative.[5] Also sought was a declaratory judgment that the resolution was "null and void on the grounds that its operation, enforcement and execution was unconstitutional on its face."[6]

Powell's attorneys also filed a memorandum in which they reviewed the case law pertaining to the convening of a three-judge court. During the 1930's, when newly enacted federal economic and social legislation was under attack in the courts, Congress enacted a statute providing for a three-judge court, including two district court judges and one court of appeals judge, and permitted direct appeal of such cases to the Supreme Court. The statute was enacted to avoid having the administration of an entire program halted pending review of a single judge's decision and to minimize delay in getting a final determination of the constitutionality of an act of Congress. Powell's attorneys wanted a three-judge court primarily so that Powell could appeal directly to the Supreme Court, hopefully gaining review during the 90th Congress; a secondary reason was that they hoped to get at least one of the three judges to respond positively to their plea.

The next day summonses were delivered to all the defendants shortly before the House met. The House leadership met, and after consulting the Justice Department, drew up a resolution authorizing the Speaker to hire an attorney to "represent the House of Representatives its members and officers named as defendants." Later in the day this resolution was presented to the House. Fully aware of the historical importance of the suit, the members debated for an hour various suggested responses to the summonses. (One congressman suggested that the Congress should pass legislation which would remove the Supreme Court's jurisdiction over cases such as the Powell litigation, thereby precluding its review of the exclusion resolution.) The question of who should represent the defendants was discussed. Under most circumstances, the Justice Department would have served as counsel to the defendants. Given the importance of the issue to Congress, said Congressman Boggs, author of the resolution to hire outside counsel, Congress should not have to rely on yet another branch of the government, the executive branch, to defend its fundamental right to judge the qualifications of its members: "It was the feeling of the leadership that this matter goes to the heart of representative government, that this body as a body should be represented independently by independent counsel to be designated and chosen by the Speaker of the House of Representatives."[7] Congressman Ford concurred:

> If it is not quite true that the Congress is the people, it is the closest thing to the people that we have—particularly here in the House of Representatives. So when we defend this House we defend the people's House. We have heard and doubtless will continue to hear much argument as to whether we have the right to exclude a Member-elect from this body. I submit that this question already has been pleaded before the only court of competent jurisdiction under the Constitution, the House of Representatives; and judgment has been passed by substantial majorities, on two roll calls, that we do have the exclusive right and power. I believe this accords with the intent of the Founding Fathers and the rules and precedents of the House. This judgment has been challenged and must be vigorously and ably defended. This is our simple duty to the past and to the future.[8]

The House approved the hiring of counsel by a voice vote. On March 14 the Speaker announced that he had retained as counsel Bruce Bromley, 73 years old, a Republican and former New York Court of Appeals judge, of the distinguished New York law firm of Cravath, Swaine & Moore. Bromley specialized in corporation law and had provided legal counsel to several major American corporations.

On March 31 Bromley filed a motion to dismiss the complaint on the grounds that, first, the court did not have jurisdiction over the subject matter in the action; second, that the court did not have jurisdiction over the persons of the defendants; and third, that the complaint failed to state a claim upon which relief could be granted. A memorandum discussing the convening of a three-judge court and a lengthier *Memorandum of Points and Authorities in Support of Defendants' Motion to Dismiss and in Opposition to Plantiffs' Motion for Preliminary Injunction* were filed.

Bromley made the following arguments, in the latter memorandum, on behalf of Congress:[9]

Point I – This Court Lacks Power
To Adjudicate This Matter
A. This Court is Barred by Article I, Section 6 of the Constitution from Questioning the Defendant Members as to the Propriety of the Action Taken in Adopting H. R. Res. 278 and Excluding Mr. Powell.

At the threshold, Article I, Section 6, clause 1 of the Constitution expressly forbids this court to proceed with this case against the defendant Members. That provision, the so-called "Speech or Debate Clause," has its roots deep in British and American constitutional history. It broadly provides that

"For any Speech or Debate in either House, they [the Senators and Representatives] shall not be questioned in any other Place."

* * *

The Speech or Debate Clause protects the Members from judicial questioning not only as to "speech" and "debate" as those terms are commonly understood, but also as to "things generally done in a session of the House by one of its members in

111

relation to the business before it." *Kilbourn* v. *Thompson*, 103 U. S. 168, 204 (1880). Accordingly, with respect to the House of Representatives, the Speech or Debate Clause extends

"... to written reports presented in that body by its committees, to resolutions offered, which, though in writing, must be reproduced in speech, and *to the act of voting*, whether it is done vocally or by passing between the tellers." Ibid. (Emphasis added.)

The very essence of the plaintiffs' complaint against the Members is that they voted for and the House passed a resolution. Clearly, the conduct complained of by plaintiffs in this case is within the coverage of the clause, and the Members hence may not be judicially questioned in this or any other court.

* * *

B. The Subject Matter of this Controversy Is a Political Question Specifically Entrusted by the Constitution to a Coordinate Branch of the Federal Government and Does Not Satisfy the Criteria for a Justiciable Controversy.

* * *

The ultimate question presented by this case is whether a court will transgress the constitutional separation between the judicial and the legislative powers and undertake to instruct the Members of the House how they should have voted or otherwise acted within the House, or how they shall vote or act, on the question of seating Mr. Powell. Courts have traditionally described such problems as political questions that are not justiciable and hence not within the power of the courts of the United States to decide.

* * *

The most recent and exhaustive analysis of the political question doctrine is contained in the Supreme Court's opinion in *Baker* v. *Carr*, 369 U. S. 186 (1962). The Court held that the state apportionment action there involved did not present political question problems for the federal judiciary, and that it was justiciable by reason of the supremacy clause of Article VI. However, the Court made clear that a non-justiciable political question would have arisen if the issue had involved coordinate branches of the federal government. As the Court put it,

"[I] n the ... 'political question' cases, it is the relationship between the judiciary and the coordinate branches of the Federal Government, and not the federal judiciary's relationship to the States, which gives rise to the 'political question.'

112

". . . The non-justiciability of a political question is primarily a function of the separation of powers." 369 U. S. at 210. The Court went on to delineate circumstances in which a political question would arise:

"Prominent on the surface of any case held to involve a political question is found a textually demonstrable constitutional commitment of the issue to a coordinate political department; *or* a lack of judicially discoverable and manageable standards for resolving it; *or* the impossibility of deciding without an initial policy determination of a kind clearly for nonjudicial discretion; *or* the impossibility of a court's undertaking independent resolution without expressing lack of the respect due coordinate branches of government; *or* an unusual need for unquestioning adherence to a political decision already made; *or* the potentiality of embarrassment from multifarious pronouncements by various departments on one question." 369 U. S. at 217. (Emphasis added.)

* * *

It was then argued that at least five of the criteria were inextricable from this case. In particular, the test that there be a "textually demonstrable constitutional commitment of the issue to a coordinate political department" was overwhelmingly satisfied here.

The fact that the Supreme Court dealt with a similar issue in *Bond* v. *Floyd* did not affect the fundamental principle of separation of powers, because in the Georgia case, the Court was dealing with a state legislature, not with a coordinate branch of the federal government.

It is fair to say that, until this Term of the Supreme Court, there has never been a decision in the state or federal courts assuming jurisdiction over this particular subject matter in the context of either a state legislature or the United States Congress. *Bond* v. *Floyd*, 385 U. S. 116 (1966), is the first such case, but it does no violence to the fundamental principle of separation of powers here under attack. As the Supreme Court earlier pointed out in *Baker* v. *Carr*,

"[I] t is the relationship between the judiciary and the coordinate branches of the Federal Government, and not the

113

federal judiciary's relationship to the states, which gives rise to the 'political question.' " 369 U. S. at 210.

For federal courts sit to vindicate federal rights under the supremacy clause, and those rights may not be impaired by the internal action of a house or a state legislature any more than by a state statute or even by a state constitution. . . .

* * *

(b) The House properly interpreted the scope of the power committed to it by the Constitution.

* * *

That language is clearly susceptible of the interpretation that the requirements for Members set forth therein are not intended to be exclusive.

In the first place, the three tests set forth in Article I, Section 2, are clearly not described as the sole qualifications for membership. Indeed, they are not even described as "qualifications." They are cast in the negative, thus strongly suggesting that they are merely meant to set forth *minimum requirements* for membership applicable to all. . . .

* * *

As we have said, we need not consider here whether the House, having interpreted its constitutional powers to permit excluding a Member on the grounds set forth in H. R. Res. 278, is legally free to exclude on any ground whatever. The grounds on which the House relied here, e.g., misuse of congressional funds and contempt of court orders, certainly fall within the ambit of proper bases for exclusion from a legislative body naturally interested in upholding its own reputation for integrity, honesty and respect for the courts. This is not a case where the House has excluded a Member on wholly arbitrary and unreasonable grounds, such as race, religion or political beliefs. Indeed, plaintiffs' complaint does not allege that Mr. Powell was excluded on any such ground, nor does it challenge the factual basis of the actual grounds on which Mr. Powell was excluded.

(c) The House action is also justified under the expulsion power committed to it.

Even if the House had erroneously added a disqualification not permitted by the Constitution, judicial intervention would not be permitted. For the House action can be alternatively justified under the expulsion power, as to which the Constitution clearly imposes no limitations, and the "error," if any there be, is thus technical at worst.

* * *

Point II — This Court Lacks Power to Grant Plaintiffs Any of the Relief Requested Against the Members of the House.

* * *

What is the result plaintiffs seek? They request that the court take all necessary action to force the House of Representatives to seat Mr. Powell. How can that result be accomplished since more than two-thirds of the members are opposed to that action? Certainly not by an order to the Speaker or to one or more of the agents of the House. They are all, even the Speaker in the final analysis, only agents of the majority of the Members of the House. Surely one cannot imagine the possibility of the Speaker, for example, administering the oath to Mr. Powell when a majority of the Members have directed him not to do so.

There is only one other way to accomplish the result plaintiffs seek; a majority of the Members must be ordered to vote to seat Mr. Powell. That must ultimately be done expressly by the court; no other relief will obtain the result plaintiffs demand. Should a Member of Congress vote in any matter as he is ordered to vote by some other branch of the government? That is a matter which each Member must settle for himself in his own conscience.

* * *

A. The Injunctive Relief Requested Against the House and its Members Is Barred by the Doctrine of Separation of Powers and by the Speech or Debate Clause.

Essentially, plaintiffs seek relief against the entire House to force the seating of Mr. Powell. It has long been clear that the judicial branch cannot entertain an action to enjoin either the legislature or the executive.

* * *

Point III — This Court Also Lacks Power to Grant Any of the Relief Requested Against Any of the Non-Member Defendant Agents of the House, Requiring them to Perform Alleged Official Duties In a Manner Contrary to an Adopted Resolution of the House.

* * *

The availability of mandamus relief is blocked by the fact that legislative action is inherently discretionary, rather than ministerial. Mandamus, of course, is only available to require a public official to perform a ministerial duty. *Marbury* v. *Madison*, 5 U.S. (1 Branch) 137, 169 (1803).

Ministerial duties of officers of the executive branch are imposed by statute. In contrast, duties of Members of the House of Representatives arising under the Constitution are not by their nature so explicit and so free from the need for interpretation as to provide a basis for mandamus. Just as an executive agency is not subject to mandamus when the "duty to act turns on matters of doubtful or highly debatable inference from large or loose statutory terms," *Panama Canal Co.* v. *Grace Line, Inc.*, 356 U. S. 309, 318 (1958), so the legislature's duty cannot be ministerial when it turns on matters requiring constitutional interpretation.

It follows that what cannot be done directly against the House cannot be done indirectly by mandamus against officers of the House. For example, to require the Speaker to administer the oath, either by a direct mandate or by an injunction restraining him from refusing to do so, is simply a way of ordering the House to cause the oath to be administered. Similarly, the sought-for mandates or injunctions against "refusal" addressed to the Clerk, the Sergeant-at-Arms and the Doorkeeper are indirect ways of ordering the House to undo an action which was within and subject to its legislative discretion. As such, they are barred by the basic principles of mandamus law.

* * *

Point IV — In Any Event, Plaintiffs Have Totally Failed To Demonstrate a Sufficiently Strong Probability of Prevailing Either as to Jurisdiction or on the Merits to Justify the Grant of a Preliminary Injunction.

* * *

A. Plaintiffs Have Failed to Make a Clear Showing of Probable Success on the Merits.

In order to establish any right to a preliminary injunction, a plaintiff must make a strong showing of probable success on the merits. . . .

Plaintiffs allege in conclusional form, without any supporting facts whatever, that numerous provisions of the Constitution have been violated by the action of the House. As we have made clear thus far, we do not believe the court should even consider these allegations in a case brought against the House and its Members. But if we are mistaken as to the court's lack of jurisdiction, plaintiffs here still are not entitled to a preliminary injunction, for they cannot show a substantial probability of ultimate success on the merits. We have already established that H. R. Res. 278 was well within the powers of the House under article I, section 5. We turn, therefore, to the alleged deprivations of federally-protected rights. As we shall now show, each of those claims is so frivolous that plaintiffs cannot possibly establish substantial probability of sustaining any one of them on the merits.

* * *

Powell's lawyers filed two memorandums in response on April 4, one dealing with the convening of the desired three-judge court and one opposing the motion to dismiss. The latter, *Memorandum of Points and Authorities in Opposition to Defendants' Motion To Dismiss and in Support of Plaintiff's Motion for Preliminary Injunction*, sought to counter Bromley's arguments point by point, as follows:

POINT I

THIS COURT HAS POWER TO ADJUDICATE THIS MATTER

* * *

A. This Court is not barred by Article I, Section 6 of the Constitution from questioning the validity of House Resolution 278.

* * *

Defendants' argument fails to acknowledge one fundamental distinction: that the "Speech or Debate Clause" protects the process of discourse and decision-making in Congress—but it does not and cannot purport to grant the same immunity to the final product of that process—whether it be an Act of Congress or a Resolution of the House. Defendants accurately state that that Clause extends protection to written reports, resolutions and even to the act of voting. But to extend that same immunity to the product that flows from that process would be to overturn the basis of judicial review established in *Marbury* v. *Madison*, 5 U. S. (1 Branch) 137 (1803).

The principle case relied upon by defendants, *Kilbourn* v. *Thompson*, 103 U. S. 168, (1880), indeed reaffirms that distinction. As *Defendants' Brief*, p. 17, properly notes:

[T]he Court drew a clear distinction between actions *within* the House, such as the debate and passage of a resolution, and *subsequent actions taken outside the House* by Members or agents of the House pursuant to a resolution as passed. . . . (Emphasis added.)

117

* * *

Primarily, the process of committee hearings, floor debate, etc., by which H. Res. 278 was produced, is material because of the constitutional infirmities in that process and its impact upon the final product of the deliberations. Had the deliberations themselves not resulted in the unconstitutional Resolution, scrutiny of the debate and hearings within the House would be academic.

But if that process, because of alleged constitutional protection, is to immunize the result, then no law which is the product of that process could possibly be attacked or subjected to judicial constitutional review.

Furthermore, the "Speech or Debate" Clause historically was intended and applied as protection against suits for damages brought against individual members for participation in discussion and debate. The purpose of the Clause was to permit debate in the House to proceed unhampered by fear of external retaliation. No such reprisal or retaliation, no personal suit for damages is here presented, but only an attack upon and application to enjoin the enforcement of the unlawful product of the debate and discussion.

* * *

In this instant matter, it is important to note that the Defendants Speaker McCormack and the Sergeant-at-Arms are not acting solely in a legislative capacity, but also as officers in carrying out and implementing the product of the legislative process. As such, they are like any other officer of the Government who must be made defendants if the authorization asserted for their acts is to be tested for constitutionality.

* * *

B. The subject matter of the controversy is not a "political question" and satisfies the criteria for a justiciable issue.

Defendants claim that the court lacks power to adjudicate this matter because it is a "political question." They cite the criteria set forth in *Baker* v. *Carr*, 369 U. S. 186 (1962), as dispositive of this issue without looking closely to the method of analysis developed and applied in that case or the context in which those criteria were enunciated.

Thus, the *Baker* court rejected the notion that such terms as "political question" were self-defining and started instead from the opposite predicate:

Deciding whether a matter has in any measure been committed by the Constitution to another branch of government, or whether the action of that branch exceeds whatever authority

118

has been committed, is itself a delicate exercise in constitutional interpretation, and is a responsibility of this court as ultimate interpreter of the Constitution. 369 U.S. at 211.

* * *

1. The criteria relied upon by defendants are necessary but not sufficient conditions to prove non-justiciability.

The conditions or characterizations cited by Defendants as dispositive are, in fact, characterized only as *necessary* but not *sufficient* to compel a conclusion of non-justiciability. As the court put it:

Unless one of these formulations is inextricable from the case at bar, there should be no dismissal for non-justiciability on the ground of a political question's presence. 369 U. S. 217.

* * *

There is indeed a textually demonstrable commitment to the House to judge those qualifications of its members which are explicitly enumerated in the Constitution. There is no such commitment of the right to create new, ad hoc qualifications or to sit in unreviewable judgment on the presence or absence of those qualifications. Nor can the power to impose discipline on a Member be treated as a power to generate and apply new qualifications to a Member-elect. The power to discipline members can hardly constitute a textually demonstrable authority to discipline non-members. Defendants' uneasiness with this position is clearest where they grudgingly indicate that, perhaps, if the House were to impose qualifications of race, religion or political belief, there might be occasion for judicial intervention. Apparently the textual commitment to the House does not extend to all unprescribed qualifications—only to those which defendants deny to be present here. *Baker* v. *Carr*, supra at 220-222.

* * *

The Court in *Baker* v. *Carr*, supra at 230, shed further light on the proper approach to a claim that a case involves a "political question":

Gomillion was lifted "out of the so-called 'political' arena and into the conventional sphere of constitutional litigation" because here was discriminatory treatment of a racial minority violating the Fifteenth Amendment.

The Court's solemn duty enunciated in *Marbury* v. *Madison*, supra, is not that easily avoided by recital of the Talismanic words "political question." At best, the involvement of a coordinate branch of government poses the issue of justiciability—it does not resolve it. *Bell* v. *Hood*, 372 U. S. 678 (1945). It cannot if there are present factors which lift this case "out of the so-called 'political arena' and into the conventional sphere of constitutional litigation." We are here once again in that conventional sphere.

* * *

Powell's attorneys then argued that Congress might have the authority to judge the three enumerated qualifications without judicial intervention, but that the Courts had the responsibility to interpret what the "judge qualifications" clause meant. The Supreme Court, not Congress, was the ultimate interpreter of the Constitution.

Whatever question of justiciability might be raised by the presence of "political factors" and the involvement of a "coordinate branch of government," is disposed of by the claim that the acts here involved transgress the Constitution. And Constitutional exegesis is the Court's domain.

* * *

POINT II

THE COURT HAS POWER TO GRANT THE RELIEF SOUGHT
BY PLAINTIFFS

Suffice it to say that plaintiffs seek only the normal available injunctive and declaratory remedies necessary to afford them relief from the unconstitutional action of defendants. What they ask for is neither novel nor unusual and courts, from one end of the land to the other, have had little difficulty in complying with similar prayers.

There can be no question whatsoever as to the power of the federal courts to restrain the unconstitutional actions of Congress. *Marbury* v. *Madison*, supra, *Ex parte Young* supra. Classically, judicial declarations of the unconstitutionality of Acts of Congress are enforced by injunctions. *Ex parte Young*, supra. Neither the doctrine of Separation of Powers nor the Speech and Debate Clause bar such relief.

The contention by defendants that relief in the nature of mandamus is likewise unavailable is equally unsound. As Chief

Justice Marshall said in *Marbury* v. *Madison*, supra, at 173, "This, then, is a plain case for a mandamus, either to deliver the commission, or a copy of it from the record." Traditionally, mandamus lies to force an officer to perform a ministerial act and is applicable when an applicant . . . has a right to execute an office of public concern, and is kept out of possession of that right. *Marbury* v. *Madison*, supra, at 169.

* * *

We are concerned here solely with a ministerial act—the swearing in and admission of Mr. Powell to the rights, powers and emoluments of the office to which he has been duly elected and for which the House itself has found that he possesses the only constitutional qualifications. There is nothing remaining but to seat him, surely a ministerial function, and it should be done. . . .

* * *

Thus a number of interesting questions were raised in the briefs submitted to the district court. First, did the court have the power to adjudicate this matter? Specifically, did the "speech and debate" clause bar the court from deciding challenges to the validity of the House resolution, or did the clause fail to grant immunity from judicial scrutiny to the products of legislative action? Did the case raise a political question that was not justiciable because of the constitutional separation of the judicial and legislative powers, or was the case justiciable because the acts complained of transgressed the Constitution?

Second, did the court have the power to grant the plaintiffs the relief requested? Did the court have the power to issue an injunction restraining the members of the House and nonmember defendants? Did the remedy (swearing in Powell) sought by the plaintiffs relate to an act which was required of Congress (ministerial) and hence subject to mandamus? Did the court have the power to grant declaratory relief?

Also on April 4, oral argument was heard before Judge George L. Hart, Jr., of the district court for the District of Columbia, to whom the case had been assigned. Judge Hart, born in Virginia in 1905, graduated from the Virginia Military Institute and received a degree from the Harvard Law School in 1930. Thereafter, he practiced law in the District of Columbia and served for a time as Republican chairman of the District. He was appointed to his judgeship in 1958 by President Eisenhower. Although Judge Hart customarily thought of himself as a liberal, many Washington lawyers regarded him as actually a conservative. All, agreed however, that he was a highly conscientious jurist.

Judge Hart gave the Powell case top priority and completed his deliberations and opinion by April 7. His opinion, which included a lengthy and eloquent development of the history of the doctrine of separation of powers, was delivered that morning. Powell's complaint was dismissed without consideration on the merits because, in Hart's view, "for the Court to decide this case on the merits and to grant any of the relief prayed for in the complaint would constitute a clear violation of the doctrine of separation of powers."[10]

After a brief review of the facts of the case, Judge Hart dealt with Powell's application for a three-judge court. The act providing for a three-judge court applied to an "act of Congress" only, he said. House Resolution 278 was clearly not an act of Congress, and in any event the decision of the court to dismiss Powell's complaint mooted the question of the right of the plaintiffs to a three-judge court.

He then analyzed the competing arguments as to whether the court should adjudicate the matter. Noting that the "speech and debate" clause "may well" bar jurisdiction of the court, he did not rest his decision on this point. Nor did he rest his decision on the "judge qualifications" clause. Said he, "It can be argued with great force and conviction that the word 'qualifications' covers any cause that the Members of the House, by majority vote, choose it to cover," including the acts alleged in the Celler report. On the other hand, it could be argued that the word "qualifications" was limited to age, citizenship, and inhabitancy, and a valid election certificate. But he did not resolve this question.

122

For Judge Hart, there was one issue of overriding importance, separation of powers:

> In this Court's view of the case, the complaint and the relief prayed for raise one issue of such transcendent importance that all other issues in the case pale into insignificance. This issue constitutes a "political question." The question facing the Court may be simply stated as follows: Would consideration of the complaint on the merits and granting any of the requested relief violate the doctrine of "separation of powers?"
>
> At first blush it might be thought that the Supreme Court answered this question in the negative in *Bond* v. *Floyd*, 385 U. S. 116 (1966). In that case the Supreme Court invalidated a resolution of one branch of the Georgia Legislature refusing to seat Bond, holding that the resolution violated Bond's right to freedom of speech guaranteed by the First Amendment of the federal Constitution. The *Bond* case did not present a "political question" nor did it raise the question of separation of powers between coordinate branches of government.
>
> The Supreme Court stated concisely when a "political question," which includes the doctrine of separation of powers, arises, and when it does not arise, in the case of *Baker* v. *Carr*, 369 U. S. 186, 210 (1962), when the Court said:
>
> "[I]n the ... 'political question' cases, it is the relationship between the judiciary and the coordinate branches of the Federal Government, and not the federal judiciary's relationship to the States, which gives rise to the 'political question.'
>
> "... The non-justiciability of a political question is primarily a function of the separation of powers." 369 U. S. at 210.
>
> As to the precise issue which I deem to be raised here, there are no cases directly in point. This Court has not found a case nor has any been cited to it where the complaint and the relief prayed therein have posed to the Court with such stark clarity the question of separation of powers between the Legislature, as represented by the House of Representatives of the United States, and the Federal Judiciary. . . .

With his decision resting squarely on this doctrine, Judge Hart reviewed the emergence of the doctrine of separation of powers, which he saw as essential to free government. He did not rely on the material presented in the briefs, but developed his own historical analysis.

123

Let us review briefly, and with a broad brush, the emergence of the doctrine of separation of powers as a principle of free government and the extent to which the doctrine had developed at the time our forefathers prepared the Constitution in 1787 for adoption by the people.

When the doctrine began to bud in ancient Greece, separation of powers referred to the division of authority between the high and the low; between the king, the aristocracy, and the masses; and between the executive and the legislature. To Solon (638?-559 B. C.), the doctrine meant increasing the power of the poor while balancing this power with aristocratic councils and magistrates. Thucydides (471?-400? B. C.) praised a fusion government of the high and the low. Plato (427?-347 B. C.) saw the need for wise aristocrats or kings, and the Statesmen.

Aristotle (384-322 B. C.) contributed the first statement of the doctrine as we now conceive it. He described government as divided into three parts—deliberators, magistrates, and judicial functionaries.

Polybius (205?-125? B. C.) said the Roman Republic was at its best when it combined democratic, aristocratic, and royal elements. Cicero (106-43 B. C.) and Machiavelli (1469-1527) praised government in which all the elements were combined.

John Locke (1632-1704), in order to prevent tyranny, would divide the government between two organs, the executive and the legislative.

Montesquieu (1689-1755) stated the doctrine as it was conceived in the early 18th century as follows:

"The political liberty of the subject is a tranquility of mind arising from the opinion each person has of his safety. In order to have this liberty, it is requisite the government be so constituted as one man need not be afraid of another.

"When the legislative and executive powers are united in the same person, or in the same body of magistrates, there can be no liberty; because apprehensions may arise, lest the same monarch or senate should enact tyrannical laws, to execute them in a tyrannical manner.

"Again, there is no liberty, if the judiciary power be not separated from the legislative and executive. Were it joined with the legislative, the life and liberty of the subject would be exposed to arbitrary control; for the judge would be then the legislator. Were it joined to the executive power, the judge might behave with violence and oppression.

"There would be an end of everything, were the same man, or the same body, whether of the nobles or of the people, to exercise those three powers, that of enacting laws, that of executing the public resolutions, and of trying the causes of individuals." Montesquieu, *The Spirit of the Laws*, 154 (6th ed., 1792).

However, Montesquieu thought the judiciary of little importance and said at p. 157, supra:

"Of the three powers above-mentioned, the judiciary is in some measure next to nothing: there remains therefore only two; and as these have need of a regulating power to moderate them, the part of the legislative body composed of the nobility, is extremely proper for this purpose."

It remained for Blackstone (1723-1780) to express the doctrine as it reached full development with the addition of a strong, independent judiciary into the threefold shield of freedom, a government separated into three parts, the legislative, the executive and the judiciary:

"It is probable, and almost certain, that in very early times, before our Constitution arrived at its full perfection, our kings, in person, often heard and determined causes between party and party. But at present, by the long and uniform usage of many ages, our kings have delegated their whole judicial power to the judges of their several courts; which are the grand depositaries of the fundamental laws of the kingdom, and have gained a known and stated jurisdiction, regulated by certain and established rules, which the crown itself can not now alter but by act of Parliament. And, in order to maintain both the dignity and independence of the judges in the superior courts, it is enacted by the statute 13 W. III., c. 2, that their commissions shall be made (not, as formerly, *durante bene placito*, but) *quamdieu bene se gesserint*, and their salaries ascertained and established, but that it may be lawful to remove them on the address of both houses of Parliament. And now, by the noble improvements of that law in the statute of 1 Geo. III., c. 23, enacted at the earnest recommendation of the king himself from the throne, the judges are continued in their offices during their good behavior, notwithstanding any demise of the crown (which was formerly held immediately to vacate their seats), and their full salaries are absolutely secured to them during the continuance of their commissions; his majesty having been pleased to declare that 'he looked upon the

125

independence and uprightness of the judges as essential to the impartial administration of justice, as one of the best securities of the rights and liberties of his subjects, and as most conducive to the honor of the crown.'

* * *

"In this distinct and separate existence of the judicial power in a peculiar body of men, nominated indeed, but not removable at pleasure, by the crown, consists one main preservative of the public liberty; which can not subsist long in any state, unless the administration of common justice be in some degree separated from the legislative and also from the executive power. Were it joined with the legislative, the life, liberty, and property of the subject would be in the hands of arbitrary judges, whose decisions would be then regulated only by their own opinions, and not by any fundamental principles of law; which, though legislators may depart from, yet judges are bound to observe. Were it joined with the executive, this union might soon be an overbalance for the legislative. For which reasons, by the statute of 16 Car I., c. 10, which abolished the Court of Star Chamber, effectual care is taken to remove all judicial power out of the hands of the king's privy council, who, as then was evident from recent instances, might soon be inclined to pronounce that for law which was most agreeable to the prince or his officers. Nothing, therefore, is more to be avoided, in a free constitution, than uniting the provinces of a judge and a minister of state." 1 Blackstone, *Commentaries on the Laws of England*, 267-68, 269 (21st American ed., 1854). By the time the members of the Constitutional Convention met in 1787 the doctrine of separation of powers between the legislative, the executive, and the judiciary had become an axiom of free government.

In the Federalist papers, which appeared in 1787 and 1788 in defense of the proposed federal Constitution, Madison was assigned the task of explaining the principle of separation of powers and proving that the framers had not disregarded it. Madison did not argue that the principle was a good one. He started with the premise that it was good and that it was a necessary doctrine to be included in the Constitution to insure a republic that guaranteed freedom to its people; this premise was accepted by the people to whom his arguments were addressed.

In The Federalist, No. 47, published January 30, 1788, Madison said:

126

"One of the principal objections inculcated by the more respectable adversaries to the constitution, is its supposed violation of the political maxim, that the legislative, executive and judiciary departments ought to be separate and distinct. In the structure of the federal government, no regard, it is said, seems to have been paid to this essential precaution in favor of liberty. The several departments of power are distributed and blended in such a manner, as at once to destroy all symmetry and beauty of form; and to expose some of the essential parts of the edifice to the danger of being crushed by the disproportionate weight of other parts.

"No political truth is certainly of greater intrinsic value or is stamped with the authority of more enlightened patrons of liberty than that on which the objection is founded. The accumulation of all powers, legislative, executive and judiciary in the same hands, whether of one, a few or many, and whether hereditary, self appointed or elective, may justly be pronounced the very definition of tyranny. Were the federal constitution therefore really chargeable with the accumulation of powers or with a mixture of powers having a dangerous tendency to such an accumulation, no further arguments would be necessary to inspire a universal reprobation of the system. I persuade myself however, that it will be made apparent to every one, that the charge cannot be supported, and that the maxim on which it relies, has been totally misconceived and misapplied. In order to form correct ideas on this important subject, it will be proper to investigate the sense, in which the preservation of liberty requires, that the three great departments of power should be separate and distinct." *The Federalist*, No. 47, 323 (Cooke ed., 1961) (Madison).

James Wilson, who was influential in obtaining the adoption of the Constitution, said:

"Though the foregoing great powers—legislative, executive, and judicial—are all necessary to a good government; yet it is of the last importance, that each of them be preserved distinct, and unmingled, in the exercise of its separate powers, with either or with both of the others. Here every degree of confusion in the plan will produce a corresponding degree of interference, opposition, combination, or perplexity in its execution." Wilson, *Works*, 407 (1804).

Thus, the doctrine, "developed over a period of two

127

millennia," was "firmly imbedded in the warp and woof of our Constitution." For the court to decide the case on the merits would be a clear violation of the separation of powers doctrine. For the court to order any member, officer, or employee of the House to perform an act related to the organization or membership of the House, to paraphrase Justice Frankfurter, would be "for the Court to crash through a political thicket into political quicksand." Therefore he ruled as follows:

1. The application for a three-judge court is denied.

2. The complaint is dismissed for want of jurisdiction of the subject matter in this court.

3. The prayer for a preliminary injunction falls with the dismissal of the complaint.

While Judge Hart allowed that the "speech and debate" clause might have precluded the court's jurisdiction in the matter, he rested his decision wholly on the constitutional principle of separation of powers. Thus, it was not necessary for him to resolve any of the other questions raised in the case. Although in his opinion he deemed it unnecessary to resolve the dispute over whether the House could add to the three expressed qualifications for membership, he later indicated that he felt the House's power was limited to judging the qualifications enumerated in the Constitution:

> I doubt if any serious lawyer, who thought about it [exclusion for other than the three stated qualifications] ever really felt that Powell should be denied his seat in view of his qualifications under the section of the Constitution mentioned.
>
> * * *
>
> However, there was a serious question as to whether the Courts could run Congress, the separation of powers doctrine.[11]

Nor was Judge Hart's opinion Powell's only reason for gloom that April 7. On April 6 his wife had filed a suit seeking support payments of $1,500 a month. Even without this added blow, Powell was in financial trouble. His only steady source of income was the royalties on the sale of his record, since he no longer received his congressional salary. And by the end of April only a little more than half the records required to cover the advance he had received—and which had immediately been paid over to Mrs. James—had been sold.

8   Aground Once More

On the same day that Judge Hart delivered his opinion, Powell's lawyers filed a notice of appeal with the court of appeals for the District of Columbia. The next day, April 8, 1967, Powell's lawyers filed a lengthy motion for summary reversal of the order and judgment of the district court and for an immediate hearing to declare the April 11 election moot. The court considered and then denied Powell's request for an immediate hearing on April 10. Powell's attorneys had filed for summary reversal of the judgment of the district court to expedite proceedings; they hoped to get an immediate decision before the 90th Congress, in which Powell hoped to be seated, elapsed.

On April 11, Powell was triumphantly reelected by his Harlem followers with 27,900 (86.1 percent) votes, to 4,091 and 427 for Mrs. Williams and Reverend Yearling, respectively. This did not mean, however, that all his backers agreed with his course. Soon after the election, John H. Young, head of the Congress Party, urged Powell to return to Harlem even at the risk of arrest and then go to Washington to demand his seat.

Not long afterward, the House finally established the Committee on Standards of Official Conduct that so many people had recommended in recent months. The formation of the 12-member bipartisan committee was approved by the unusual unanimous roll-call vote of 400-0. The committee was authorized to recommend procedures to establish and enforce standards of official conduct, but was not given authority to investigate the activities of individual members.

While action on the Standards Committee was being completed, the House members were also considering their strategy in the event that Powell appeared to take his seat on the basis of the new election. Several proposals for seating him were advanced. Representative Celler suggested that Powell be seated with a mild censure (which would not be read in his presence). A group of House liberals proposed a similar plan, with the added provision that after Powell was seated his expulsion (requiring a two-thirds vote) be moved and defeated. Other members suggested that the matter be referred to the new Standards Committee. And yet another group urged that the House delay action pending the resolution of the issue in the courts. Despite public appeals to their colleagues, the House leadership was forced to admit that the votes necessary to seat Powell could not be found. Opposition to Powell was as great as, or greater than, it had been on March 1.

At the same time the Justice Department announced that it had begun a full-scale investigation of Powell's alleged wrongdoing. The ex-congressman made no comment on any of these developments. On the advice of his lawyers, he once again announced a policy of strict silence.

The motion for summary reversal was argued before Chief Judge David L. Bazelon and circuit judges Warren E. Burger and Harold Leventhal of the District of Columbia Court of Appeals on April 27. Later in the day the three judges issued a per curiam order[1] denying the motion for summary reversal and directing that briefs be filed in preparation for a complete consideration of the case.

Although the House received a notice on May 1 from the State of New York officially certifying Powell's election,

Powell made no effort to take his seat. Frank Reeves, one of Powell's attorneys, indicated that their understanding of the rules and precedents was that Powell was not to present himself in Washington until the House indicated its readiness to swear him in. Indeed, the question, raised by Congressman Celler during the debates on March 1, had not been resolved. When Celler had asked if H. Res. 278 would bar Powell from membership in the entire 90th Congress, even if he were reelected, Speaker McCormack had stated: "This is a matter which the Chair cannot pass upon at the present time. That is a matter which, if it arises, would require consideration in the future by the House."[2] On May 1, McCormack again indicated that the House would consider the question only when Powell presented himself.[3]

After the court of appeals denied the motion for summary reversal, Powell's lawyers concluded that it would be early 1968 before Supreme Court review of the eventual decision of the court of appeals could be obtained. Consequently they informed the court of appeals on May 4 that they intended to apply directly to the Supreme Court for a writ of certiorari. (A writ of certiorari directs the lower court to send up the record of the case for review.) Supreme Court rules provide for such a procedure "upon a showing that the case is of such imperative public importance as to justify the deviation from normal appellate processes and to require immediate settlement in [the Supreme] Court."[4] The petition for certiorari was filed on May 13. Motions for leave to file amicus curiae[5] briefs were filed by some 12 organizations and individuals within the next two weeks.

The petition for certiorari, like Powell's earlier arguments, attacked the House action on several points, including the claim that the exclusion of Powell violated the rights of his Negro constituents guaranteed in the 14th and 15th Amendments. Thus far the Powell lawyers had been hard-pressed to substantiate this point—hard-pressed, that is, until Emanuel Celler came to their aid.

133

On May 14 Celler appeared on "Searchlight," an NBC-TV interview show. Celler was asked what he thought of Powell's charge that his exclusion was motivated by racism. "I believe there was an element of racism in the vote in the House that rejected the resolution which I as Chairman of the Select Committee offered," replied Celler. "It was racism accompanied by the hysteria that had resulted from the climate of public opinion due to Mr. Powell's antics and peculiarities and swagger and defiance." Celler was then asked if the House would again vote to exclude Powell if he attempted to take his seat. Celler said that he feared the House would "repeat its error again," for the same reasons as before: "racism, hysteria, and so forth and fear, because there's an avalanche of mail received by the Congressmen which is all hostile to Powell." Asked if the House had erred from the standpoint of policy or the standpoint of law, he said: "Well, the House is a law unto itself. I can't say it's an error in law because what the House does is something that cannot be challenged in my opinion in the court."

Celler's comment that "the House is a law unto itself" was interesting, in view of his past agreement with Powell that the exclusion was unconstitutional and his suggestion that Powell take the case to court. On the program he suggested that the House's action, although unconstitutional, was not reviewable by the courts.

Powell's lawyers hurriedly embodied the transcript of this program in an "Emergency Supplement to the Petition for Writ of Certiorari" and filed it with the Supreme Court. But their efforts were in vain. The court denied the petition on May 29.[6] The lawyers for the two parties then spent the remainder of the "long hot summer" of 1967 wrangling over the forms and schedule for filing briefs in the court of appeals.

The ex-congressman's summer, spent on Bimini, got off to a bad start. On June 1, the highest New York court, the court of appeals, unanimously upheld the rulings of the lower courts that Powell must first return to New York State and suffer arrest before review of Judge Markewich's arrest order would be granted.

Powell's second blow of the summer was the comparatively mild censure administered on June 23 to Senator Thomas Dodd of Connecticut for misuse of political funds. At a Bimini news conference a few days later, Powell was extremely bitter about the difference between the harsh treatment he had received and the rebuke received by Dodd. The punishment accorded Dodd magnified, Powell said, "the obscene distinction between the justice for white men and justice for black men in America." But there was more on Powell's mind than just that. He was ready to bargain for his seat. "Although my conscience is clear and my heart untroubled," the erstwhile Representative said, "I would nevertheless accept with reluctance the same punishment meted to Senator Dodd. For this purpose I would accordingly present myself before the bar of the House of Representatives at any time the House Democrat and Republican leaders deem appropriate." But if the House did not agree to punish him in the same manner as Dodd, he would wait for the federal courts to order his seating. Powell's proposition was a major concession on his part, and it held out a possible solution for those congressmen who had qualms about the constitutionality of H. Res. 278 or who feared a confrontation between the courts and Congress.

But there were no takers. Democratic leaders let it be known that Powell would be "lucky to get into the House under any circumstances." Emanuel Celler reasoned that "his statement doesn't enhance his chances of more favorable consideration in the House, particularly when he refers to the action of the House as obscene. I doubt very much whether the House, as he suggests, would accept anything less than the recommendations made by the Select Committee. . . . . It's a vain hope that the House would milden the sanctions."[7] Gerald Ford said flatly, "I don't think the House should make any deals with Mr. Powell."[8]

Powell did not attend a black power Conference held in Newark on July 20-24, although he was listed as honorary cochairman with Dr. Nathan Wright, Jr. His lawyers explained that their client ws anxious to return to the United States and to Harlem, but feared that his arrest would touch off riots in racially tense America. The reaction of the conference delegates to the former congressman's nonappearance was mixed. Some plastered the convention area with stickers reading "Keep the Faith: Kennedy-Powell '68." These were quickly removed by other delegates, for many of them were angered by Powell's failure to attend. When his son, Adam Clayton Powell III, tried to speak in his father's stead, many delegates voiced vigorous objections and others walked out. The conference did agree, however, on a resolution calling for the censure of all congressmen who voted for Powell's exclusion.

This discontent at the conference only reflected the growing discontent in Powell's constituency. The Alfred E. Isaacs Club constituency office, manned by volunteers, looked after local problems, and a pair of Powell's former secretaries, now on the House payroll, tried to handle matters in Washington, with the volunteer help of his former administrative assistant, Odell Clark. But Powell's constituents were understandably angered by the lack of real representation, and many placed the blame for this lack on Powell's failure to return. Their anger toward him had risen steadily during the summer. A delegate to the Newark conference spoke for this group when he said, "You saw what happened to his son—if he [Powell] stays away much longer it will happen to the big man himself."

A few days after the Newark conference, Powell held another Bimini news conference to emphasize his view that the riots in Detroit and other cities were a "necessary phase of the black revolution." He predicted that new riots would occur in 12 American cities unless Negroes were nominated to Congress by September 1. He also singled out Representative Conyers as being due for replacement.

In early September, while on Bimini, Powell was served with a subpoena to appear before the federal grand jury for the District of Columbia. Powell's lawyers doubted the validity of the subpoena but felt it was wiser to appear and avoid adding a federal contempt suit to their other problems. Powell accordingly appeared before the grand jury for 65 minutes on September 11, accompanied by two new lawyers, one of them Edward Bennett Williams, who had defended Powell during his income tax troubles in 1960. Neither Powell nor the Justice Department made any comment on what the inquiry was about. After a brief visit to his old office in the Rayburn Building, Powell returned to Bimini.

On September 15, *Powell v. McCormack* was reargued before the Court of Appeals for the District of Columbia. The case was heard by Circuit Judges Warren E. Burger, Carl McGowan, and Harold Leventhal. Judge Burger presided. Judge Burger was born in St. Paul, Minnesota, in 1907. He graduated from the University of Minnesota and earned his LL.B. in 1931. He received an LL.D. in 1964. Judge Burger was admitted to the bar in 1931 and engaged thereafter in private practice in Minnesota. From 1931 to 1946 he was a member of the faculty of the St. Paul College of Law. He became an assistant U.S. attorney general in 1953, was appointed to the court of appeals by President Eisenhower in 1956, and was nominated chief justice of the Supreme Court by President Nixon on May 21, 1969, and confirmed by the Senate on June 9, 1969. Judge McGowan was born in Hymera, Indiana, in 1911. He received an A.B. from Dartmouth in 1932 and an LL.B. from Columbia in 1936. Thereafter he engaged in private practice in New York, Washington, and Chicago. He also served three years on the faculty of the Northwestern University Law School. Judge McGowan was appointed by President Kennedy in 1963. Judge Leventhal was born in New York City in 1915 and graduated from Columbia in 1934. He graduated from Columbia Law School in 1936. Judge Leventhal served as law clerk to Supreme Court Justices Stone and Reed and then served as counsel for a number of federal offices. He served on the staff of Justice Jackson at the Nuremberg trials and thereafter was engaged primarily in private practice. He was a visiting lecturer at Yale for five years. Judge Leventhal was appointed to the bench by President Johnson in 1965.

The brief submitted by the appellants differed from the brief presented to the district court in that the arguments that Powell's exclusion had violated his constitutional rights had been greatly expanded. Apparently there had been some discussion among Powell's attorneys as to what lines of argument should be pursued. The Howard Law School group, Reid and Reeves, believed that the argument that Powell had been denied basic constitutional rights during the hearings before the Select Committee and in subsequent congressional review of his conduct deserved prominence in the brief to the court of appeals. On the other hand, other attorneys, particularly Kinoy, wanted to base their major argument on the qualifications issue. The resulting compromise produced extensive discussion in the brief of the due process argument. One tactical advantage was that the court was offered the opportunity to reverse the decision of the House on the grounds that Powell's due process rights had been violated without the court's having to determine the scope of the House's power to judge the qualifications of members-elect. Such a decision on the due process question, however, would only have postponed a decision on the fundamental issue—qualifications—since there was little indication that the House could be dissuaded from excluding Powell.

In their brief to the court of appeals, Powell's attorneys argued that the district court should not have dismissed the complaint for "want of jurisdiction of the subject matter."[9] The arguments supporting their claim that the subject matter of the suit was justiciable were in essence the same as those advanced in the brief filed in the district court. What was new in this brief (and what merits additional comment here) were a lengthy discussion of the intent of the framers with regard

138

to the power of the legislature to judge the qualifications for membership; a discussion of the alleged violation of Powell's constitutional rights; and a brief discussion of the "speech or debate" clause, requested by the court in light of the unanimous per curiam opinion of the Supreme Court in *Dombrowski et al. v. Eastland et al.*, 387 U. S. 82 (1967).

The history of the proceedings at the Constitutional Convention revealed, Powell's attorneys claimed, "the unmistakable intention of the Framers that neither branch of the Legislature was to have any power to alter, add to, vary or ignore the constitutional qualifications." The power to judge the qualifications was "restricted solely to these qualifications set forth in the Constitution itself." Relying upon Charles Warren's study of the convention, *The Making of Our Constitution* (1928), they noted that the convention defeated a proposal to give the Congress power to establish qualifications in general and defeated a proposal for a property qualification. And certainly the convention "did not intend that a single branch of Congress should possess a power which the Convention had expressly refused to vest in the whole Congress." Thus, since the Constitution expressly stated three qualifications for membership, "the elimination of all power in Congress to fix qualifications clearly left the provisions of the Constitution itself as the sole source of qualifications." Also noted was Alexander Hamilton's analysis in the Federalist Papers: "The qualifications of the persons who may choose or be chosen, as has been remarked upon other occasions, are defined and fixed in the Constitution, and are unalterable by the Legislature."

The punishment of exclusion and the process by which this punishment was obtained violated Powell's constitutional rights, his attorneys argued. The resolution imposing the punishment of exclusion was, they said, "a classic Bill of Attainder," prohibited by the Constitution. It was a legislative act imposing penalty without a judicial trial and represented, in the words of Chief Justice Warren, in *United*

States v. *Brown*, 381 U. S. 437 (1965), "the evil the framers had sought to bar; legislative punishment, of any form or severity, of specifically designated persons or groups." Furthermore, it was argued, the action of the House during committee proceedings and on the floor of the House violated Powell's substantive and procedural due process guarantees. He was denied these rights on the erroneous theory that the proceeding was not adversary in nature but merely an inquiry. It was significant, they thought, that in the hearings involving Senator Dodd, the senator was allowed, among other things, to cross-examine witnesses and offer evidence on his own behalf. Finally, the attorneys argued, the court had power to grant whatever relief was necessary to remedy the claimed violations of constitutional rights, for as the court said in 1803 in *Marbury* v. *Madison*, ours is a "government of laws and not of men," and "the very essence of civil liberty consists in the right of every individual to claim the protection of the laws, whenever he receives an injury."

The per curiam opinion in *Dombrowski* did not support "the extraordinary contention that the Speech or Debate Clause repeals the historic function of judicial review firmly grounded in our jurisprudence since *Marbury*," said the brief. The Supreme Court said in *Dombrowski*:

> It is the purpose and office of the doctrine of legislative immunity, having its roots as it does in the Speech or Debate Clause of the Constitution, *Kilbourn* v. *Thompson*, 103 U. S. 168, 204 (1881), that legislators engaged "in the sphere of legitimate legislative activity," *Tenny* v. *Brandhove*, supra, 341 U.S. at 376, should be protected not only from the consequences of litigation's results but also from the burden of defending themselves.

Powell's attorney's interpreted the language to mean that legislative immunity was not absolute, but related solely to "legitimate legislative activity." Moreover, the clause was intended to protect legislators only from punitive actions, not from the remedial action sought here.

140

The brief submitted by Bromley for the defendants was also noteworthy for its development of historical material regarding the legislature's power to judge qualifications for membership. The question of justiciability was argued, as it had been before the district court, but again, the issues that require additional comment here are the historical development of the legislature's power to judge qualifications, the alleged violation of Powell's constitutional rights, and the "speech or debate" clause in light of *Dombrowski.*

In the brief itself, the attorneys for the House traced the development of the legislature's power to judge the qualifications of its membership: in England the right of the legislature to be the sole judge developed as a part of the struggle for legislative independence from the monarch; likewise, in the legislatures in the American colonies the power to judge qualifications was exclusive and never a part of the jurisdiction of the courts. By not specifying otherwise, the framers intended that this power should remain solely with the legislature:

> Thus, at the time of the Constitutional Convention, the phrase "judge the qualifications" had become a term of art with a well-defined and widely understood meaning, which entailed the exclusive delegation of that power to the legislative body. At least since the sixteenth century, no court, either in England, the colonies or the new nation, had ever assumed the power to review the judgments made by the legislative branch. . . .
>
> Nothing at the Convention itself supports any conclusion other than that the framers intended to allocate power between the legislature and the judiciary in what was to them a familiar English judicial practice, they wrote into the Constitution explicit provisions to that effect. . . .

And no court had ever passed upon the scope of the power of the House or Senate to judge the qualifications of its members since the Constitution was written.

Also submitted as a supplementary compilation of historical practice to 1787,[10] in which the attorneys cited others who had reached a conclusion different from that of Professor Warren. There was a historical basis for a middle ground that would provide Congress some latitude in judging the qualifications of its members but at the same time would uphold Madison's view that Congress could not exclude for reasons capricious or arbitrary. Cited approvingly was Professor Zachariah Chafee's analysis in *Free Speech in the United States* (1941):

> We are not forced to choose between giving the House absolute power to unseat whomever it dislikes, and giving the voters absolute power to seat whomever they elect. A third alternative has been adopted, fairly close to the second view. The constitutional qualifications ordinarily suffice; but Congress has rather cautiously imposed some additional tests by statute, and the House of Representatives or the Senate has probably added a very few more qualifications by established usage (a sort of legislative common law) to cover certain obvious cases of unfitness.

In Blackstone's *Commentaries* (4th ed., 1770), the three "standing incapacities" for membership in Parliament were set forth in "precisely the negative language" used in our Constitution. But Blackstone allowed that there might be other reasons for which the House of Commons might wish to judge a member incapable of sitting. The brief stated:

> Under Blackstone's analysis there are two separate and distinct powers involved in determining qualifications of a member to sit in a legislative body. The *first* power is that of creating by legislation "standing incapacities," which operate prospectively to exclude groups or classes of persons from membership in the legislative body. The statements and arguments of the framers at the Constitutional Convention quoted in Warren and by appellants, and the action taken by the Convention, are on their face directed toward depriving the houses of Congress of that power to create additional "standing incapacities." The *second* power is that to "adjudge [a person] disabled and incapable to sit as a member" for the duration of a particular Congress, for reasons going to the character or conduct of the individual involved. The members of the Convention took other actions (not cited by

142

Warren) which, when read against the historical background with which the framers were familiar, indicate in our view an intent to preserve for each house that entirely different power.

Thus, the supplement urged the position that the House could judge the three enumerated qualifications as well as the suitability of a member to sit during a particular session of Congress based on some proven misdeeds.

The defendants argued that Powell's "ancillary allegations" regarding denial of his constitutional rights did not confer jurisdiction on the courts and, in any event, were without merit. The House had not denied Powell substantive due process, for, contrary to Mr. Powell's claim, he was aware of the standards of conduct by which he was to be judged. He should have been aware of the "legislative common law" described by Professor Chafee that has allowed both houses to exclude members-elect in cases of obvious unfitness. Powell's acceptance of the power to exclude was evidenced by his vote in the House in 1965 against the seating of the entire Mississippi delegation. Regarding procedural due process, Powell mistakenly claimed that only triallike procedures met the demands of due process. Bromley argued that the Supreme Court emphasized on several occasions that due process was not an immutable concept; if the proceedings were essentially investigatory rather than adjudicatory in nature, the full range of judicial procedures was not required. And, Bromley urged, the proceedings of the Select Committee were investigatory, since the committee's function was merely to report to the House the results of the investigations and its recommendations. Finally, Bromley argued that H. Res. 278 was not a bill of attainder. Powell erroneously assumed that all adjudicatory powers were assigned to the courts; on the contrary, Congress was expressly granted the power to judge the qualifications of its members.

The defendants' claim that the "speech and debate" clause was an absolute bar to the court's consideration of this action was reinforced, said Bromley, by the *Dombrowski* opinion. Bromley interpreted the opinion as barring Powell's claim against members of the House and noted that the court had also held that the immunity, although less absolute, was applicable to employees and officers of the Congress.

In sum, as was the case in the arguments before the district court, the overriding issue was justiciability. Was the subject matter of the suit justiciable because the acts complained of were in violation of various sections of the Constitution, as the appellants argued, or did the case present a political question that was not justiciable because it would necessarily involve a confrontation between coequal branches of government? Both briefs contained rich historical material bearing on the power of the House to be the judge of the qualifications of its members and the question of whether the three enumerated qualifications were the exclusive qualifications for membership. There was additional discussion of the "speech and debate" clause in light of the *Dombrowski* case. The clause, the appellants maintained, was designed to protect legislators only from punitive actions arising out of "legitimate legislative activity," not from remedial action, which Powell sought. Defendants read *Dombrowski* as precluding judicial relief. Included was a fuller discussion of alleged denial of substantive and procedural due process than had appeared in the earlier briefs. Appellants argued that the punishment of exclusion constituted a bill of attainder and that in proceedings leading up to punishment, denial of due process was based upon the erroneous notion that the proceedings were not adversary in nature but merely an inquiry. The defendants maintained that since the proceedings were investigatory rather tha adjudicatory, the full panoply of judicial procedures was not required.

After oral argument, the three judges took the case under advisement. Meanwhile the grand jury investigation of Powell's activities continued.

The revolt against Powell in Harlem grew stronger as

winter approached. The *New York Times* reported on October 30 that Dr. Eugene Callendar, director of the Greater New York Urban League, had urged the people of Harlem to "cut out the sentimentality" and "seek someone else to represent them." His sentiments were echoed by Whitney Young. Powell, declared Young, "ought to resign or come home. . . . As for the arrest order, he should stand up and face it and not leave this community."

But Powell still had many supporters. Three days later William Booth, chairman of the New York City Commission on Human Rights, criticized statements that Powell should resign or be replaced by the Harlem voters. "Such talk plays right into the hands of those in the white community who opposed Powell's election," he said. Soon afterward, the Black People's Party of North America, a recently formed group of young people headquartered in Harlem, designated November as Adam Clayton Powell Month in Harlem. During a four-hour rally addressed by H. Rap Brown and LeRoi Jones, the group vowed to boycott elections and refuse to pay taxes until Powell was seated. Other Negroes were warned not to run for his seat. A few days later, James Meredith announced he would run again for Congress from Harlem in 1968.

In late December, several congressmen, among them two Negroes, Conyers and Diggs, introduced a bill to provide for a special staff to provide services for constituents of districts not represented in Congress by a sitting member. Powell reacted violently to the proposal. He denounced it on December 21 as "white colonialism" and a "return to slavery." Of cosponsor Conyers, he said, "His consistent actions against my return to Congress have only played into the hands of white racists." Powell made no comment on the fact that Diggs was also a cosponsor. Conyer's office replied that Odell Clark, who had been helping to look after Powell's constituents, approved the measure.

On January 8, 1968, Powell flew to Los Angeles. There he

toured the Watts area and delivered a number of speeches, both there and at California universities. He announced that if the District of Columbia grand jury brought in an indictment against him, he would "blow the whistle" on members of the House.

Powell also taped a show in mid-January for the CBS program "Face The Nation." He declared through that medium that the courts were "filibustering against him" and that he would return to the House "when the Supreme Court gets enough guts to rule one way or another." But he said he was no longer willing to reenter Congress as the most junior member and would not attempt to get back in, either by running again or on the basis of the April election, if the courts ruled against him.

Powell made the West Coast trip at least partially because of the honorarium he received from UCLA. He was in serious financial trouble. His only source of income came from occasionally renting his boat. This was supplemented by a small amount he won by betting on a Bimini fishing contest. On the debit side, however, in addition to his legal costs, he owed his wife $1,500 a month in support payments. The situation became even more serious when a New York Supreme Court judge ruled Powell was liable for additional expenses incurred by Mrs. James stemming from the transfer-of-assets case.

On February 28, 1968, almost one year to the day after Powell's exclusion, the court of appeals rendered its opinion.[11] This delay, due partially to Powell's attempt to gain direct appeal to the Supreme Court, turned out to be very costly to Powell and helpful to the Supreme Court, for the 90th Congress had elapsed by the time the Supreme Court eventually decided to review the case. Each of the three court of appeals justices agreed that ex-Congressman Powell was not entitled to relief from the court, although they invoked different reasons to support this conclusion.

The opinion of Judge Burger was extremely sensitive to

the role of the federal courts in the political system; he was keenly aware that the courts possessed neither the power of the purse nor that of the sword. Burger began by indicating the novelty of the question before the court: "This case presents for the first time the question of whether courts can consider claims that a Member-elect has been improperly excluded from his seat in the United States House of Representatives." In the 16 pages that followed, Judge Burger set forth the rather complicated facts of the case and reviewed the issues raised by the appellants and the relevant constitutional provisions.

Burger's opinion was divided into four parts. Part I raised the question of whether the court had jurisdiction in this case. After citing the relevant criteria for federal jurisdiction, as set forth by Mr. Justice Brennan in *Baker* v. *Carr*, Judge Burger found that these criteria were met and the federal courts had jurisdiction, a point of agreement among all three members of the court.[12]

Judge Burger then proceeded to the second part of the opinion: Should the courts act? This section of the opinion dealt with "the appropriateness or inappropriateness of the subject matter of Appellants' claim for judicial consideration," the "political question" doctrine on which district Court Judge Hart had based his refusal to hear the case. Judge Burger suggested that "the term 'political' has been used to distinguish questions which are essentially for decision by the political branches from those which are essentially for adjudication by the judicial branch."

The judge then set forth the rationale behind the political question doctrine:

> Nonjusticiability of a question because it is found to be essentially political is declared by *Baker* to be a doctrine peculiar to confrontations within the *federal* establishment and derives from the fundamental structure of our system of divided and separate powers.

Citing Justice Brennan's catalogue of six factors developed in

Baker which bear on the question of whether a case presents a political question, Burger based his conclusion that the case was not justiciable on the fourth of the *Baker* criteria, "the impossibility of a court's undertaking independent resolution without expressing lack of the respect due coordinate branches of government." Burger said:

> Any judgment which enjoined execution of House Resolution 278, or commanded the Speaker of the House to administer the oath, or commanded Members of the House as to any action or vote within the Chamber would inevitably bring about a direct confrontation with a co-equal branch and if that did not indicate lack of respect due that Branch, it would at best be a gesture hardly comporting with our ideas of separate co-equal branches of the federal establishment. These circumstances would give rise to a classic political question and fall within the definition of such a question under *Baker*.

Judge Burger had concluded that the court could not order Congress to seat Powell; but could the court decide whether Powell had been unconstitutionally excluded, even though relief for such an action could not be ordered? Burger's analysis was that the issues raised by Powell could not be decided for the same reasons that the relief sought could not be rendered, for to do so would put the court in the position of deciding the underlying issues which the judge held to involve a political question. In addition, Judge Burger considered whether the claims of the voters could be decided independently of the rights of Powell. He ruled:

> The right to vote is not an academic right; its primary objective is frustrated when the person elected cannot assume the powers and responsibilities of office. Nevertheless, the subject matter of Mr. Powell's claim and the voting claims of the class Appellants are so interrelated that neither can be regarded as having an existence entirely independent of the other; in the context of this case, they stand or fall together. It must follow that as Mr. Powell's claims are inappropriate for judicial consideration, so also are those of the class Appellants.

148

Part III of the opinion was in response to one of the major issues raised by the House's attorneys, that the "speech and debate" clause barred

> . . .any court from questioning Members of the House of Representatives, individually or collectively, with respect to legitimate legislative activities and that this includes the exercise of their constitutional responsibility to vote on the seating of a Member-elect.

Burger held that the clause did bar Powell's actions:

> If the Members of the House who are Appellees here cannot be "questioned in any other place," it would seem that they need not *answer* in any other place, including courts. . . .
> Having in mind the breadth accorded the Clause in *Kilbourn, Tenney* and *Dombrowski*, and the "prophylatic purposes of the clause," *United States v. Johnson*, . . it would seem that, however characterized, the Clause operates as a bar to the maintenance of this suit.

In Part IV, regarding the question of whether Powell should have been granted a hearing before a three-judge court, Judge Burger supported the finding of the district court that the statutory language providing for a three-man court does not encompass an appeal to such a body from a congressional resolution, as was here being challenged.

Judge Burger than argued that the court does not have to decide the merits of the case:

> Our disposition of this appeal on the ground that the claims are nonjusticiable
> because of the inappropriateness of the subject matter for judicial consideration, makes
> it unnecessary to reach the claims of the merits.

However, even though refusing to decide the actual issue presented to the court as to the constitutionality of the exclusion of Powell, Judge Burger noted that there is historical disagreement as to whether Article I, Sec. 2, cl. 2 set forth the only grounds for excluding a member-elect from Congress. Concluding his opinion, Judge Burger argued that there were certain costs to our political system; one cost could be that some errors would go unchallenged in order to maintain the delicate balance between the various branches of government:

> Conflicts between our co-equal federal branches are not merely unseemly but often destructive of important values. . . .
>
> That each branch may thus occasionally make errors for which there may be no effective remedy is one of the prices we pay for this independence, this separateness, of each co-equal branch and for the desired supremacy of each within its own assigned sphere. When the focus is on the particular acts of one branch, it is not difficult to conjure the parade of horrors which can flow from unreviewable power. Inevitably, in a case with large consequences and a paucity of legal precedents, the advocates tend to raise the spectre of the hypothetical situations which would be permitted by the result they oppose. Our history shows scant evidence that such dire predictions eventuate and the occasional departures in each branch have been thought more tolerable than any alternatives that would give any one branch domination over another. That courts encounter some problems for which they can supply no solution is not invariably an occasion for regret or concern; this is an essential limitation in a system of divided powers. That courts cannot *compel* the acts sought to be ordered in this case recedes into relative insignificance alongside the blow to representative government were they either so rash or so sure of their infallibility as to think they should command an elected co-equal branch in these circumstances.
>
> We should resist the temptation to speculate whether and under what circumstances courts might find claims to a seat in Congress which would be justiciable. . . .

The concurring opinion by Judge McGowan was noteworthy because even though he denied that he was deciding the underlying issue of whether Congress had constitutional authority to exclude Powell from Congress, he clearly suggested that Congress could exclude a member-elect from Congress for the same reasons and by the same vote on which a member could be expelled. He seemed to merge the requirements of the power to expel, requiring a two-thirds vote, with the power to exclude. Judge McGowan's analysis of the issue before the Court was the following:

> Appellant Powell's cause of action for a judicially compelled seating thus boils down, in my view, to the narrow issue of whether a member found by his colleagues, after notice and opportunity for hearing, to have engaged in official misconduct must, because of the accidents of timing, be formally admitted before he can be either investigated or expelled. The sponsor of the motion to exclude stated on the floor that he was proceeding on the theory that the power to expel included the power to exclude, provided a 2/3 vote was forthcoming. It was. Therefore, success for Mr. Powell on the merits would mean that the District Court must admonish the House that it is form, not substance, that should govern in great affairs, and accordingly command the House members to act out a charade.[13]

Although accepting that Congress may be able to exclude on the same grounds on which it can expel a member, Judge McGowan refrained from resting his opinion on that point:

> The question is one of whether, under all the circumstances and with a wise regard for the nature and capabilities of judicial power and for the respect it must always command, the court is bound to hear and determine a complaint on its merits.[14]

Judge McGowan was impressed with the fact that even though Speaker McCormack did not rule that a two-thirds vote was required for exclusion, in fact a two-thirds vote was obtained. However, he felt the court should not intervene in the House's determination that exclusion and expulsion can be done for the same reasons because that judgment "presents no impelling occasion for judicial scrutiny."

In a separate concurring opinion, Judge Leventhal assumed that Powell was correct in asserting that the three grounds of eligibility were exclusive. But, he said, "That does not mean that appellant Powell was immune from exclusion on grounds that would justify expulsion." Leventhal was willing to follow Congressman Curtis' position that Powell could be excluded on the same grounds on which he could be expelled, provided that such exclusion was by a two-thirds vote. Even if the procedure used to exclude Powell might have been improper, the court could decline to entertain an action based on a procedural defect:

> The fact that the House voted exclusion by a 2/3 vote is not irrelevant, even assuming the majority ground rule was improper, for it at least generates a substantial doubt that a court declaration would provide Powell his seat—even assuming as I think we should, that the House would respect the court's declaratory judgment. Compare *Bond v. Floyd*, 385 U.S. 116 (1966). The House could immediately exclude on the same ground, by the same vote.
>
> True, the House could do this, by hypothesis, only if the "ground rule" were that a 2/3 vote was necessary. But it does not appear that appellant Powell ever staked his position on the need for a 2/3 ground rule.

For Leventhal, it was significant that Powell had not availed himself of his legislative remedy by asserting his claim to his seat after his reelection. Powell's attorneys had indicated that he had not invoked the legislative remedy because it would not have restored his seniority and chairmanship. But Leventhal thought that it was doubtful that the claim to senority could be pursued before a court: "A court would be going to the extreme edge of its authority if it were to declare his status as a Congressman."

Since Powell did not proceed on the "premise of permissible exclusion," that is, that the House could exclude on the same grounds and vote required for expulsion, and therefore did not attempt to defend himself before the Celler committee or to claim his seat after relection, Judge Leventhal thought that the court should not decide some of the issues raised by Powell, particularly those relating to the denial of due process during the committee hearings:

152

The key point, to me, is that Congressman Powell erred in his assumption that his satisfaction of the Constitutional requirements (of residence, citizenship and age) meant that he had to be seated, and that grounds justifying expulsion could only be applied to those who had already been seated. My ruling on the merits of this Constitutional issue leads to the conclusion that the House had legislative jurisdiction to consider and appraise the activities and fitness of appellant Powell at the time he presented his credentials. It is not a full adjudication of the merits of the claim of appellant Powell that he was wronged. It does not necessarily mean either that the House acted properly when it failed to heed the ground rule of a 2/3 vote put forward by Congressman Curtis as the assumption of his motion to exclude, or that a court considering a different prayer for relief would be disabled from saying so upon a full consideration of Powell's case on its merits.

The case before us presents problems of confrontation with a coordinate branch and of molding relief. These are considerations that lead a court in some instances to find non-justiciability of the issue for any court. They may also properly be invoked, I think, as backdrop and perspective for a ruling to decline to provide a full adjudication on the merits, even assuming justiciability. My reasoning is that the confrontations would likely have evolved in a quite different way if appellant Powell had recognized a power to exclude on grounds of misconduct (albeit on 2/3 vote) and had conducted himself on this premise from the start. Hence I do not think it mandatory for a court to consider and determine the Constitutional issue as he has chosen to frame it, from an erroneous premise; and specifically, I think it proper to refrain from a full determination of the merits in a case where petitioner is seeking an extraordinary remedy yet has failed to invoke to the fullest extent the remedies and procedures available within the legislative branch.

Judge Leventhal suggested that had Powell framed the issue differently and had he invoked legislative remedies fully, by recognizing the power to exclude on grounds of misconduct and defending himself before the Select Committee, the court might have reached a different conclusion about determining the merits of the case.

153

9   Powell Mends His Fences

Powell had boasted and threatened that he would return to Harlem time and again, but he had never done so. Hence, perhaps, it should have been expected that when the unpredictable ex-congressman finally returned, he would do so without warning, in silence. At any rate, that was the way it happened.

It all began during a visit by H. R. Williams, Powell's New York lawyer, who had handled Powell's legal difficulties with Mrs. James. Williams added his own pleas to the urgings of the many others who wanted Powell to return to Harlem. There were a number of reasons that inspired, perhaps even invited, Powell to return to Harlem at this time: the Federal court of appeals ruling of February 28 that his exclusion had not been unconstitutional; concern over the impending primary and election; a growing feeling in his district that he should either return and run or withdraw; and, anticipating an election victory in November, the need to clear up some of his legal problems in New York because the qualification of residency might be in dispute if Powell could not legally enter his state without being subject to arrest.

On March 21 Powell finally agreed to return. Williams flew to New York from Bimini and phoned Justice Arthur Markewich, who said he would entertain an application for parole. Williams then contacted the sheriff, who was happy to hear of Powell's intention to return and surrender.

The next day Powell flew to Newark and then was driven to the sheriff's office. There he surrendered. He was taken immediately to Markewich's apartment, where he arrived about 11:30 P. M. Parole was granted on the condition that his appeal of the original arrest order be reinstated with the appellate division by April 8.

Powell then went to a rally of his supporters, who had gathered quickly as word spread that he was back. He was greeted that night by shouts of "Keep the faith, baby" and "Fight, baby, fight." Powell told his supporters, "They've [the law] never seen a scene like they're gonna have if they try to touch Big Daddy. I don't call for any violence and I don't call for any riots, but the non-violent days are over and if we must die, let us not die like hogs in some inglorious spot." He told his supporters he was "almost beginning to lose faith."[1]

On Saturday the 23rd, Powell and over 1,000 cheering followers marched down Seventh Avenue in the rain to the Abyssinian Baptist Church. In the basement of the church Powell delivered an impassioned address attacking moderate civil rights organizations and urging a more militant approach. He also denounced Martin Luther King and his strategy of nonviolence.

Early on Sunday, Powell held a news conference at his church, where he repeated his sentiments. He also told the reporters that he believed the United States should get out of Vietnam. Later in the day he preached in his church for the first time in over a year. His sermon was entitled "If a Man Falls, He Shall Rise Again." He was surrounded at the pulpit by a bodyguard of young militants. Powell ordered the replacement of a white image of Jesus in a stained glass window with a black one, and then lashed out at the antipoverty program which he had helped establish. He told his congregation, who, he declared, had become "fat and comfortable" on antipoverty funds, that they "must now reject them." It was "up to black people," he said, "to lead the revolution with any white people who will follow us as troops. And if this doesn't happen black Africans and colored people of Asia and South America will rise up against the United States."[2] After the service he led another march up Seventh Avenue.

It was well for Powell that he returned to Harlem when he did, for dissatisfaction with him there was mounting steadily. A movement had begun among his parishioners to oust him as minister of the Abyssinian Baptist Church, and he was in political trouble as well, facing a fight in the June 18 primary for the first time in ten years. His opponent was a former aide, John H. Young. James Meredith was also planning to run as an independent Democrat. Both Young and Meredith announced that Powell's return did not alter their plans. Young called Powell "a dictator deluded by the thought that he is God" and said that the people "want a new Harlem of dignity and self-respect, a young Harlem of courage and foresight, and most of all, a new Congressman."[3] When the New York County Executive Committee of the Democratic Party met on March 25 and decided not to oppose Powell in the Democratic primary, both challengers were deprived of whatever help the party might have lent. Sometime thereafter Meredith withdrew from the race.

Young's statement reflected the views of a fair portion of Powell's constituents. The dissatisfaction had come first from his long sojourn in Bimini and his failure to attempt to take his seat in Washington. As one local Democratic official noted, "A lot of people began thinking Adam was taking a Harlem-be-damned attitude and maybe the time had come to elect someone else." Others were disturbed by his efforts to embrace the new militancy, and particularly his association with the activist Charles Kenyatta's Harlem Mau Mau group. Powell's association with the militants cost him the support of the *Amsterdam News*, Harlem's largest and most influential newspaper. It said on March 29 in an editorial that it was "sorely troubled" by Powell's actions and statements.

Powell's parole was upheld on March 27 over the objections of Raymond Rubin, who claimed Markewich had not been told of an arrest order issued in Puerto Rico on March 20 when Powell failed to appear in court there in connection with the illegal transfer of assets case. Williams also began an action to have the civil contempt orders vacated because most of the judgment had been paid. Powell meanwhile flew back to Bimini, planning to return on April 7.

Powell had intended to address students at Duke University before returning to Harlem, but he ended up instead in the Duke University Hospital. His doctors explained he was suffering from exhaustion. After his release from the hospital, Powell returned to Bimini. There he held a news conference on April 19. He formally announced his candidacy for renomination and said he would begin his campaign on May 4. He was a candidate, he said, against "white racism," and added that it was this white racism which had been responsible for the April 4 murder of Martin Luther King and for his own exclusion from the House of Representatives. Assailing Mayor Richard J. Daley for his order instructing Chicago police to shoot arsonists and looters, he said the order "sounded like the beginning of officially sanctioned genocide in America. First we shoot to kill looters and shoot to kill arsonists, then we shoot to maim persons for disorderly conduct, then breach of the peace, and finally we shoot niggers just for being niggers."[4] Powell said he was neutral about the Democratic presidential contest but indicated that he might endorse New York's Governor Rockefeller for president. Powell also announced that his lawyers were preparing an appeal to the U. S. Supreme Court.

As promised, Powell returned to Harlem on May 4 to begin his campaign. He preached in his church on the 5th, and told his parishioners, "Whether you like it or not, you're looking at a new Adam." The change he referred to was his growing

158

show of militancy. Powell told the congregation that Humphrey, Robert Kennedy, McCarthy, and Rockefeller should be considered as presidential possibilities.

A news conference was held the same day. Powell claimed that he had almost received the Republican nomination in the current campaign. Negro Republican leaders, he said, wanted to nominate him to avoid a campaign against him, "a massive exercise in futility," as he called it. He charged that white leaders had blocked the move. He also explained that he had not attempted to take his seat after the special election because H. Res. 278 excluded him from the entire 90th Congress. "If they'd rescind the resolution," he said, "I'd walk down that aisle tomorrow, and I'd say 'Mr. Speaker, here ah is, suh.' I'd sooner be low man on the totem pole, and in Congress, because the nation needs me." Taken seriously, his comment was a withdrawal from his previous insistence that his seniority be returned. As was the case the preceding summer, no move was made to take Powell up on his offer.

Powell visited Harlem once more during the campaign, near the end of May, and urged his congregation to join student pickets at Columbia. After his supporters dropped a legal effort to bar Young from the primary ballot, the campaign passed without incident. Barely 11,000 of the 80,000 registered Democrats in Harlem turned out for the election on June 18, and Powell won the nomination by an unusually small margin of 6,665 to 4,387. Both the low vote and the small (3-2) margin of victory were cited by Harlem Democratic leaders as indications that Powell's hold over the electorate was deteriorating. The growing "disenchantment" among voters was attributed to his inactivity in Washington, resulting in Harlem's being largely without representation, and his residency in Bimini.[5]

Powell's Republican opponent, Henry L. Hall, was heartened by the outcome of the primary. "The vote was more anti-Powell than pro-Young," Hall said, "because John

Young had been so closely identified with Adam to make much of a candidate on his own." Hall, a 48-year-old free-lance writer active in civil rights work, said he would win in November, "because Adam these days is just an occasional overnight visitor from Bimini. His real home is Bimini and the Harlem voters know it. Thinking people in Harlem resent the fact that the community is not represented in Congress, that Mr. Powell does not even make a move to claim his seat, that he would be without influence in Washington even if he were seated."[6]

Meanwhile, the battle over the defamation suit continued. Williams appeared in court on June 20 to contest Rubin's attempt to collect $1 million in cost-of-chase damages and to attach Powell's property in Puerto Rico. He also succeeded in having the civil contempt convictions vacated. However, on July 11 the appellate division upheld 3-2 the 30-day jail sentence and the $500 fine imposed on Powell for criminal contempt. The ruling, which lacked the caustic criticism of Powell's conduct that had been included in the opinions of other New York judges, immediately terminated Powell's parole and made him once again subject to arrest on entering the state. After Williams filed notice of appeal on July 16, Justice Markewich extended Powell's parole until after the court of appeals decision.

Able to move freely again, Powell paid a surprise visit to New York on July 20. He conferred with aides about the November election and confidently told newsmen he had already won. The next day he preached in his church. He told the congregation America was "a wilderness of prejudice, a wilderness of hatred. . . . It's almost a disgrace to be an American today," Powell declared. "There has never been anyone who has tried to do something for the Negro who hasn't been assassinated—beginning with Abraham Lincoln—imprisoned, exiled, or died because of broken hopes and dreams."

Even the "new Adam," however, was not sufficiently

160

militant to satisfy some members of the Negro community. The Black Panthers planned to oppose Powell, the *New York Times* reported on July 28. Eldridge Cleaver said of Powell, "Adam's a political prostitute and we're going to get rid of him. He's not militant enough and represents only the black middle class, not the masses."

In mid-August Powell praised President Johnson and Vice-President Humphrey before reporters, but indicated he was somewhat disillusioned with the latter's performance. He said he expected Humphrey to win the nomination and announced he would support him if he chose an acceptable running mate. Powell indicated that Edward Kennedy would meet his requirements. Although Powell was willing to support the vice-president, he let it be known that he personally endorsed the policies of the vice-president's rivals, McCarthy and McGovern.

Powell paid relatively little attention to his own reelection. He never bothered to campaign and was out of town, either in Bimini or on lecture tours, most of the time. Powell promised, however, to return to Washington to attempt to take his seat if reelected. Actually, after the withdrawal of Meredith, Powell had little formidable opposition. Hall was hampered by a lack of money and volunteers and was not well-known. Joseph McGuire, the Conservative candidate, made little effort in the campaign.

The ex-chairman did of course express some interesting views on the presidential race. "We are living in a most troublesome time," he told his congregation on September 22, "and we don't know what is going to happen in the United States. The next President may be the former Governor of Alabama, and if that happens I'll leave the country." Powell felt that "regardless of who wins, we're [Negroes] not going to get anywhere." Nonetheless, he told another audience barely a week later that he respected Governor Wallace. "This may come as a shock to my 'soul brothers,'" he said, "but Wallace is the only one of the bunch that's got guts."[7] Powell never announced his unqualified support for Humphrey, on the grounds that the vice-president did not divorce himself completely from Johnson.

Despite the indications to the contrary at the time of the primary, the vote on November 5 showed that Powell had not lost his hold on the electorate. Powell received 36,973 votes (80.6 percent) to 7,290 (15.9 percent) and 1,616 (3.5 percent) for Hall and McGuire, respectively.

Powell returned to Harlem from Bimini on November 9 and announced that he would try to take his seat in the 91st Congress regardless of seniority. He had been the victim of "white power," he said. "I was Number 7 in seniority on the Democratic side," Powell explained, "and everybody ahead of me was 80 years or older. I figure that it would have taken about six years, if they hadn't cut me off, to be Speaker of the House, and Speaker is Number 3 in line for the President of the United States. They don't want a black man to be President." Powell left in a few days to continue his lecture tour.

On November 18, 1968, some six weeks after the 90th Congress had adjourned and after Powell had been reelected, the Supreme Court granted certiorari on *Powell* v. *McCormack*.[8] Elated, Powell called the court's decision to review the appellate court decision on his case "a monumental moment in American history." The grant of a writ of certiorari directing the lower courts to send up the record of the case so that the decision could be "made more certain" indicated that at least four justices had felt that there were "special and important reasons" for review and that the issues raised were of sufficient public importance to merit their consideration.

Why did the court grant certiorari? The court had waited almost six months since the petition for certiorari was first filed; yet in another six weeks the court would know whether Powell would be seated. There was a strong possibility that

162

he would be sworn in, and he had indicated his willingness to take his seat even if denied his seniority. The most impelling question, his right to sit in Congress, would in all likelihood be settled. Why did the court not use its opportunity to avoid the issues posed by the case? The court's action tended to suggest that the court in fact welcomed the opportunity to deal with the merits of the case, for, if after hearing argument, it were to rule that the case was not justiciable because of the separation of powers doctrine, it could have achieved the same effect simply by allowing the lower court decision to stand. The case presented the court with the opportunity to deal with the merits of the case—the constitutionality of the exclusion—without risking a direct confrontation with Congress. Powell's attorneys had reason to rejoice.

The decision reaffirmed, said Powell on November 18, "that we do have three branches of Government." He would try to take his seat, he said, and he had already received an invitation to attend the Democratic caucus.

Bad news came on November 20, however, when the New York court of appeals upheld, 7-0, Powell's convictions for criminal contempt. Williams decided to appeal to the U. S. Supreme Court, and Powell's parole was extended pending the outcome of the appeal.

Powell had acted circumspectly during 1968, in an obvious attempt to appease his former colleagues in Congress and thus enhance his chances of being seated. That his efforts had not beem completely successful became apparent in early December, when Rep. H. R. Gross announced that he would demand that the "high-flying, whiskey-drinking" Powell (as Gross described him) be denied a seat in the 91st Congress. His reason, Gross said, was that "nothing has changed in the record which shows that Powell defrauded the Government of at least $40,000."[9]

Not long after Gross' announcement, on December 9, the Justice Department issued a statement on the grand jury that had investigated Powell. The statement read:

The grand jury which investigated the allegations against Mr. Powell expired today.

The Department of Justice did not recommend an indictment and none was returned.

The Department concluded that available evidence did not warrant prosecution.

The Department is studying the matter to determine whether there is civil liability.[10]

The Justice Department announcement had not told the whole story, however. The inquiry had been begun on April 14, 1967, by a sitting grand jury. When it expired, an "extra grand jury" had been impaneled on October 9, 1967, and sworn in the next day. The extra grand jury had a statutory life of 18 months, unless dismissed sooner. It considered the Powell matter until March, 1968, and then turned to other cases. On December 9, 1968, the extra grand jury was dismissed by an order of the chief justice of the district court for the District of Columbia without ever voting on the Powell case, although it had four months to go before it would expire.

The Justice Department's action enraged Gross. On December 10 he said he would ask the Nixon administration to reopen the case when it took office, and declared, "Congress and the American people have a right to know the reasons for this strange and unusual action, this whitewash, of the very serious charges against Powell."

At first the Justice Department had no comment. Finally, on January 1, 1969, a department spokesman admitted that the four attorneys working on the case had been unable to reach any unanimous recommendation, although some had favored indicting Powell on several counts which could have carried total penalties of 25 years in jail and $25,000 in fines. The head of the Criminal Division, Assistant Attorney General Fred M. Vinson, Jr., had recommended against an indictment, however, a position sustained by his chief, Attorney General Ramsay Clark. This explanation led to increased criticism of the department's action.

164

Thus, with the 91st Congress due to meet on January 3, 1969, a new grievance had been added to those already held against Powell by many members. However, it was apparent that the overall feeling against Powell had moderated considerably. Van Deerlin, for example, said, "I feel the circumstances have changed [from 1966]. He's no longer a fugitive from justice and apparently is moving to resolve his legal difficulties in New York. I can't conceive of his not being seated now."[11] In addition, there was no deluge of mail such as had influenced many members two years before.

No organized opposition to Powell's seating made itself known. The only representative to announce publicly that he would challenge Powell's seating was Gross, three days before the opening of Congress. However, he did not campaign for Powell's ouster among his colleagues, having concluded that "They know what the story is. So I intend to try to see to it they get an opportunity to vote on whether they want this character among us—I don't."

Two Negro members, Conyers and Charles C. Diggs, Jr. (D-Mich.), began to lay the groundwork for Powell's seating several days before Congress met. Both contacted other members to urge them to support a motion to seat Powell, and conferences were held with the leadership of both parties and aides of President-elect Nixon.

On January 2, the Republican caucus debated the Powell matter and decided to take no collective stand. The matter was not even brought up in the Democratic caucus, which Powell attended. The Democratic Study Group discussed the question and found an overwhelming consensus in favor of seating Powell.

By January 2, it had become apparent that one of the key figures in the debates would be Rep. MacGregor, who had gained considerable exposure and experience since his Select Committee service as a top-ranking member of Nixon's campaign team. He showed himself willing to cooperate with strong Powell supporters, and conferred on the 2nd with Conyers. MacGregor also supplied Conyers with a copy of the

165

substitute resolution he intended to present regarding Powell's seating.

The proceedings when the 91st Congress assembled resembled those of 1967.[12] As before, John McCormack was elected speaker amid lengthy speeches. He then announced that he would administer the oath to the members. Again an objection to the seating of Powell was raised, this time by Gross, who announced that he intended to offer a resolution to exclude the representative-elect. However, after the oath had been administered to the remaining members, Celler was recognized by the speaker. He offered a resolution which simply said:

> Resolved, that the gentleman from New York, Mr. Powell, be now permitted to take the oath of office.

Celler spoke at some length in support of his resolution, recounting the history of the controversy and emphasizing changes in the situation since Powell had been excluded. He placed particular stress on the fact that no indictment had been returned by the federal grand jury, and on the conclusion of the Justice Department that the evidence did not warrant prosecution. When challenged on this point by Gerald Ford, Celler responded that although he still subscribed to the Select Committee findings, he had been persuaded by the Justice Department that a conviction could not be obtained on the evidence.

The debate which followed was highly reminiscent of those of two years before. MacGregor and Ford, each of whom spoke several times, emphasized that they took a middle ground, in favor of some modification of the Select Committee's recommendations. MacGregor levied special criticism at the dismissal of the grand jury.

At the expiration of the hour of debate, a roll-call vote was taken on the previous question. This failed 176 to 248. MacGregor then immediately presented his resolution, in the form of a substitute to that offered by Celler. The MacGregor substitute referred in its whereas clauses to Powell's possession of the three requirements of age, citizenship, and inhabitancy, the maintenance of his wife on the payroll, his improper expenditures, and his behavior in regard to the Hays and Celler investigations. It proposed the following action:

Resolved—
(1) That the speaker administer the oath of office to the said Adam Clayton Powell. . . .
(2) That as punishment Adam Clayton Powell be and he hereby is fined the sum of $30,000 . . . the sergeant-at-arms of the House is directed to deduct $1,250 per month from the salary otherwise due to said Adam Clayton Powell . . . until said $30,000 fine is fully paid.
(3) That as further punishment the seniority of the said Adam Clayton Powell commence as of the date he takes the oath as a member of the 91st Congress.
(4) That if the said Adam Clayton Powell does not present himself to take the oath of office on or before January 15, 1969, the seat of the Eighteenth District of the state of New York shall be deemed vacant and the Speaker shall notify the Governor of the state of New York of the existing vacancy.

Before MacGregor could proceed, Celler was on his feet with a point of order. He charged that MacGregor's substitute was not germane to his original resolution, since the original had made no provision for a fine. After a brief debate, Mc-Cormack sustained the point with the explanation that "the punishment of Mr. Powell for acts committed in the 88th or 89th Congresses, or declaring his seat vacant in the 91st Congress, is not germane to the proposition that he be now sworn in." A second roll-call vote was taken on the previous question, and it was defeated 172 to 252. MacGregor then submitted as a substitute the resolution offered by Ford on the first day of the 90th Congress, having changed the five-week study period to three weeks. Previous question was ordered on this substitute and the resolution after a brief debate, and it was rejected by a vote of 131 to 290. Celler's original resolution was rejected by a voice vote.

Celler then introduced a resolution which was the result of negotiation among MacGregor, Ford, Conyers, and Carl Albert. It retained the text of the MacGregor substitute but reduced the fine to $25,000 and decreased the monthly deduction to $1,150. Celler moved the previous question immediately, and the previous question passed on a roll-call vote, 248 to 171. Representatives Gross and Watson then spoke at length, rehearsing the various charges levied against Powell at one time or another. When they were done, the compromise resolution was adopted 252 to 160, with six voting "present."

Powell, who had waited out the debates in and about the House chamber, immediately took the oath. He then held a press conference, where he told reporters, "I'll behave as I always have." Powell played down the role of Conyers in reaching the compromise on his seating, saying more credit was due to two other Negro members, Diggs and Robert N. C. Nix (D-Pa.). Of the fine itself, Powell said, "Well, maybe I'm an emancipated slave. . . . It wouldn't be a bad idea if everyone had to pay $25,000 to get in here." He said he felt the punishment imposed on him by the House was racially motivated, but he refused to comment on whether he would challenge the fine in the courts.

Back in Harlem the next day, Powell repeated that he felt the fine was racially motivated and said he was discussing it with his lawyers. He also announced that he would introduce a resolution to establish a task force, chaired by himself and supported by a staff and appropriation, to conduct a nationwide in-depth study of the poverty program. Because the poverty program was attracting considerable attention at this time, the chairmanship of such a task force would afford Powell some of the influence and power he had once wielded as head of the Education and Labor Committee.

Powell's task force resolution, introduced on January 7, was his major legislative effort.[13] He was reassigned to the Education and Labor Committee (where he was ranked last on the Democratic side) and was listed as a cosponsor of several committee bills. The remainder of his efforts during the first session consisted of introducing numerous relief bills and proposing the creation of two additional Select Committees. The committees, to be chaired by himself, would investigate combat deaths of Negro soldiers and a controversial army court-martial.[14] No action was taken on any of the proposed committees. Powell also signed two letters addressed to President Nixon. A letter signed in April by Powell and seven other black congressmen expressed concern about a ranking Republican official's attacks on the Equal Employment Commission and challenged government contract awards to companies which allegedly practiced racial discrimination. The other letter, written in the same month, invited President Nixon to use his good offices on behalf of Charleston, South Carolina, hospital workers who were attempting to unionize. The ex-chairman did not speak on the floor, however, until April 29, when he joined briefly in a tribute to A. Philip Randolph's 80th birthday. His voting record for the session was the worst in the House; he answered to only 5 percent of the roll calls. Only Michael Kirwan, who was hospitalized most of the time, came close to Powell's record (with 6 percent). The next lowest percentage was 29 percent.

Instead of attending congressional sessions, Powell spent his time lecturing and mending his fences at home. The latter activity was carried on in his usual style. He resumed his regular preaching at his church and became heavily involved in local affairs. Powell's concerns ranged from the New York teacher's strike to an art exhibit at the Metropolitan Museum of Art portraying Harlem's history. In February, Powell attacked the city and the Nixon administration for having "raped" the antipoverty program in Harlem and Bedford-

Stuyvesant. He claimed that evidence he had "borrowed" from files of the local OEO office showed that cuts in funds for those areas were disproportionately large compared with those in other areas of the city. He also participated in an "informal citizens' hearing" on school and antipoverty problems. In March he demanded state-financed programs in Puerto Rican and Afro-American history and became involved in a dispute over the closing of Harlem Hospital for lack of funds.

Powell also flirted for nearly a month with the idea of running for mayor of New York City. In the end, he made no public announcement one way or the other, but rumors of his intentions had left Negro state legislators confused and angered, and had blocked their plans to present their own Negro candidate.

The final step in repairing Powell's situation occurred April 10. After a rehearing, the appellate division revoked by a unanimous vote the jail sentence for criminal contempt, changed the finding against Powell to civil contempt, and sustained the $250 fine. Since most of the judgment had been paid to Mrs. James, this brought to an apparent end the nine-year defamation litigation. Powell could then fix his attention on his challenge to his exclusion and the impending oral argument before the Supreme Court.

10   Oral Argument

When the Supreme Court granted certiorari, thereby agreeing
to consider Powell's appeal, on November 18, 1968, Congress
had already adjourned and Powell had been elected overwhelmingly by his constituents. By the time the justices
heard the oral argument on the case, Powell had been seated
in the 91st Congress and the three issues of continuing
importance were his loss of seniority, the $25,000 fine, and
his claim to back salary.

On a sunny day, the visitor who walks across the street
from the Capitol and climbs the white marble steps of the
Supreme Court building is almost blinded by the reflected
sunlight. The architecture of the building is Greek, patterned
after the Temple of Diana at Ephesus; the words "Equal
Justice Under Law" are carved above the columned entrance.
Inside the high-ceilinged courtroom, amid more columns,
carved walls depicting judicial figures, and red velvet hang-
ings, the nine robed justices sit in high-backed black swivel
chairs of varying size and description to listen to oral
argument, to ask questions of counsel, and, generally on
Mondays, to deliver opinions. By the time the justices hear
the oral arguments, printed briefs have already been submitted; most, but not all, of the justices have read the briefs
before the oral argument. Counsel is expected not to read the

argument, for as the now-famous remark of Justice Frankfurter so aptly put it, the court does not see itself as "a dozing audience for the reading of soliloquies, but as a questioning body, utilizing oral argument as a means for exposing the difficulties of a case with a view to meeting them."[1] Whether or not oral argument is the deciding factor in a justice's decision is open to debate, but certainly some of Bromley's assertions must have had a negative impact on certain of the justices. Ordinarily the court allows half an hour or an hour to each side in the case; in the Powell case, each side had an hour. The party losing the case in the lower court argues first and may reserve part of the time for rebuttal. Although the physical setting is formal and awesome, when oral argument begins the atmosphere becomes more intimate as the justices probe to learn the facts and to buttress or demolish the logic of the arguments presented by counsel.

In a packed courtroom—only 300 people can be seated—Chief Justice Earl Warren called the Powell case at 10:52 A. M. on April 21, 1969. Representing Powell were Arthur Kinoy and Herbert O. Reid; Bruce Bromley was to speak on behalf of the defendants. With Powell sitting among the spectators in the first row, Arthur Kinoy rose to address the nine justices. At the center sat Earl Warren, 78, serving the last term of his 16-year tenure as the nation's chief judge. He had presided over the court during one of its most controversial periods, when it took new stands regarding equal rights for minorities, the rights of the criminally accused, apportionment of state legislatures, and school prayers. Before being named to the court by Eisenhower, he had been district attorney, state attorney general, and governor of California. The other justices were seated on either side of the chief justice in descending order of length of service.

To the left of Warren sat Hugo L. Black, 83, the senior justice in length of service and former U. S. Senator (D-Ala.). Named to the court by Roosevelt in 1937, he became on the court a consistent liberal, particularly regarding the First Amendment guarantee of free speech. Speaking with a soft Alabama drawl, he was noted for his searching questions put to lawyers arguing before the court.

To the right of Warren sat William O. Douglas, 70, law school professor at Yale and Columbia and New Deal official, who was appointed by Roosevelt in 1939. With a reputation as an outdoorsman and conservationist, his opinions have been consistently on the side of freedom for the individual and in opposition to governmental curtailment of that freedom.

On the other side of Black was John Marshall Harlan, 69, appointed by President Eisenhower in 1954. A New York lawyer who had served as U. S. attorney and chief counsel to the New York State Crime Commission, he was picked by Eisenhower for the court of appeals and advanced to the Supreme Court in 1955. He was known for his carefully researched and scholarly opinions and tended to take a more restrained view of the court's role than did some of his colleagues.

On the other side of Douglas sat William J. Brennan, Jr., 62, who had developed a reputation as a liberal judge on the New Jersey Supreme Court when appointed by Eisenhower to the court in 1956. One of eight children of an Irish immigrant couple, he had won a scholarship to Harvard Law School, was the only Catholic on the Court, and was usually aligned with the judicial activists on the bench.

Potter Stewart, 54, appointed to the court by Eisenhower in 1958, had been court of appeals judge, had practiced law in New York and Cincinnati, and had served on the city council and as vice-mayor in Cincinnati. A Phi Beta Kappa at Yale, Stewart was an independent thinker, aligning himself with neither the liberal nor the conservative groups on the court.

Byron R. White, 51, deputy attorney general when named to the court by President Kennedy in 1962, had been Phi

Beta Kappa and Rhodes Scholar, and had played professional football to help finance his legal education. On the bench, he was usually aligned with the conservative group.

Abe Fortas, 57, was nominated by President Johnson in 1965 to fill the vacancy left by Arthur J. Goldberg (Kennedy's only other appointee). Also Phi Beta Kappa, he had served as government counsel during the New Deal and as undersecretary of the interior, and had helped to found one of the most successful law firms in Washington, Arnold, Fortas and Porter. Fortas had been nominated by Johnson as chief justice after Warren's announced resignation, but on October 1, 1968, the Senate had refused to vote on confirmation. Fortas heard the oral argument in the Powell case, but on May 14, 1969, resigned from the court amid criticism for extrajudicial behavior; hence, he did not take part in the decision.

Thurgood Marshall, 60, had been named by Johnson as U. S. solicitor general before being named to the court in 1967. The first Negro named to the court, Marshall had argued cases before the Supreme Court many times (and had lost only three) as counsel for the NAACP and the NAACP Legal Defense and Educational Fund. His victory as counsel in *Brown* v. *Board of Education* (1954) set the court on a new direction in cases involving rights of minorities.

Kinoy began his eloquent argument by reviewing the action of the House on March 1, 1967, in refusing to seat Powell, despite the warning of the chairman of the Judiciary Committee (Celler) that such action would be unconstitutional.[2] On a brief summation of the facts, he began to build his legal argument. The case presented a fundamental constitutional issue, "whether the Legislature has any constitutional power to refuse to seat a duly elected representative of the people who meets all the qualifications for membership in the Legislature set forth in the Constitution." For him, that question was key to the questions of jurisdiction, justiciability, and remedy. In urging the people of New York to ratify the Constitution, Alexander Hamilton and Robert Livingston had said that the Constitution was grounded on the principle "that the people are the best judges of whom ought to represent them. . . ."

> It was upon this understanding that the people of the State of New York ratified the Constitution. Today, the people of the 18th Congressional District of the State of New York stand here and ask this Court to enforce this understanding. This principle, written as a bedrock into our Constitution, stands as a rock against the possibilities that waves of hysteria will take place in which a majority, temporarily, can overrule the free choice of the minority of citizens.

Kinoy argued that the defendants (as represented by Bromley), who had some "difficulty" with the writings of Madison and Hamilton, with the constitutional opinion of their own Select Committee, and with the court's decision in *Bond* v. *Floyd*, had built their "entire constitutional edifice" upon the Wilkes case, the exclusion of John Wilkes by the British Parliament and Blackstone's rationale and justification for the parliamentary action.

> But I suggest to the Court this is fantastic, that it turns history upon its head, that the Wilkes case was the very lesson Madison said in Philadelphia was what we must prevent in the new republic, in this Republic. Blackstone's justification for the action of the British parliament, upon which their entire constitutional case rests, they do not inform the Court was first of all not included in his first commentaries. He was very embarrassed on the Floor of Parliament when he appeared as a special pleader for His Majesty's government to justify the Wilkes exclusion when his own commentaries were read against him.
> So he revised his opinion to justify the Wilkes exclusion, and he was then attacked on both sides of the Atlantic by the leading spokesman for the colonial cause as evidencing the precise theory of legislative tyranny which the colonists were rising against. . . .

The precedent was further discredited by the fact that Parliament itself repudiated the exclusion resolution.

The question of justiciability was easily resolved by looking at the teachings of *Baker* v. *Carr*: "The test of nonjusticiability in the political question doctrine is deciding whether a matter has been in any way committed by the Constitution to another branch of Government, or whether the action of that branch exceeds whatever authority has been committed." Kinoy argued that the Congress had indeed exceeded the authority committed to it and that since there had been a violation of a federal constitutional right, judicial power must be exercised. The court must step in to protect the rights of the people of Harlem to be represented by a congressman of their choice. He suggested that relief here would not violate separation of powers, contrary to the assertion of the lower courts:

> Let me speak frankly at this point: What is at the heart of the reluctance of the lower courts to grant relief here? It is their fear of a confrontation with the House. But this fear, in itself unreal, since in the words of this Court, it is an inadmissible suggestion that the House would not accept this Court's role as the ultimate interpreter of the Constitution. This fear would paralyze the Court in its most important function—to preserve a rule of law. . . .
>
> * * *
>
> The reaffirmation that this is a government of laws and not men, that representative government means that ultimate power remains with the people, is particularly necessary when the crisis arises in a context in which black citizens are denied the right to elect their own black representative who had risen to great heights of legislative leadership. It is difficult, indeed, to demand law and order of American citizens if the Legislative Branch itself denies the first assumptions of an ordered society, the right of people to govern themselves.
>
> Thus, to grant relief here would not only be to reaffirm the fundamentals of a representative government, but it would reaffirm the fact that the principles of popular sovereignty are equally applicable to citizens black and white.
>
> Such a decision, in Justice Clark's words, concurring in *Baker* v. *Carr*, would be in the greatest tradition of this Court.

At this point Herbert Reid, law professor at Howard University, took up the argument that not only did the Congress not have the power to exclude Powell (nor the power to expel for conduct during a prior session of Congress) but that the way it had done so raised other constitutional objections. He was questioned about his assertion that a member could not be expelled for conduct occurring during a prior session of Congress. Admitting that there was no judicial opinion supporting this claim, because no matter had ever come before the court, Reid said:

There is judicial power there [in the House] to seat and to remove one who has been seated. However, where one was never seated, and punishment was legislated, as it was here, after a legislative finding that at no time was there any semblance of due process hearing held, we contend then that the manner in which this was accomplished in the House violates first the due process clause, its substantive and procedural requirements, and in addition that it amounts to a bill of attainder.

He then suggested that the predicates of the House's action in refusing to seat Powell had been removed: (1) the findings in the Hays report (the report of the Subcommittee on Contracts) were mere legislative findings; Hays himself pointed out on January 3, 1969, that these facts had been found insufficient by a grand jury and that they were also insufficient for the House to act on; (2) Powell's difficulties in the New York courts had been resolved; and (3) his "contumacious" conduct toward the Select Committee could not be a basis for punishment, for by refusing to participate in the hearings, Powell was exercising a constitutional right.

Reid returned to the question of procedural guarantees and was questioned about the requirements of due process:

Q. I want to be sure I understand your position. You would say, then, that the House could constitutionally expel a Member after a due process hearing for the misappropriation of House funds, and I assume that everything happened during a single session.

177

A. Well, misappropriation of funds, yes, sir. However, in terms of such a proceeding and defense to that, the conduct of other Members of the House would be highly relevant, and this is one of the reasons, I am sure, that the House did not want to afford him a due process hearing, because they did not want any comparative study made, and this is indicated also by the January 3, 1969 record when Chairman Celler said, as to nepotism, judge not lest you be judged.

Q. You mean you can't expel one person for misappropriation of House funds unless you expel everybody?

A. No, sir; I am not saying that, Mr. Justice Fortas. What I am saying, relevant to the expulsion of the one is the conduct of others, and whether or not, he has an equal protection argument because of being singled out. This was highly relevant in the particular case, as well as the conduct of other Members, and I think there is no other justification for the House's failure to accord him a due process hearing requiring the attendance of witnesses, and the like, other than they wanted to avoid this comparative study, to which I think he was entitled.

The assertion by the House that the seating of Powell on January 3, 1969, has mooted the controversy was countered by Reid, who argued that Powell was entitled to the back pay for the two years in which he was not allowed to sit and that the House action in fining Powell $25,000 amounted to a continuation of the unconstitutional exclusion.[3] He noted that certain leaders in the House, including Albert, Celler, and Udall, suggested that the House could not punish Powell prior to seating him, because to do so was to add to the qualifications.

A discussion of the rather difficult question of remedy ensued. Reid noted that "the big stumbling block" had been "whether the Court could enforce its mandate." Since the congressman had been seated, the "remedy problem becomes much, much easier to handle and to direct here in terms of declaring Resolution 278 of March 1, 1967 and the resolution of January 3, 1969 unconstitutional." Reid was interrupted in mid-sentence:

Q. The 1969 resolution is not before us, is it, for adjudication?

A. Well, we feel that it is. Number 1, we feel that this is a part of the illegal, unconstitutional conduct for which we had complained about in the original suit; that is, the predicate, sir, for the passage of the resolution on January 3rd was the same conduct. The fact of the matter is, it is in the same language.

Q. But there is a difference between our taking notice of that for whatever bearing it may have on the mootness question, and our granting relief, because that has not been adjudicated in the lower courts, has it?

A. No, it has not, sir, because this action took place while the matter was pending here. Of course, also implicit in any notion of mootness is the validity of this action.

* * *

Q. Do I understand you then that your position now is that all you seek is a declaratory judgment?

A. No, sir; we argue that we are entitled to declaratory judgment, injunctive relief, and we press for mandamus.

Q. What injunctive relief are you asking for?

A. Well, mandatory relief, sir, in the sense of the only disability to the paying of the back pay of $55,000 is, of course, a resolution of the House which has directed, in effect, that he not be paid because he was not seated.

* * *

A. ... We are merely suggesting here that everything indicates to us that if this Court exercises its historical judicial function and declares this resolution unconstitutional, that the House would abide by it.

Q. Well, that sounds to me as if you would be content with just a declaratory judgment that Resolution 278 was unconstitutional. Is that what you are talking about?

A. Yes, I think that effective here by declaration of unconstitutionality of 278.

Apparently Reid assumed that all other remedies sought by Powell would flow from a declaration of the unconstitutionality of H. Res. 278.

The chief justice turned to Mr. Bromley, a 76-year-old, white-haired former judge of the New York Court of Appeals. Bromley, whose law firm had been paid more than

$200,000 to represent the House before the case reached the Supreme Court, spoke confidently. "There are at least four undisputed matters before us to which my two friends have paid scant attention." He then proceeded to counter certain arguments offered by Kinoy and Reid. First, the court had no power to entertain this action against members of Congress questioning their action in their official capacity, any more than the court could order the members to pass or repeal a statute. Second, there was no dispute about the correctness of the findings of the Select Committee of the 90th Congress (Celler committee); the serious charges against Powell were not denied by him at any time. Third, the complaint did not allege that Powell was excluded because of race, and the record of the House did not support such allegation; thus, the issue of race had no proper place in the case. Fourth, the action of the House on January 3, 1969, in punishing Powell was not before the court.

The crux of the argument, Bromley urged, was that the court could not review a decision of the members of Congress acting pursuant to their constitutional powers to judge the qualifications of their own members, "to exclude a member-elect solely for reasons of personal misconduct. . . ." At this point Mr. Justice Black intervened:

> Q. Suppose he had been excluded because of his race in the form of a resolution. Would you say he would have any judicial remedy?
> A. I should say, sir, in answer to that question, that the action of the House would be clearly unconstitutional.
> Q. Would he have judicial remedy?
> A. As I read the speech or debate clause, he would not, sir.
> So our position is that what the House did in this matter was for the House, and the House alone, to decide, and its actions should not and is not subject to judicial review.

From this point on, Bromley's argument was punctuated by frequent questions. He argued that the action was clearly moot. "The House of the 90th Congress, against which relief is sought, has terminated. Mr. Powell can no longer be seated in that House. There is now a new house. He now sits in that House, and I believe for that reason, and that simple reason, the case is moot." Bromley then declared his intention to devote the rest of his time to substantive issues. He never got that chance. A barrage of questions followed: "How about his back salary...."

A. Back salary is so incidental to the main prayer for relief that I do not feel it can justify the jurisdiction of the Court. It is completely de minimis. He was paid up to March 1, 1967, the date on which he was expelled. He was reelected very promptly, and he could have presented himself to the House in April of the same year and, as the Speaker said twice, the matter would be considered again in light of the very important new factor that he had been reelected, as it was last January.

But Mr. Powell chose to stay away. He never presented himself. He never came near the House. So I say he clearly has no claim for any salary except maybe a month's salary.

* * *

Q. Well, I suppose you might concede that he might have an action in the Court of Claims.

A. I certainly would, sir, and in that court, the United States should have the opportunity, which it might very well seize, of pleading a counterclaim or a set-off for the $50,000 or so of its funds which Mr. Powell had taken unlawfully.

* * *

Q. Judge Bromley, on your question of mootness, if the Court should be of the opinion that this action was justiciable originally, if it had been timely, do you think that it would be moot now?

A. I think so, clearly, sir.

Q. Why?

A. Because he has been seated. There is nothing you can do about the 90th Congress, I respectfully submit. It is gone. You can't seat him in that Congress, and the present Congress is the one in which he has been seated. That action, the propriety of the fine which he got, and the loss of seniority which he got in company with his seating, is not attacked in the complaint and is not here.

Q. What happens, Mr. Bromley, if he does attack it? Then two years from now that will be moot.

181

A. Not if he proceeded promptly it wouldn't be.

* * *

A. Of course, my point about the salary is, after he was paid to March 1st, he could have come back and the result might have been entirely different, as it was last January. The reason he didn't get his salary after April 1967, until January 1969, was because he never presented himself. He never asked the House to reconsider in the light of the important fact that he had been overwhelmingly reelected in Harlem.

But the question of back salary was not the only question on the justices' minds. Bromley committed a tactical error in responding to a question concerning a more fundamental issue:

Q. Could I ask you a question about your nonjusticiability argument?

To put an extreme case, do you find that if the Congress had expelled Mr. Powell, saying, "Well, we will lay aside a majority vote required for exclusion and the two-thirds vote for expulsion. We will just take a general consensus and expel him." Would you say that was nonjusticiable?

A. I think so. Of course, it was improper and unconstitutional.

Q. No relief?

A. No relief, because the power to judge includes the power to judge erroneously [and the power to judge] has been confided to the House.

This admission led Chief Justice Warren to inquire whether a majority party controlling two-thirds or three-fourths of the House could refuse to seat all members of the minority party on the ground that their views were dangerous to the country. Bromley replied that the court could move against such action in spite of the "speech and debate" clause. But, asked Warren, "Suppose they did it one by one, just one by one. They take a Mr. Powell today and a Mr. Smith and a Mr. Jones the next day, and did it one by one. Where would the remedy lie?" "That would be a harder case," said Bromley. To which Warren countered, "No, it isn't a harder case if we have no jurisdiction whatsoever." Bromley admitted that "there are some perversions which this Court must be ingenious enough to find a way around the speech or debate clause, or else we will be confronted with revolution or worse." When Bromley suggested that somebody had to draw the line and was asked who, he replied, "The House draws that line, sir," except in case of utter perversion. "What could be more perverse," asked Warren, than excluding a member for racial reasons, which Bromley had said could be done without recourse to the courts when questioned earlier by Justice Black. "Well, a great many things," he answered, such as "seizing the President and dragging him into the well of the House under a resolution that he be beheaded."

At this juncture Warren called a recess and the justices rose for lunch. Bromley had pushed the "speech and debate" clause farther than he needed for the purposes of this case. He could have drawn some limitations to the argument, saying that if a specific provision of the Constitution was violated, such as the First, Fifth, or Fourteenth Amendment, and someone were expelled for religious or political beliefs or for reasons of race, that the court clearly could move against such action.

When the argument resumed at 12:30, Bromley attempted to pull together his argument, which relied primarily on the constitutional provision that "for any speech or debate in either house, [members] shall not be questioned in any other place." He began:

I recognize that it has a strange sound coming from any lawyer to tell this Court that something unconstitutional may have occurred, and yet you have no power to intervene, but I make that contention in this posture and I rest it squarely on the speech or debate clause as interpreted by at least three cases decided here under that clause.

That clause, providing that for any speech or debate in the House, its Members shall not be questioned in any place, underscores and enforces the separation of powers doctrine

183

embedded in our Constitution. It has the broad purpose, I submit, of protecting the integrity of independence of the Federal Legislative Branch from any interference whatsoever by the Executive or Judicial Branches, even to the extent of imposing upon the Members the inconvenience and expense of defending themselves.

No longer does anyone question the fact that speech or debate is not limited to words spoken in debate in the House, but includes everything done in the House in connection with its business, such as the act of voting, the passage of a resolution, directing the activities of its agents.

From then on, Bromley was deluged with questions.

Q. If you follow that to its logical conclusion, why doesn't that vitiate the whole power of judicial review? review?

A. Because it is confined only, Your Honor, to the actions which the Members take in connection with the regulation of their own proceedings within the House.

Q. Their own business?

A. And mind you, that is why I emphasized at the outset, in a suit against the Members, it doesn't vitiate the broad area at all, sir. It only vitiates a very narrow area.

* * *

Now, the only possible limitation, as I said before, on the speech or debate clause is what this Court said in Kilbourne and what it described as "possible utter perversions," and the example that gave of beheading the what it described as "possible utter perversions," and the example that I gave of beheading the President was given by this Court in the opinion in Kilbourne as an example of an utter perversion. I didn't make it up.

What other cases would be included in this doctrine of utter perversion? That is a very difficult question but I am willing to say, I think, for what it is worth, that probably if all blacks were excluded in any fashion, either seriatim or by the passage of a rule, that would be an utter perversion possibly. I am sure if all Republicans were excluded, it would clearly be an utter perversion.

But I say probably not if only one black were excluded, such as here, assuming, contrary to the fact, that Mr. Powell was excluded because of his race.

Justice Fortas wanted to know if Bromley believed the courts could reverse an action of the House excluding ten blacks. Bromley replied: "Well, ten at one time, and if there were only ten in the House, I can't tell you. I don't know." The questioning then turned to the matter of qualifications for members. Bromley argued that while the House could not add any additional standing qualifications (besides age, citizenship, and inhabitancy), the House could judge the qualifications regarding personal conduct and that such legislative judgment was beyond judicial review. Bromley and the justices had some difficulty in understanding one another here.

Q. What I mean to say is that if I correctly understand your last statement, you are saying that the House may adopt its own standards as to what are requisite qualifications of Members, subject to only one limitation, and that is this perversion, or whatever the correct words are. Is that right?
A. Adopt its own standards? They can't adopt any additional standing disqualifications.
Q. I am trying to understand your position.
A. I know it is difficult.
Q. It is; yes, it is, Judge.
Q. Judge, suppose we had the situation they had in New York after World War I, the case in which Chief Justice Hughes, then out of office, interceded for five men who were denied admission to the New York Legislature just because they were Socialists. Now, suppose that same thing happened in the Congress today under your argument. Would there be any remedy for that?
A. Under speech or debate, I do not believe so; no, sir.

Bromley then addressed himself to the argument of Powell's attorneys, that the "speech and debate" clause barred imposition of criminal or civil penalties but did not bar the relief sought by Powell: injunctive relief, a writ of mandamus, or a declaratory judgment. "In order to effectuate the immunity afforded by the speech or debate clause," said Bromley, "it must apply to injunction, mandamus, or declaratory judgment, because it is far simpler to intimidate critical legislators by direct order of a court with its attendant sanctions than it is by the indirect threat of subsequent criminal or civil proceedings." And, getting to the crux of the question of remedy, he suggested that Powell's attorneys had not overcome this problem simply by limiting their request to a declaratory judgment. Declaratory judgment was itself a "questioning of speech or debate taken in the House." And, "insofar as a declaratory judgment would be given force and effect by the Members' voluntary acquiescence, it would be, I submit, as effective an impingement and interference with legislative proceedings as a flat injunction would be." He thus anticipated the narrow grounds upon which the court chose to act.

When the questioning returned to whether Congress could determine what the qualifications were and judge whether a congressman complies with them, Bromley summed up his argument in simple language. Congressmen "have the right to judge whether the man's character and action is worthy of a Member of their body, or whether the man is a crook and ought to be thrown out." But when he said, incredibly, that the principle was "so deeply embedded in our whole system that I really don't see how anybody can question it," he immediately challenged: "Where has it been explored, either in our Constitution or in our cases, if it is so clear?" Bromley referred to precedents listed in an appendix filed with the court, but had to concede that there were no precedents where the House expelled members for conduct prior to that term of the House. Then he was asked if the court should attach any significance to the conclusions of the Select Committee that Congress could not expel for prior conduct. He adhered to his basic argument that only the House could decide: "No, no. This is a legal conclusion which no matter what the recommendation of the report was, was decided as a legal matter by the House on March 1st, and they did not accept that."

Bromley let himself be drawn into a real quagmire when he

suggested that although Powell had misappropriated funds during a prior Congress, he was still guilty of something since he still had the funds in his possession and had not offered to give them back. When Bromley said Powell had taken $50,000, he was forced to acknowledge, "Well, I upped it a little," and "maybe I should have said $44,892.12."

* * *

Q. Mr. Bromley, it sounds to me like, from what you say, they charged him with the crime of embezzlement.
A. They found that he misappropriated, their finding was. I suppose that is a crime.
Q. When it belonged to the United States.
A. Yes, I suppose that is a crime.
Q. Well, wouldn't that be embezzlement?
A. It might be embezzlement; yes, sir.
Q. Were they punishing him for that, or what were they doing when they fined him?
A. He wasn't fined in the 90th Congress. He was fined in the present Congress, which is not before your Honors. But what were they doing? They were exercising their constitutional power to punish him.

* * *

Q. But it seems to me like what they have done is try him for a criminal offense, thereby denying him the opportunity to be tried before a judge and jury.

* * *

When Bromley asserted that Powell had admitted his guilt because he had not denied it, he was asked, "Well, he is not required to deny it, is he, under the Constitution?" Bromley was not dissuaded: "I should think in this posture that we ought to come here with some statement from him, if he didn't do it, saying 'I didn't do it,' but they are very careful not to say that and they have never said it." Powell should have been indicted, said Bromley. Said Mr. Justice Black: "That is what I was thinking. That would probably be a better place to try him."

Bromley noted that Congress had seated Powell in 1969,

after the voters had again expressed their preference for Powell; since the congressmen felt that they could not let him go "scot-free" they had punished him by loss of seniority and fine. The justices then pursued the question of punishment:

> Q. Well, there is quite a difference between those two, isn't there, quite a difference between taking away his seniority, which I presume nobody would decline to say the Congress didn't have a right to do, and fining him for a crime?
>
> A. I don't see the difference, sir, fining him for appropriating the money, making him pay it back in part. I think it was a very mild sanction, myself.

He was asked, "Is there any power to commit him to prison . . .?" Bromley said he assumed Congress had the power to punish a member for disorderly behavior, including the power to have him imprisoned. Then came the clincher:

> Q. And in that event, would he be entitled to—is it your position that he wouldn't be entitled to any judicial review?
>
> A. That is my position; yes, sir.

With guarded understatement, Kinoy began his rebuttal argument: "May it please the Court, there have been some rather unusual statements made in Court this morning which we would like to respond to very briefly." Kinoy argued that the precedent established in the case of Congressman Lyons in the 5th Congress was still pertinent. The House had debated the issue and had concluded that the House had no constitutional power to expel for alleged acts prior to the election, for the same reason advanced by Madison and Hamilton—that the ultimate tribunal as to the fitness of a member was not Congress but was the people.

Contending that the "speech and debate" clause had nothing to do with this case, Kinoy said that the clause did not vitiate the power of judicial review, but that it merely protected legislators in legitimate legislative business from criminal or civil sanctions. There were no criminal or civil sanctions here.

Then he dealt with Bromley's accusation that Powell's silence betrayed his guilt:

> Now I have to say one thing: I think it is outrageous that before this Court assertions are made that the petitioner was guilty of certain acts, that the petitioner never denied his guilt of certain acts. The record hasn't an ounce of evidence of that in it, and I want to make it very clear.

Powell's attorneys had made their position clear to the Select Committee, Kinoy said when questioned by Mr. Justice Black; their position was that Congress had the power to inquire into the three enumerated qualifications for membership, but had no power to inquire beyond that.

Justice Fortas asked whether, if Powell had been seated, the House would have had the power to punish him. Kinoy said that it could punish and expel, subject to the constitutional requirement that the House could not punish or expel for alleged acts occurring prior to Powell's election and subject to Powell's being accorded the rights of an adversary proceeding. Then, in a question getting to the heart of the matter, Kinoy was asked if his argument depended "upon the distinction between the exclusion and the expulsion procedures, or the exclusion and the punishment procedures." Replied Kinoy:

> I would put it this way, Your Honor: Fundamentally the constitutional argument, the constitutional position, is the same. If the expulsion power were used, in effect, to do what the House cannot do under the exclusion power, that is, to add a qualification to membership, that would equally fall as unconstitutional.

Kinoy concluded his argument by saying that to argue a doctrine, as the defendants did, "which says that the Legislature can transcend the boundaries placed in the

Constitution is to subvert the very meaning of a written Constitution."

Outside the courtroom Powell had no comment for reporters, but to Kinoy he said, "Beautiful."

11   Pyrrhic Victory?

Just one week before the end of the final term of the Warren court, the landmark Poweil decision was announced on June 16, 1969. Writing his last opinion for the court, Chief Justice Warren said that there were occasions when the courts might be required to give an interpretation of the Constitution that was at variance with the interpretation given by another branch of Government. The case of Adam Clayton Powell was one of these occasions. The House was without power to exclude him from membership in the 90th Congress, said the court.[1]

Warren's last year as chief justice had begun and ended in controversy. Criticism of court decisions was combined with controversy over the extrajudicial activities of Justices Abe Fortas and William O. Douglas.

The October 1968 term of the court might have been very different. When Warren announced on June 13, 1968, his intention to retire contingent upon the confirmation of a successor, he hardly envisioned serving another full term. Had the nomination of Abe Fortas been blessed by the Senate, Warren in all likelihood would not have been on the court to hear the Powell case. Yet President Johnson, who nominated his long-time friend and confidant, Fortas, as chief justice, had not reckoned with Senatorial ire. There were those who objected to recent decisions of the court, particularly decisions in the areas of criminal procedure and obscenity, and to the judicial philosophy which Fortas had evidenced in his three years as associate justice. During the hearings before the Judiciary Committee, Senator Sam Ervin (D-N.C.) expressed doubts about Fortas' ability to "exercise judicial restraint." Senators Ervin and Strom Thurmond (R–S.C.) questioned Fortas about specific court decisions. Fortas declined to comment on the decisions. Senator Robert Griffin (R-Mich.), who was to lead the opposition to the nomination, objected to the timing and wording of Warren's resignation, which he said created a vacancy so that a "lame duck" president could fill it before the election of Nixon anticipated by Griffin. Questioning before the Judiciary Committee also dwelt on Fortas' role as participant in conferences at the White House. Fortas, the first nominee as chief justice ever to be questioned by the committee, said that these conferences were only on matters of very critical importance and that his role was only to summarize for the president what others had said. Significant opposition coalesced when it was disclosed that Fortas had received a fee of $15,000 for a series of lectures at American University during the summer of 1968. The funds had been raised by a partner in Fortas' former law firm from five former business associates. Opponents charged that such extrajudicial activities by a potential chief justice should not be countenanced. A five-day filibuster on a motion to take up the nomination began on September 25, 1968, and during it there were strident attacks on the Warren court. Mansfield managed to obtain 26 signatures on a petition for cloture, but when the roll-call vote was taken on October 1, the Senate refused 45-43 to invoke cloture. The next day Fortas wrote to the president, requesting that his nomination be withdrawn to avoid further attacks on the court.

The following week, on October 7, the Supreme Court began a new term with Warren as chief justice and Fortas still sitting as associate justice. Warren continued to serve after President Nixon asked him to remain on the court throughout the term which ended on June 23, 1969. But Fortas, although a member of the court during the oral argument on the Powell case, when he asked several searching questions, was no longer on the court by the time the decision was announced. In May, 1969, *Life* disclosed that Fortas had received $20,000 in January, 1966, from a foundation established by Louis Wolfson; Fortas was to receive $20,000 annually for research and writing connected with the work of the foundation, and in the event of his death the payment would be made to his wife, an outstanding Washington tax lawyer. Wolfson was indicted in September 1966 for selling unregistered securities, and two months later Fortas returned his fee. Wolfson was subsequently convicted and sentenced to one year in prison. His appeal to the Supreme Court in April 1969, a case in which Fortas did not participate because his former law firm had represented Wolfson, was denied. Denying any wrongdoings, Fortas replied to the *Life* charges, stating that since becoming a member of the court he had accepted no fee, given no legal services, nor made any representations on behalf of Mr. Wolfson. There were calls by certain senators for his resignation, and threats that impeachment proceedings would be initiated unless he resigned from the court. On May 7, an extraordinary meeting between Attorney General John Mitchell and Chief Justice Warren took place; it was rumored that the Justice Department had information more damaging to Fortas than that revealed in the *Life* story. No evidence indicated that Warren placed any pressure on Fortas. One week later, however, Fortas sent a letter of resignation to Warren in which he concluded that there had been "no default in the performance of my judicial duties in accordance with the high standards of the office I hold." But, said he, "the welfare and maximum effectiveness of the Court to perform its critical role in our system of government are factors that are paramount to all others." He was resigning to terminate the public controversy and to "permit the Court to proceed with its work without the harassment of debate concerning one of its members."

But the debate did not subside, for in the meantime, senators had begun to look into the activities of Justice Douglas. It was disclosed that Douglas had received about $12,000 a year as president and director of the Albert Parvin Foundation, whose philanthropic activities were in the field of international education and cultural exchange, and which allegedly owned stock in another company owning Las Vegas gambling casinos. Douglas' resignation from the foundation in May did not quiet the furor, nor did his subsequent publishing of a book, *Points of Rebellion.* Criticism in Congress was accompanied by the introduction of legislation which would discourage future involvement by justices in outside activities. Warren called the Judicial Conference, the administrative and policy-making arm of the federal judiciary, into special session on June 10 to consider a code of conduct for federal judges. Rules were adopted requiring annual reports of income, investments, and assets and forbidding the acceptance of outside fees for all federal judges, with the exception of the Supreme Court justices, who were not governed by the Judicial Conference. The court itself voted to postpone consideration of a voluntary code until the next term.[2]

Several months before the beginning of the last term of the Warren court, the Congress had acted on its disagreement with court decisions by attempting to overturn three decisions in the field of criminal law. The Omnibus Crime Control and Safe Streets Act was passed with amendments regarding the admissibility in evidence of confessions by suspects in certain situations and the right to counsel when a suspect was identified in a police lineup.[3] A provision that would have specifically denied the Supreme Court jurisdiction to review a determination by a state court judge that a confession was "voluntary" if that decision had been upheld by the state's highest court was deleted from the bill in the Senate only after extensive deliberations.

In mid-May 1969, President Nixon nominated Warren Earl Burger to succeed Warren as chief justice. It quickly became apparent that he would be confirmed, and in fact he was on June 9, just a week before the Powell decision was announced. The sitting justices found themselves in the awkward position of reviewing a decision of an appellate court judge, Burger, who was to become their colleague.

Thus, amid the political and personal turmoil of the 1968 term, the court considered the issues in the Powell case. The briefs by both parties were characterized by extraordinary legal craftsmanship. The brief on behalf of the House was competently researched and written under the tutelage of an outstanding New York law firm. Powell had had excellent legal scholarship undertaken for him by his coterie of attorneys, although by this time Frank Reid and Arthur Kinoy were almost totally responsible. It was rare when a case before the Supreme Court was so well briefed. Two short amicus curiae briefs were filed, one by the American Civil Liberties Union and the other by George Meader, who was chief counsel for the Joint Committee on the Organization of the Congress but filed as an individual.

The Court's determination that Powell had been unconstitutionally excluded from the 90th Congress was more a victory for the principle of representative government—the right of the people to have their elected representative seated—than a personal victory for Adam Clayton Powell. For while Warren's 61-page opinion proclaimed with clarity that the "judge the qualifications" clause permitted Congress to decide only whether a member-elect possessed the three enumerated qualifications of age, inhabitancy, and citizenship, the court deliberately left unanswered the matter of intense concern to the Harlem congressman: the question of the remedies available to him. Warren mustered all but one of the eight sitting justices to join in the precedent-setting decision. Only Justice Stewart dissented, his dissent being based upon his conviction that the case was moot and that the court should therefore refrain from deciding "the novel, difficult, and delicate" constitutional issues raised by Powell.

After an extended review of the facts, the chief justice rejected the Government's contention that the case was moot because Powell had been seated in the 91st Congress. Bromley had argued before the court that the only remaining claim Powell might have was for back salary and that this claim was a "mere incident" of his main claim relating to his exclusion; accordingly, there was no real controversy between the litigants. The court held, however, that "Powell's claim for back salary remains viable," and that the case was not moot and could be considered by the court. Yet Warren made it clear that Powell's claim to back salary had not been decided, but would be remanded to the lower court for consideration.

Nor was the "speech and debate" clause a bar to judicial review of the case, said the court. The clause protects a legislator for the burden of defending himself, but does not preclude review of the underlying legislative decision. The purpose of the clause was to insure that the legislators were not hindered in their legislative duties by being forced to defend their actions in court; the court's decision to dismiss the action against the named congressmen was consistent with this purpose, particularly since Powell could maintain the action against the agents of the House. The question of whether Powell could maintain this action against the congressmen if there were no agents to sue and no other remedy was available was not decided.

Warren also rejected a third argument raised by the House as a bar to judicial review, the contention that Powell's failure to be seated could be treated as a permissible expulsion because the final vote on exclusion was passed by a two-thirds majority. No grounds for expulsion were listed in the Constitution. Yet Warren suggested that there were three distinctions between exclusion and expulsion proceedings. Most important of the distinguishing characteristics was the two-thirds vote requirement for expulsion placed in the Constitution by the framers because they considered the act so serious that it should receive substantial House support. Since Speaker McCormack had ruled on March 1, 1967, that the vote required only a simple majority, this indicated to Warren that the House was acting on an exclusion. The court would not speculate on what the results might have been if McCormack had announced that the House was proceeding on an expulsion, but implied was the speculation that the anti-Powell forces might not have been able to muster the necessary two-thirds vote in such a context. Congressman Curtis had stated at the time that he thought a two-thirds vote should be required and that Congress could exclude on the same grounds as those permitted for expulsion as long as the two-thirds vote was obtained.

A second distinction involved the question of whether a member could be expelled for acts committed during a prior session of Congress. Since the House's own manual stated that "both Houses have distrusted their power to punish in such cases," the court stated that this was an additional reason for not treating Powell's removal as an expulsion. The court did not rule, however, on the question of whether expulsion for acts during a prior session would be permissible.

Finally, in an expulsion proceeding, the charged member has the right to address the House and participate in the debate. Present during the January 10, 1967, debate, Powell did not participate in the exclusion deliberations on March 1. Although no one said he could not attend, he was not invited.

The court did not explore the matter regarding what limits, if any, governed the House's power to expel and punish. Justice Douglas, in a concurring opinion, stated his belief that the House had authority to punish its members on any grounds in expulsion proceedings, and that the courts could not review challenges to expulsion. Thus, had Powell been seated and then expelled, as some congressmen had advocated, Powell's challenge might have met a different response from the court.

The court sustained the court of appeals decision that the federal courts do have jurisdiction over the Powell matter and then raised two crucial questions: whether the claim presented and the relief sought were of the type admitting of judicial resolution, and whether the issue presented a "political question" which was not justiciable in federal courts because of separation of powers provided for in the Constitution.

Regarding the question of relief sought, the court noted that the petitioners sought only a declaratory judgment as to whether Powell was properly excluded from the 90th Congress, not coercive relief. Such a judgment could be "considered independently of whether other forms of relief are appropriate," and hence the court could decide the question of the constitutionality of Powell's exclusion. Thus, the court avoided the question of whether the courts could consider coercive relief—whether the courts could or should order Congress to reimburse Powell for back salary. However, under normal circumstances a declaratory judgment setting forth the rights of the parties would not be given unless it could be followed by relief which would implement the legal relationship declared.

Did the case raise a political question which would bar adjudication? As the lower courts had done, Warren cited the six formulations from *Baker*, the presence of any one of which would indicate that the case presented a political question. Justice Burger on the court of appeals had relied primarily upon the fourth formulation, "the impossibility of a court's undertaking independent resolution without expressing lack of the respect due coordinate branches of government," in his decision that his court should not review the case. He was deeply troubled by the possible confrontation with Congress, which he foresaw in the event that Congress might choose to disregard a court order:

> Conflicts between our co-equal federal branches are not merely unseemly but often destructive of important values. In the interpretation of provisions which are pregnant with such conflicts the unavailability of a remedy and the consequences of any unresolved confrontation between coordinate branches weigh heavily in pointing to a conclusion either that no jurisdiction was intended or that if jurisdiction exists it should not be exercised.[4]

Framing the issue somewhat differently, Warren reduced the issue here to just one of the *Baker* formulations, the first, whether "a textually demonstrable constitutional commitment of the issue to a co-ordinate political department," had been made. He answered the House's contention that the "judge the qualifications" clause had committed to the House the sole power to determine the qualifications of its members-elect by citing *Baker* again:

> Deciding whether a matter has in any measure been committed by the Constitution to another branch of government, or whether the action of that branch exceeds whatever authority has been committed, is itself a delicate exercise in constitutional interpretation and is the responsibility of this Court as the ultimate interpreter of the Constitution.

This interpretation was precisely what Powell's attorneys had been saying the court should do.

To determine the scope of the commitment to the House, the court had to determine the meaning of the phrase "judge the qualifications," which involved in turn a lengthy historical analysis of the clause. While conceding that the historical record was subject to interpretation, the court found that the record of proceedings during and immediately following the Constitutional Convention suggested that the Congress was not to have the power to exclude for reasons other than the three enumerated qualifications, contrary to the claim of the House in this case. In its deliberations, the convention had first dealt with exclusion, and then with expulsion. The court found:

> The Convention's decision to increase the vote required to expel, because that power was 'too important to be exercised by a bare majority,' while at the same time not similarly restricting the power to judge qualifications, is compelling evidence that they considered the latter already limited by the standing qualifications previously adopted.

Precedents cited by the House in which Congress had excluded members on grounds other than those enumerated were not given favorable consideration by the court, since, said Warren, many of these exclusions occurred during periods of national hysteria. And an interesting rule of historical construction was developed:

> Particularly in view of the Congress' own doubts in those few cases where it did exclude members-elect, we are not inclined to give its precedents controlling weight. The relevancy of prior exclusion cases is limited largely to the insight they afford in correctly ascertaining the draftsmen's intent. Obviously, therefore, the precedential value of these cases tends to increase in proportion to their proximity to the Convention in 1787. . . .

Since for almost the first 100 years, the Congress had limited itself to the three enumerated qualifications in exclusion proceedings, the court concluded:

> What evidence we have of Congress' early understanding confirms our conclusion that the House is without power to exclude any member-elect who meets the Constitution's requirements for membership.

Even if certain precedents supported the House's theory that Congress can add to the qualifications required, the court declared that a past unconstitutional action "surely does not render that same action any less unconstitutional at a later date." Here the court apparently agreed with the argument put forward in the amicus curiae brief submitted by the ACLU: subjective criteria for eligibility were supposed to have been eliminated by the "judge the qualifications" clause. The Powell case demonstrated the very kind of action the clause was designed to prevent, said the brief, for "the debates on the petitioner's eligibility leave no doubt that his conduct coupled with assorted political pressures were the basis for his exclusion from the House."

Even if the historical materials has been less clear, said Warren, "we would nevertheless have been compelled to resolve any ambiguity in favor of a narrow construction of the scope of Congress' power to exclude members-elect." At the heart of the opinion was the policy question involved, the very question that the Warren court had dealt with in its reapportionment decisions, the question of how best to achieve representative democracy. Hamilton's comment was compelling: "The people should choose whom they please to govern themselves." It was that simple. Said Justice Douglas in his concurring opinion, "When that principle [one man, one vote] is followed and the electors choose a person who is repulsive to the Establishment in Congress, by what constitutional authority can that group of electors be disenfranchised?" The right of Congress to protect its institutional integrity can be "sufficiently safeguarded," said the court, by the exercise of its power to punish and expel.

Thus, the "political question" prohibition to adjudication did not apply. There was no textual commitment to Congress to judge beyond the three qualifications specifically enumerated.

The court had found that the case was not moot; the action could be maintained against the agents of the House but not against the named congressmen; the denial of membership to Powell had to be treated as an exclusion; the court had jurisdiction; the case was justiciable; and the House had no power to exclude Powell from membership. A direct confrontation with Congress was avoided for the moment, however. In a final short paragraph the court directed:

> Petitioners seek additional forms of equitable relief, including mandamus for the release of Petitioner Powell's back pay. The propriety of such remedies, however, is more appropriately considered in the first instance by the courts below. . . .the case is remanded to the United States District Court for the District of Columbia with instructions to enter a declaratory judgment and for further proceedings consistent with this opinion.

The opinion was noteworthy for what was left unsaid. Nothing was said about Powell's claims to back salary, restitution of the fine imposed as a condition for his being seated in the 91st Congress, or seniority. Nor did the court offer any guidelines to Powell or to Congress as to what, if any, due process guarantees must be afforded a member-elect during an exclusion proceedings. The court did not need to consider the due process issue; only if the court had accepted—either explicitly or implicitly—the power of Congress to exclude Powell, would it have needed to rule on the question.

There were other unanswered questions, in addition to those raised by Powell himself.

1. Would the "speech and debate" clause bar a suit against congressmen if there were no congressional agents to be sued or if there were no other remedy? In the Powell case, there were congressional agents against whom Powell could maintain his action.

2. Were there limitations on Congress' power to expel? The court did not delineate perimeters of the expulsion power, for it held that Powell had been excluded. However, Justice Douglas suggested in his concurring opinion that Congress could expel and punish, without such action being reviewed in the courts.

3. Could a congressman be expelled prior to being sworn

in? Since the court held that Speaker McCormack had ruled that the House was voting on an exclusion, the court did not answer the question of whether Congress could have expelled Powell if a two-thirds vote were obtained.

4. Could the court review the grounds for exclusion if the exclusion rested on one of the three standing qualifications? The court hinted that it might lack the authority to review such action.

5. Could Congress expel a member for acts committed during a prior Congress? Although the court noted that Congress itself had expressed some apprehension about doing so, the court did not directly answer this question.

6. Were challenges to the seniority system in Congress reviewable by the courts? Although the court did not direct itself to this question, Justice Stewart noted his belief that the courts could not review decisions about seniority, which were solely within the governance of Congress.

7. Was the decision reached in *Powell* applicable to the Senate's authority to exclude a member-elect? In all likelihood, this was the case, but the court did not directly address itself to this question.

Justice Stewart's lone dissent sprang from his belief that since the case was moot, the Supreme Court should not decide the thorny constitutional issues raised. Powell's main claim was to his seat in the 90th Congress. But that Congress was no longer in existence, and Powell had been seated in the 91st Congress. Thus, in Stewart's view, Powell's only remaining claims were to back salary and to restitution of his fine. These claims would be more appropriately litigated in a court of claims, where the monetary claims could be settled without deciding the constitutional issues, particularly the question of Congressional immunity under the "speech and debate" clause. His opinion was not inconsistent with his general view of the court, that consideration of broad constitutional questions should be avoided if a conflict could be resolved in a narrower context. Nor was it advisable for the court to consider constitutional issues in this case if it was doubtful that the relief sought could be obtained:

> If this lawsuit is to be prolonged, I would at the very least not reach the merits without ascertaining that a decision can lead to some effective relief. The Court's remand for determination of that question [relief] implicitly recognizes that there may be no remaining controversy. . .redressable by a court, and that its opinion may be wholly advisory.

But Stewart's view of the court as a political institution is somewhat at variance with that of the chief justice and, in varying degrees, with the views of several of the other Justices. In *Powell*, the court saw the opportunity to enhance the court's authority to review actions of Congress and to establish the principle that a member-elect can be judged only on the three enumerated qualifications. By ordering only that a declaratory judgment be issued, the court avoided the confrontation with Congress which might have been provoked had the court ordered the specific remedies sought by Powell.

The similarities between *Powell* and *Marbury* v. *Madison* (1803) were manifest. The most obvious was the forceful restatement in *Powell* of the principle established in *Marbury* that the Supreme Court was the ultimate interpreter of the Constitution. Where *Marbury* overturned an act of Congress, *Powell* invalidated the action of one house. *Marbury* was in fact cited in *Powell*, regarding the court's assertion that legislative immunity afforded by the "speech and debate" clause did not bar judicial review of all legislative acts. A second similarity was in the judicial craftsmanship exercised to avoid a conflict between another coequal branch of government and the court. In *Marbury*, the court asserted its power to review acts of the executive officers—the act in question was Secretary of State Madison's refusal to deliver Marbury's commission as justice of the peace for the District of Columbia—but did not directly order him to deliver the commission. Madison probably would have refused to implement the order. Instead, Chief Justice John Marshall held that the portion of the Judiciary Act (1789) giving the court original (first instance) jurisdiction to issue writs of mandamus was unconstitutional, since such jurisdiction was not one of the areas of original jurisdiction conferred on the Supreme Court by the Constitution. Here, as in *Powell*, the Court established fundamental principle while avoiding the confrontation.[5]

The great ambiguity in *Powell*, however, was not resolved as neatly as in *Marbury*, for the court directed the district court to consider the other issues, issues which the Supreme Court itself had refused to decide because of this risk of confrontation. Indeed, much of the criticism of the decision by legal scholars was directed at this ambiguity. "In short, *Powell* is not very helpful; far from being a triumph of clarity, judicial or otherwise, it is a Pandora's Box of unanswered, potentially significant queries."[6]

Although most legal scholars affirmed the correctness of the court's strict interpretation of the constitutional provisions on House membership, criticism was leveled at the court for taking the case, particularly since the court might have denied review because of mootness or lack of justiciability. For some critics, it was yet another example where "the Warren Court once again followed its activist approach and, once again, assumed a primary position of power."[7]

It appeared that Warren had anticipated this criticism when he wrote in the opinion:

> Our system of government requires that federal courts on occasion interpret the Constitution in a manner at variance with the construction given the document by another branch. The alleged conflict that such an adjudication may cause cannot justify the courts' avoiding their constitutional responsibility.

This paragraph was footnoted: "In fact, the Court has noted that it is an 'inadmissible suggestion' that action might be taken in disregard of a judicial determination. . . ."

Warren's public statements had indicated that he felt that the integrity of the electoral process was one of the most important issues which had been considered by the court. In July 1968, he had said that *Baker* v. *Carr* was the most important case to be decided in his tenure on the court, because other problems would have been solved if every man's vote was worth the same as anyone else's. The *Powell* decision a year later, affirming the right of constituents to have their duly elected representative seated in Congress, was not inconsistent with the court's previous opinions on the electoral process.

When reflecting at a press conference in July 1968 upon the role that the court had assumed in the last decade and a half, Warren had said that there were great adjustments occurring in the life of our society. "The Court lives in an era," he said, "and must play its part." He said, however, that every man with whom he had been associated on the court "basically practices judicial restraint, believes he should not try to do the work of the Executive Branch of the Government or the Legislative Branch of the Government." How had the United States changed since he took office, he was asked.

All I can say to you is for a long, long time, we have been sweeping under the rug a great many problems basic to American life. We have failed to face them squarely, and they have piled up on us, and now they are causing a great deal of dissension and controversy of all kinds. Efforts on the part of people to remedy those things eventually reach the Court for adjustment.[8]

Warren's inclination, in general, had been to allow adjudication of those problems.

Although the *New York Times* editorially embraced *Powell* as "a strong reaffirmation of the Constitution and of the democratic process of electing Congressmen to represent the people,"[9] the paper's executive editor and columnist, James Reston, evidenced skepticism. He noted:

The argument against the Warren Supreme Court was that it was too eager to intervene, that it had lost the art of judicial restraint, and was too inclined to reach out for supremacy over the other two co-equal branches of the Federal Government.

In his farewell opinions after a remarkable and historic career as the nation's foremost judge, Chief Justice Warren almost seemed to go out of his way to provide evidence for the charge.[10]

His criticism was based not on the merits of the decision but on the political implications. He argued that the decision would lend greater credence to those who were urging President Nixon to appoint another justice of Burger's judicial termperament, one who could be counted upon to exercise judicial restraint, to fill the seat vacated by Fortas.

Yet, even though Burger refused to pass judgment on the Powell case, it cannot be assumed that he would have done the same thing if he had been sitting on the Supreme Court. The lower courts in the federal system tend to decide cases in line with available legal principle; they act primarily as courts of law. However, the Supreme Court, political institution as well as court of law, having assumed the role of ultimate interpreter of the Constitution, does from time to time make decisions that are essentially political as well as judicial. The *Powell* decision is part of the tradition of the political development of the court.

Did the *Powell* decision, coinciding as it did with the end of the Warren court, mark the end of an era and the beginning of a more cautious court under Burger? No doubt President Nixon had pondered this question before June 23, when he climbed the steps to the Supreme Court building, in an act without precedent, to praise the retiring chief justice and to witness the swearing in of his own nominee. As a candidate in 1968, in obvious reference to the opinions spawned by the Warren court, Nixon had indicated that he would appoint men to the court who saw themselves as "caretakers of the Constitution and servants of the people, not super-legislators with a free hand to impose their social and political viewpoints upon the American people." He had called for a court that looked upon its "function as being that of interpretation, rather than of breaking through into new areas that are really the prerogative of the Congress. . . ." Warren Burger, court of appeals judge since 1956, appeared to be congruent with Nixon's preference for a "strict constructionist." Particularly in matters concerning the rights of accused or suspected persons, he had the reputation of a conservative, and his rulings at the appellate level frequently had differed from those of the Warren court.

But on this day, when the chief justice recognized the president, Nixon expressed the appreciation of the nation for the example of dignity, integrity, and fairness which Warren had shown.[11] The 16 years that Warren had served were years of momentous change and were characterized by "great debates" and "some disagreements even within this Court," said the president. "No institution of the three great institutions of our government has been more responsible for that continuity with change [so important for progress] than the Supreme Court."

In response, Warren noted that the court was similar to the presidency, in that many times it had the "awesome responsibility" for speaking the last word for "not only 200 million people, but those who follow us." The responsibility was made more difficult for the court because the court had no constituency. "We serve only the public interest," said Warren, "guided only by the Constitution and by our own consciences. And conscience sometimes is a very severe taskmaster." He said that if the members of the court ever agreed on all things, "its virility will have been sapped." He wished his successor well and administered the oath of office:

I, Warren Earl Burger, do solemnly swear that I will administer justice without respect to persons, and do equal right to the poor and to the rich . . . and that I will support and defend the Constitution of the United States . . . and that I will well and faithfully discharge the duties of the office on which I am about to enter.

208

To a letter written by his colleagues in which they expressed their admiration of his "unswerving devotion to liberty and justice," Warren answered simply: "To have been able to serve with you through these many eventful years is one of the great satisfactions of my life, and to retire with the friendship of all of you fills my cup to overflowing."

12   I Have Kept the Faith

"I am particularly happy and overwhelmed," said Powell at a news conference on Bimini on the day following the announcement of the decision. The significance of the decision was the reinstitution of the principle of coequal branches of government. His personal triumph was of less importance than the principle resulting. "I would not say it's a personal victory because Adam Powell does not matter," he said. "It is a victory for the American people, because if anything like that could be done to me it could be done to any of you from the States." He was not bitter. Said he, expansively:

> I'm overwhelmingly grateful with humility that I have been able to fight through this landmark decision that will be hard to revoke and will be good for the 220 million American people. From now on, America will know the Supreme Court is the place where you can get justice.

Arthur Kinoy, acting as Powell's legal representative and spokesman for the group of eight lawyers who had donated their services to Powell for the case, remarked briefly that the court had "told the entire country that the written Constitution is the supreme law of the land, and that this is a government of laws and not men."

Powell was uncertain and therefore noncommittal about the unsettled aspects of the case: his back pay and allowances, the fine imposed by the 91st Congress, and his seniority. He did note, however, that he thought the decision was a mandate "to go back and see what they are going to do." He was going to discuss these matters with Democratic leaders in Washington the next day, to "test the mood and the temperature." Subsequently his lawyers would determine whether to pursue the case any further. Asked by a reporter why he had not used the familiar phrase "Keep the faith, baby," he said gently that the phrase had been changed: "I have kept the faith."

On Capitol Hill, the mood ranged from respect for the decision to threatened nonobservance. Some who had voted against exclusion saw the court's decision as a vindication of their own stance that such action by the House was illegal. Reticent to comment, Speaker McCormack and Majority Leader Carl Albert sought a cooling-off period. The ruling required, said McCormack, "no immediate response on the part of the House." He urged congressmen to study the situation, so that they might, "in their good time resolve the matter as their wisdom dictates," and he proposed that the matter be transferred to the Judiciary Committee, which is "composed of some of the outstanding lawyers in the House."[1] It was thought that consideration by the committee would blunt any possible allegations that a decision had been reached on political or personal, rather than legal, grounds.

Emanuel Celler (D-N. Y.) tried to frame the issue so that a potential conflict between the Congress and the court over Powell's claims could be avoided. The essence of the decision was that Powell "satisfied the constitutional qualifications for admission." Said he, optimistically, "That is the guts of the decision. The rest is housekeeping, on the matters of salary and so on."[2]

There were others who were less restrained in their

reactions. Clark MacGregor (R-Minn.) foresaw "some trouble down the road."[3] Minority leader Gerald Ford stated that he was "shocked" by the decision, which was an "unfortunate transgression" by the court on congressional authority. The House, he thought, might reject any court order directing payment of back salary. Did he think that disregard of the court might promote legal defiance if offenders believed principles to be involved, he was asked. "No," he said, "I don't think so at all."[4] He felt that the American people could differentiate between a constitutional conflict involving branches of government and a criminal matter concerning citizens who act in defiance of the recognized legal authorities.

Others forewarned defiance. Said Sam Gibbons (D-Fla.) flatly, "I hardly think that the House will bow to the wishes of the Court on this most important question."[5] William Colmer (D-Miss.), chairman of the House Rules Committee, met applause in the House when he recalled the words of President Andrew Jackson, who had said after the court had overturned an act of Congress, "John Marshall has made a decision. Now let him enforce it." Rep. John R. Rarick (D-La.) said bitterly, "Chief Justice Warren in his swan song has given the American people his final insult, a license to any member of this body to misappropriate public tax funds under judicial protection from the wrath of honest men."[6]

While prominent Harlemites welcomed the decision, it was evident that many were most concerned about the decision's implementation. Many leaders expressed the hope that the "law-and-order" Congress would restore to Powell all that was rightfully his. They were particularly concerned about his seniority. Said Livingston Wingate, director of the New York branch of the Urban League, in what was obviously a political overstatement, "If they don't give him back his chairmanship, the Democrats will have forfeited the black vote forever."[7]

Powell's statements on Bimini on June 17 seemed to

213

indicate a willingness to compromise with the House. The possibility of avoiding a confrontation between the court and Congress was appealing to many congressmen. Thus, there was talk that Powell might dispense with court action to secure back salary if he were to recover some degree of seniority. Few foresaw Powell's regaining his chairmanship, through which he had controlled important legislation and considerable patronage. An alternative might be offering him the chairmanship of a subcommittee, with a staff and operating funds. There was consensus among legal authorities that Powell could regain seniority only through political compromise, since seniority was an internal House affair—custom, really—and was immune from legal action. On the other hand, the reclamation of back salary and restoration of his fine were considered ripe for litigation.

Yet the talk of compromise never amounted to more than speculation. In preparation for a meeting with Powell, House Democratic leaders met on June 18 and rejected the possibility of compromise. Rather than offer partial concessions, such as a portion of his back salary or some measure of seniority, they hoped to persuade him to suspend court action so as to avoid a potentially dangerous clash between the court and the House. The terms suggested by the House leaders, which conceded nothing to Powell, accurately reflected the mood of the House. Most congressmen were in agreement that Powell could not win if the salary issue came to a floor vote. Unexpectedly, Powell canceled his trip to Washington to confer with the leadership; his absence was attributed to exhaustion and low blood pressure.

In the absence of any other plan by the House leadership, what resulted in Congress was a series of bills, the majority of which were punitive. On June 18, Representative Bob Casey (D-Tex.) introduced, with nine cosponsors, a resolution (H. Res. 442) requiring Powell to restore to the government the money that he had allegedly misappropriated, an amount set by the Select Committee of the 90th Congress at $44,936.56.

Casey said this sum would be a repayment of what Powell owed the taxpayers, over and above the $25,000 fine. Another resolution introduced was designed to render House officials incapable of reimbursing Powell for salary "lost" through exclusion.

In the interim, Senator James O. Eastland (D-Miss.), chairman of the Senate Judiciary Committee, introduced a joint resolution (S. J. Res. 125) that, if approved by Congress, would prohibit the federal courts from hearing suits involving either house of Congress, its members, committees, or congressional employees if they were operating in their official capacities. In effect, the resolution extended to congressional employees the legal immunity already enjoyed by members under the "speech and debate" clause. The resolution was proposed in response to the distinction drawn by the court in *Powell* v. *McCormack* between the immunity of members and the lack of such protection for employees. The Senate "cannot afford to allow this arrogation of power" by the court, said Eastland.[8]

Only Rep. Charles C. Diggs, Jr. (D-Mich.), one of ten blacks in the House, introduced a bill (H. Res. 443) to restore Powell's back salary and his 22-year seniority. His action on June 19 was unanticipated by the House leadership. He pleaded with congressmen to transcend their own personal feelings and their indignation about the court's ruling. "The integrity of this body is now spotlighted. If the House follows the suggestions of those who would defy this edict, its reputation as the citadel of law and order and justice will be sorely tarnished."[9] But feeling on the question was intense, and Diggs remarked a few days later, "We will have to let the first wave of reaction to the Supreme Court decision pass over, before the bill can be seriously considered."[10]

But nothing happened, on the Diggs resolution or any of the others. None was ever brought to a vote, and no real bargaining between Powell and the House leaders ever occurred. It appeared that the Congress had no intention of reimbursing back salary or fine voluntarily, and there was speculation that even if ordered by the district court to pay Powell, Congress might not authorize the clerk to do this. It was difficult to see how Powell's seniority could be restored. In the unlikely event that his name would be reintroduced near the top of the Democratic seniority list, his party would not grant him the chairmanship he had once held, a position which in his colleagues' eyes he had abused; in effect, he would be left with signal seniority, existent but unexercisable.

It was clear, then, that if Powell wanted a restoration of his salary and fine, he had no recourse but to return to the courts. Since there had been no political settlement of Powell's claims by late July, the next move was Judge Hart's.

13 Framed in an Enigma

Judge Hart must have read the opinion of the Supreme Court with amazement and bafflement. The court had overruled him by holding that Powell's exclusion could be reviewed by the courts. In ruling that Powell had been unconstitutionally excluded, the court had remanded the case to the district court "to enter a declaratory judgment and for further proceedings consistent with the opinion." The court also had ordered that the action be dismissed against the defendant congressmen, who were protected by the "speech and debate" clause from litigation, and that the appellants be issued an order for the court costs of Supreme Court litigation in the amount of $1,363.42. Yet the court had not specified what Judge Hart was to do about the questions of back salary, fine, and seniority, the very questions that might place the courts in confrontation with the United States Congress. It had merely said that "the propriety of such remedies, however, is more appropriately considered in the courts below." And public statements by congressmen indicated considerable resistance to Powell's being paid anything. The outlook for a political compromise was bleak.

Judge Hart's own copy of the Supreme Court opinion was revealing. There were markings in the margin beside a number of important passages: the sentence on page 29, "We need express no opinion about the appropriateness of coercive relief in this case, for petitioners sought a declaratory judgment, a form of relief the District Court could have issued"; on the following page, "A request for a declaratory relief may be considered independently of whether other forms of relief are appropriate", and on page 62, the concluding part of the opinion regarding what was ordered by the court.

In late July, Hart began what turned out to be a very catalytic round four, by writing to the attorneys for Powell and the House.[1] He requested that both parties submit (1) a proposed form of order or orders to comply with the Supreme Court's mandate and (2) suggestions as to what further proceedings, if any, were required to conform to the opinion of the court.

Answering for Powell, Herbert O. Reid sent to Judge Hart on August 15 a proposed declaratory judgment to the effect that (1) Powell was illegally and unconstitutionally excluded from the 90th Congress and that accordingly he was "entitled to the rights, privileges, and emoluments" of his office; (2) the resolution of January 3, 1969, in which Powell was fined and divested of his seniority, was a continuation of the illegal activity and was therefore "null and void, and without legal force and effect"; and (3) the remaining defendants, in their official capacities, pay the costs of Supreme Court litigation. Reid also requested that oral argument be set on the proposed declaratory judgment.

On August 18, Bruce Bromley responded, saying that he had been "instructed" to inform Hart that "the House, with all due respect, does not agree with the decision of the Supreme Court in this matter." The House considered the court's mandate "an unwarranted action inconsistent with the separation of powers provided by the Constitution." As Hart had requested, Bromley submitted a proposed court order which, he noted, did "not constitute any acceptance or acquiescence on the part of the House with respect to the

Supreme Court's decision." He proposed (1) that the action against the defendant congressmen should be dismissed; (2) that costs for the Supreme Court litigation be ordered for the appellants; and (3) that a declaratory judgment should be issued to the effect that Powell had met the qualifications as provided for in the Constitution and had been entitled to be seated as a member of the 90th Congress. The House's position was that Powell was not entitled to any further relief and that the action should be dismissed. If the appellants wanted to make additional claims, Bromley said that these claims should be briefed and then all of the claims could be answered by the defendants. Indeed, Bromley suggested, the House might not implement any order against the remaining defendants: "I am not able to state what action the House might take with respect to any order which any court might direct. . . ."

It was clear that there was little sympathy in the House for Powell's claim to back salary. Bromley had been instructed to apprise Judge Hart of the intensity of feeling on the part of many congressmen and indirectly to suggest the possibility that if the court were to force a confrontation with Congress, the House might stick to its ground and refuse payment. An order for salary would precipitate a confrontation which all of the courts, including the Supreme Court, wanted to avoid. In effect, a vote against payment of Powell's salary was one way the congressmen could show their antipathy to the opinion of the Supreme Court.

Not surprisingly, Bromley's letter apprising Hart of the political considerations in the case did not go unchallenged. Two days later, Reid and Arthur Kinoy sent a second letter to Hart. They said:

> Counsel for the defendants in his letter of August 18th, to the Court advances an extraordinary suggestion that the House of Representatives may possibly not comply with orders entered in this case pursuant to the decision and mandate of the Supreme Court of the United States. We have carefully considered this

letter. It is our responsibility as officers of the Court and members of the profession to point out at once that it is impermissible and improper to even suggest that possible noncompliance with decisions of the highest Court of the land is a relevant consideration in determining the scope of relief required by the opinion of that Court. As the Court itself noted in its opinion in this case, "it is an 'inadmissible suggestion' that action might be taken in disregard of a judicial determination" [footnote 86 to opinion].

Our system of government rejects as "inadmissible" any suggestion that the House of Representatives will not comply with the decisions of the Supreme Court of the United States. The highest court in the land has spoken in this case. A system of law requires acceptance of such a decision by everyone no matter how high their station.

The suggestion in the letter of counsel for the defendants that the House of Representatives may possibly not comply with orders to be entered in this case is impermissible. It is a suggestion, which once made, raises implications dangerous to the security and stability of a democratic government grounded upon a rule of law. The overwhelming public interest in the reaffirmation of the principle that the rule of law demands compliance by all, regardless of their station, with the decisions of the highest court of the law now requires that the resolution of the questions raised in the letter of counsel for the defendants not be protracted or delayed. This is no ordinary law suit. In its present posture, it now touches upon the most fundamental concept upon which the Republic rests—namely whether the rule of law applies to all or is to be invoked only when poor and powerless citizens are involved. The constitutional liberties of all of us depend upon the acceptance of the rule of law by every organ of government, no matter how exalted its status.

But Bromley held fast. The next day he wrote:

1. We submit that it is not inadmissible, or in derogation of the rule of law, for one branch of Government to call attention to the principle of separation of powers with its attendant system of checks and balances which is designed to insure that no one branch becomes dominant. That principle is fundamental to our system of law and essential to the preservation of our liberties. Our history, accordingly, is not lacking in instances where each

branch was invoked the principle where it has believed that one of the other branches has departed from it. To do so implies no lack of the respect due to another branch. That is particularly true in the present posture of this case, where, as developed in paragraph 3 below, no order has been or can be entered by the court against the House or any of its members.

In June, there had been a report in the press that Powell might drop his claim for $55,000 in back salary in return for reinstatement of his seniority. Powell had denied the report. This was not the time to make deals, he had said, at a press conference on June 22. "I couldn't make a deal if I wanted to." Such reports were to surface repeatedly during the summer. Yet Powell clearly would not accept any compromise that involved a humiliation or an admission of any wrongdoing on his part. To do so would be to lose more than he would gain. He might have accepted a settlement for back salary if the government were to give up any threat of counterclaims for funds allegedly misappropriated. Reid stated, as late as August 27, that there was a possibility for resolving the prolonged litigation but that he didn't know whether a proposal was still being considered by the attorneys for the House.[2]

Yet it was evident that a political settlement between Powell and the House was not to be forthcoming when Judge Hart began the hearing in the district court with Bromley, Kinoy, and Reid on the same day.[3] He first set forth the points of agreement among the parties: that a declaratory judgment should be issued against the remaining defendants; that Powell had been entitled to his seat in the 90th Congress; that the defendant congressmen should be dismissed as parties to the litigation; and that Powell was entitled to a judgment for the court costs of Supreme Court litigation, to be paid by the remaining defendants. Kinoy pressed that the declaratory judgment should be entered against the House employees in their individual and official capacities. His reason was that in the event that the House would not approve a claim for back salary or reimbursement of the fine, Powell could have a claim against the employees as individuals. Not surprisingly, Judge Hart denied this request: "Surely, individually, they have been guilty of no wrong."

The remainder of the hour and 20 minute hearing involved a debate between Hart and Powell's attorneys about the mandate of the Supreme Court, with only occasional comments from Bromley. Two basic issues surfaced repeatedly in the deliberations: payment of back salary and reimbursement of the fine imposed by the 91st Congress. In the hearings, Kinoy and Reid did not press Powell's claim to seniority because of the widely accepted notion that seniority was not subject to legal enforcement, but was a matter of congressional prerogative. As Powell himself knew, mere restoration of his seniority would not restore the power he had wielded as chairman of the Education and Labor Committee. He once had noted, "Unless you're a chairman, or a party leader, seniority does not mean a thing."

Hart asked the plaintiffs to tell him what further proceedings should be undertaken consistent with the Supreme Court opinion. Kinoy sought for his client an order directing the officers of the House to reimburse Powell for his salary due from the 90th Congress, which would be $55,000, since he had already been paid $5,000 for the first two months. Kinoy thought it "perfectly obvious that if the exclusion was unconstitutional, then the plaintiff is entitled to a declaration that he is entitled to what he would have received monetarily if the unconstitutional conduct had not occurred." And, he noted, "it was perfectly clear" that "the High Court expects that the declaratory judgment will so state."

But it was not perfectly clear to either Judge Hart or to Bruce Bromley. It was even arguable whether the court had intended to be so clear. Hart asked incredulously, "What is before me that would justify such relief that was not before the Supreme Court?" And if the court thought that Powell was entitled to his salary, "why did not the Supreme Court say that the Court shall issue a judgment for salary and costs?" Hart hit on the nub of the problem. "Are you suggesting to me that they did not have the courage [to say so]?"

"No," said Kinoy, "I am not suggesting that at all, Your Honor." If a declaratory judgment was not to be rendered meaningless, it "must state what are the legal relationships which flow from a given act or occurrence."

But, asked Hart, if it was so perfectly clear that Powell was entitled to his salary that no one should even question it, then why are you "saying that for everybody to understand it, I have to issue an order saying that he is entitled to his salary?" He observed, "that is just a bit on the inconsistent side."

Kinoy answered that although the unconstitutionality of the exclusion was clear to Powell, Congress did not agree; and Powell had to go to the courts to get an adjudication of his rights. And "If a man is illegally and unconstitutionally deprived of his seat, he must be treated as if he was not deprived of his seat." Kinoy wanted Hart to issue a specific order for salary because of the clamor that had arisen in the House. This was the first time, he said, since Andrew Jackson raised the question, "that a high official of the United States has raised the question that it will not accept the decision and opinion of the Supreme Court of the United States." It was important, he said, "if the rule of law is to be sustained, that a meaningful decree be entered, so that in fairness to the Congress and to the people of the United States, one knows what it is that the Congress is supposed to do."

Judge Hart was candid. He said he had felt that Powell should not have been excluded from the House: "I doubt if any serious lawyer, who thought about it, ever really felt that Powell should be denied his seat in view of his qualifications. . . ." What had bothered him at the time he had first ruled on the case was the separation of powers doctrine. It bothered him still:

Now, the Court has said that, well, at least to some degree, that the separation of powers no longer exists and the Court can direct Congress in certain ways. But it is up to us to find out how far and in what way. That is what is so puzzling.

The Supreme Court could have, in its opinion, quite easily cleared the whole matter up by saying exactly what judgment this Court could issue. Somehow it shrank from it. I do not know why, but it did. It puts us in our present dilemma, framed in an enigma.

Kinoy understood. "I appreciate Your Honor's quandary. This is a most unusual and difficult case. It has been with all of us."

Kinoy persisted, however, in urging Hart to issue a specific order for salary. "Otherwise," he said, "there is not an iota, a scintilla of sense to the entry of a declaratory judgment; we are merely going through a useless charade." When he allowed that "counsel for the defendants may not like the opinion of the High Court. They may not like the issuance of a declaratory judgment. . . ." he was interrupted by Hart: "Counsel, do not give speeches to me. Let us have arguments on the issues."

Inextricable from this debate was the question of counter-claims which the government might have against Powell's claim to back salary. The position taken by the House was that Powell's claim to salary (as well as his claim to reimbursement for the fine) had not been fully litigated; the defendants wanted further proceedings on this issue, at which time they intended to try to recover funds allegedly misappropriated. Hart asked whether the Supreme Court had meant him to hold a hearing to see whether Powell came to the court "with clean hands," or to see whether the House had a "counterclaim against Powell for funds that he may have misappropriated or improperly spent?. . ." Kinoy said, "No, I would suggest that it is not a possibility, Your Honor." Reid emphasized that a countersuit by the House would be inappropriate. And if there was a judicial hearing to determine whether Powell had misappropriated funds, "we are entitled to a showing of the comparative conduct of other Members of Congress in order to determine whether or not he has been singled out and discriminated against."

Judge Hart found that an "extraordinary doctrine."

The Court: Suppose you are a member of a corporation and two auditors steal money and you only prosecute one. Can he come in and file a defense and say: Well, you only prosecuted me; you did not prosecute the other auditor who stole money; therefore, it is discrimination under the Thirteenth Amendment.

Mr. Reid: I will make the same reply to you, sir, that I made to Justice Fortas in oral argument before the Supreme Court:

"Now, you can punish one without punishing all. But the one that you punish is entitled to a showing of whether or not he has been discriminated against in the prosecution of this isolated one."

I cite to you the *Yick Wo. v. Hopkins*, 119 U.S. 356, a case from California. As Your Honor may remember, the Court held that the statute regulating laundries in San Francisco was fair and valid on its face, but its discriminatory application to people of Chinese descent was enough to declare the prosecution unconstitutional.

So we have no problem with that, Your Honor. And there are cases.

We would be entitled to a showing of fairness of treatment. Whether or not we may get that showing, is a question of fact.

Thank you, Your Honor.

The Court: I trust that Justice Fortas was better satisfied with your answer than I am.

Mr. Reid: Well, they probably may have been, sir.

The Court: All right.

At this point, Bromley, silent during most of the proceedings, presented the House's position. He agreed with Hart that there were still questions to be litigated regarding Powell's right to salary. Since Congress had determined that Powell had misappropriated at least $46,000.00, he "certainly, then, comes before this Court with unclean hands." He noted:

The House, surely, or the United States, is entitled to offset that amount, to say the least, and maybe affirmatively to recover it, since it is entirely arguable that Mr. Powell is owed no salary, at all, save for two months, during which time he succeeded in being reelected, and the certificate from the Governor came down to the House.

Thereafter, Mr. Powell did nothing, although the Speaker was quite definite in stating to him that the matter would be reconsidered if he were to present himself again. He never did.

Thus, if Powell were entitled only to the two months' salary from the time of his exclusion, March 1, 1967, to the time when his election certificate was presented to the House on May 1, then Powell owed the government money. Judge Hart anticipated such a possibility when he asked Powell's attorneys whether they wanted to dismiss the 13 other petitioners, Powell's constituents who had filed with Powell, so that the constituents would not be liable for costs in the event that Powell lost. Powell's attorneys did not wish to do so. Bromley asked that the defense be allowed to litigate the question of counterclaims before Judge Hart issued any order about salary.

In passing, Bromley commented: "We gather, incidentally, that Mr. Kinoy and Mr. Reid, on behalf of Mr. Powell, are no longer interested in such matters as the restoration of his seniority," because of their "repeated use of the words 'monetary emoluments'. . . ." Judge Hart interrupted: "I do not know that that is a fair representation of their argument, because you could not restore his seniority in a body that ceased to exist. . . . I do not know whether they have or not." The interchange continued:

Mr. Bromley: Maybe I was confusing it with his appearance on television, in which he said, as I remember, that his seniority had automatically been restored and he had no further complaint in that direction.

The Court: Mr. Bromley, I do not look at television on those matters, so I do not know anything about that.

Mr. Bromley: Well, I do not either. But I listened to this one by accident. Of course, I turned it off when I found who was speaking.

The Court: Well, let us stick to the issues.

* * *

Mr. Kinoy: Well, if it please the Court, I will not take the occasion to reply to the comments of counsel concerning our client, which I think were inappropriate and ill-advised. This is a serious matter. It is not. . . .

The Court: Counsel, I have said that we will not talk about personalities here. We will talk about the issues. Let's get at them.

When Reid sought to have the resolution of January 3, 1969, which fined Powell and divested him of his seniority, declared unconstituional, Judge Hart answered emphatically: "That is not before this Court. That is nowhere in your pleadings. . . . there is nothing involving the 91st Congress before this Court, and the Court will not hear argument on it."

Reid countered that the mootness argument before the Supreme Court was based on the grounds that the 90th Congress had expired and that the defendants were no longer officers. But, he said, "the opinion, itself, rejects this motion."

Hart was not persuaded. Said he, "Had you wished to bring those matters up, I think you have practiced law long enough to know that you should have come in with a petition to amend your complaint sometime ago. You did not do it."

Dryly, Reid said, "Well, I hope, sir, that I have practiced long enough to follow the Supreme Court's opinion if a question arose."

"I will hear no further arguments on that point," Hart said flatly.

Near the end of the hearing Hart asked, "What is the Supreme Court talking about when it says, 'further proceedings consistent with this opinion?' "

Ever hopeful, Kinoy suggested again that additional relief

should include, among other things, a declaratory judgment to the effect that the resolution of the 91st Congress was unconstitutional. He insisted that the Supreme Court had directed Hart to rule on the issue. The law had been settled already, "because the Supreme Court has said that no conditions may be placed on the seating, other than the constitutional qualifications. You cannot seat a man subject to a fine."

At this point Hart declared that he was ready to issue a ruling, but only to the effect that the case against the congressmen defendants was dismissed. He allowed the plaintiffs until October 1 to file an amended complaint setting forth additional claims which had not been briefed thus far, and he allowed the defendants until November 1 to file answers. Proceedings would follow.

He would be willing he said, to issue a judgment immediately that Powell had been unconstitutionally excluded and that he was entitled to costs, but only if the attorneys were willing to sign a consent that the issuance of orders would not prejudice further proceedings. He admitted candidly, "That as I sit here with no law books available, I have some question about my authority to issue a declaratory judgment and continue with the case." He did not want to have removed further proceedings in the case from his jurisdiction. If the attorneys were not willing to sign, then he would issue the declaratory judgment only after the entire proceedings were terminated.

Kinoy stated that he would consent to there being further proceedings, "pursuant to the order and mandate of the Supreme Court of the United States." Kinoy's word choice would effectively exclude proceedings about counterclaims the government might have.

"That, sir, is begging the question," Hart asserted, "and I will not be bamboozled in such a fashion." What he wanted, he said was consent in writing that the issuance of a judgment would not prevent any future action which "may arise under present complaint and amended complaint and answer."

228

Kinoy said he would agree to it, although Judge Hart observed Reid shaking his head. Hart returned to his chambers to prepare the proposed order.

Two days later attorneys Kinoy, Reid, and John H. Pickering (for the defendants) met Judge Hart, this time in his chambers, for a 15-minute hearing.[4] Powell's attorneys would stipulate only that the issuance of a declaratory judgment would not prejudice future proceedings pursuant to the opinion of the Supreme Court. Hence, Judge Hart ordered (1) that the defendant congressmen were dismissed, (2) that there were to be further proceedings, and (3) that a declaratory judgment that Powell's exclusion was unconstitutional and that Powell was entitled to costs would be issued later, in the final order of the court.

Kinoy objected to the delay in entering the declaratory judgment, for "there is no discretion on the part of the District Court to withhold the entry of that judgment for any period of time. There is nothing to be considered or litigated."

"However," said Hart, "the Supreme Court did not state the time of issuing, as it could have had it stated 'would enter forthwith.'" Kinoy also noted for the record that the plaintiffs did not consider Judge Hart's proposed declaratory judgment as fulfilling the mandate of the Supreme Court. Judge Hart entered the order, concluded the hearing, and left for vacation.

If the order left Powell's attorneys unsatisfied, the attorneys for the House had few complaints. Pickering had noted in the second hearing, on August 29, that the government was willing to accept Judge Hart's proposed judgment and, in fact, would not have objected if Hart had chosen to issue it that day. The House attorneys had agreed with Hart from the beginning that Powell had to argue and brief the claims for salary and fine before the issues could be decided. Judge Hart had given them the opportunity to file counterclaims against Powell.

An alternate procedure, which the House would have embraced, was a transferral of the action from the district court to the court of claims. Some congressmen had argued that Powell's claim for back salary was properly against the United States government, since the 90th Congress no longer existed. In his dissent, Justice Stewart noted that he thought this the proper procedure; the procedure would have avoided the constitutional issues posed by the "speech and debate" clause and there would have been no need for a declaratory judgment against Congress.

Kinoy and Reid found themselves in a disquieting situation. They had won their case before the highest court in the land. Yet after almost three years of litigation, they had not produced any compensation for their client's illegal exclusion. They had not even been reimbursed for costs. If there were further proceedings before Judge Hart, there was a possibility that the government would make a substantial counterclaim against Powell. Their client, meanwhile, had shown himself in the Congress only infrequently and had not attended any meetings of the Education and Labor Committee. His salary for the two year session—$42,500 per year—was reduced by the deduction of the $25,000 fine and his health was poor. In September, the Justice Department disclosed that the Internal Revenue Service had begun an investigation of Powell's returns, but declined to comment on the extent of the investigation. It appeared, however, that the case dismissed by Ramsey Clark in 1968 was being reopened by the new administration. In a letter to Speaker McCormack, Assistant Attorney General Wile R. Wilson asked the House's permission to have certain records that had previously been made available in the federal grand jury investigation of 1967. The matter was referred to the House Judiciary Committee.

In a dramatic move, Powell flew to Washington from New York to announce that his attorneys would appeal Judge Hart's preliminary order to the Supreme Court. It was to be

Powell v. *Hart.* He was questioning whether the Supreme Court order was being fully carried out by Judge Hart. "I've fought too long for many things," he said. "I told my attorneys, 'Let's fight this thing right down to the wire.' Then we'll find out if this land is a democracy or if it's a fake." When asked by reporters if he intended to become more active in Congress, he replied glibly, "Part-time pay, part-time work,"[5] a comment that was to haunt him in his fight to hold the allegiance of his Harlem constituents.

On the theory that Judge Hart had refused to carry out the order of the Supreme Court, Powell's attorneys on November 1 petitioned the court for a writ of mandamus directing Hart (1) to issue a declaratory judgment that Powell had been unconstitutionally excluded and that he was entitled to whatever salaries and monetary emoluments he would otherwise have been entitled to; (2) to enter a judgment for costs to be paid by the defendants; and (3) to decide Powell's claim for a declaratory judgment that the resolution of the 91st Congress imposing a fine was a continuation of the unconstitutional exclusion. The brief petition, which included elaborate appendixes reproducing the correspondence and proceedings before Judge Hart, opened:[6]

> We do not believe that extensive argument beyond the uncontested facts which the record presents is necessary. All the Nation acknowledges that this is a landmark case, the issues in which go to the very fabric of our society. If the opinion and the mandate of this Court is not enforced the rule of law upon which the Republic must rest is shaken. . . .

If the declaratory judgment were entered, coercive relief would not be necessary, for it was, in the court's words, "an inadmissible suggestion" that the House would not comply. Should the judgment not be accepted by the House, then Powell's attorneys might return for an order from the district court that Powell be paid. There was no mention in the brief of Powell's claim to seniority. The petition concluded:

Today, every sober citizen recognizes that we are at a turning point in our country's history. If "law and order," if "the rule of law," are mandates of conduct solely to be applied to black citizens, to the poor, to the disenfranchised, if the concept of constitutional supremacy is flaunted, then the essential premises upon which a democratic society rests are placed in issue.

Representing Judge Hart in the mandamus action was Solicitor General Erwin Griswold. The solicitor general and the members of his small staff argue most of the federal government cases before the Supreme Court and, with regular appearances before the court, have developed considerable expertise. Normally the Justice Department represents the federal government at the lower levels.

The solicitor general's memorandum, filed December 1, argued that since the district court had proposed to do everything required by the Supreme Court mandate, there was no basis for a mandamus action. Hart had said he would issue a declaratory judgment as to the unconstitutional nature of Powell's exclusion and would order a judgment for costs; the only point in dispute involved the timing of the judgments. Failure to issue the orders immediately did not prejudice Powell, since he would be entitled to interest on any monentary claim involved.

The petitioners were asking, in essence, "that the District Court now be ordered to do those things that this Court, only a few months ago, refused to require it to do": order payment of back salary and reimbursement of fine.

Contrary to Powell's contention, the court did not resolve the question of Powell's right to back salary, but specifically said it was "a question which is inappropriate to treat at this stage of the litigation." Regarding the fine, there was no request for such relief in the original complaint, and the district court in fact has allowed Powell to amend the complaint so that the claim could be considered. The district court should be permitted to conduct further proceedings on the outstanding issues: "There is no occasion for interrupting the normal progress of the case." If Powell was not satisfied with the outcome of further proceedings before Judge Hart, then there would be the "opportunity for further review in this Court. ...."

In a final effort to persuade the court to hear the mandamus action, Powell's attorneys filed a *Memorandum for the Petitioners in Reply to the Opposition*. Their plea that a declaratory judgment for salary be issued immediately was reiterated; they hoped that Congress would abide by the order and that no coercive relief would be required. They asked an order for costs immediately, citing in a footnote the fact that Congress had paid Bromley's law firm in excess of $200,000, while Powell's attorneys, who had expended $30,000 in costs alone, had not recovered, although they had won the litigation.

The greater part of the memorandum, however, dealt with the question of Congress' implementation of any court order:

> Respondents' position during the entire proceedings before the District Court consistently reflected this implied threat that there might well be no compliance with any orders of any court. Effort to evade or forestall the finality of this Court's opinion in respect to the fundamental constitutional issues adjudicated and settled in the decision can only be understood within the complicated context of the reiterated implied threat of what this Court has termed an "inadmissible suggestion that action might be taken in disregard of a judicial determination." *Powell* v. *McCormack*, 395 U. S. 586 at 549.

> * * *

> The plain fact of the matter is that there was no conceivable justification in law for the District Court's hesitancy to issue the declaratory judgment. The only inference possible is that the District Court was attempting to punish the petitioners because they would not agree in advance to participate voluntarily in a long drawn out proceeding which had every potentiality of being ultimately evasive of this Court's constitutional conclusions, and the forum for the institution and litigation of issues wholly unrelated to the constitutional questions which the respondents have sought to avoid for more than two years.

233

* * *

The Solicitor asks what prejudice would flow from the refusal of the District Court to comply at once with the commands of this Court? We would suggest that this failure to carry out the mandate in *Powell*, perhaps more than in any other case in the entire system and philosophy of government by law. It would undermine among the citizens, and particularly among the black population of this country any confidence that this Court is indeed the ultimate interpreter of the Constitution and the guardian of the fundamental liberties of the people. It would undermine any confidence that the command of obedience to law applies to the high and powerful as well as to the low and powerless. It is dangerous indeed to the fabric of a constitutional democracy to admonish citizens with deep grievances to pursue the remedies of a system of law and then to permit commands of that system of law which uphold the grievances to be ignored, evaded and delayed in execution. The lessons of the years following *Brown* v. *Board of Education* are only too clear. Any tolerance of the open evasion of the mandate of this Court in *Powell* would be a repudiation of the promise of the efficacy of a system of law.

At a news conference on November 30, the day preceding the filing of the solicitor general's brief, a restrained Powell disclosed that he had been suffering from enlarged lymph glands. He was accompanied by his doctor, Aaron O. Wells, who said that Powell would undergo tests in the hospital for a week to determine the extent of the illness, which Wells described as "proliferating lymph glands." "It could be cancerous and it could be a cold," said Powell. "It may just be a matter of time until the Old Man will knock on my door." Wells cautioned, "Powell is not a physician." No matter what the results of the examination, said Powell, he would run for Congress again the next year and he would lead a boycott of downtown department stores, "a militant and massive boycott and picket campaign to wipe out tokenism."[7]

The week that Powell spent in the hospital saw the surfacing of an incipient movement to depose him. There had been rumors that he was ill and was considering resigning.

234

Repeatedly, the need of Harlem's citizens for a full-time congressman was voiced. Yet the growing group of Harlem Democrats and community leaders that was quietly attempting to coalesce support for an alternate candidate was careful not to attack Powell personally. "The man was my inspiration in my youth," said Assemblyman Charles B. Rangel, "but the seat must be filled because Congress is the place where problems of the inner cities must be effectively fought."[8] John Young, who had received 40 percent of the votes cast in the 1968 Democratic primary, had already expressed his intention of running. There were many other possible candidates, since Powell had not brought along any young politician as a logical successor. Powell was released from the hospital on December 5, when his doctor said that Powell was suffering from "proliferating diseased lymph glands" but would continue his speaking engagements.

The quiet movement to replace Powell became public when Percy E. Sutton, borough president of Manhattan, called on Powell to relinquish his seat. Powell's recent record, said Sutton, "is doing injury to the memory of him when he was a great leader." He paid deference to Powell's past achievements but noted, "Our needs are too great in Harlem and in the 18th Congressional district to survive on memories alone. Many of us in public life have to give attention to problems that are his." Referring to Powell's statement a month earlier, Sutton noted, "We need a voice in Congress, and Mr. Powell has admittedly said that he did not plan to serve full time." Should Powell not resign, Sutton urged that Assemblyman Rangel be "drafted" to run against Powell.[9] Asked about Sutton's statement, Powell appeared unperturbed: "No comment. I'll make my comment when I feel like it." And referring to his health, he said: "As Mark Twain said, 'the reports of my death are greatly exaggerated.' "[10]

Unfortunately for Powell, the Supreme Court denied his motion for mandamus on February 2, 1970. Powell's attorneys had no alternative but to return to their nemesis,

Judge Hart in the district court. The proceedings before Judge Hart had been suspended pending the outcome of the mandamus action. Here they faced a new battery of attorneys, for the Justice Department had taken over the case in December 1969, Bromley having been replaced because of the controversy over the large fee paid to his law firm and because the fundamental constitutional issue had been resolved. Under normal circumstances, the Justice Department would have represented the House from the beginning. The cost of representation by Justice would be absorbed in the departmental budget and would be less visible (than the Bromley fee). Irwin Goldbloom had assumed direction of the case for the Justice Department. Named as defendants were Jennings, Johnson, and Miller, clerk, sergeant-at-arms, and doorkeeper, respectively. The unresolved issues were salary, fine, and seniority. The issue of salary was already before the court in the original complaint, filed in the district court on March 8, 1967, in which the plaintiffs had argued that Powell had been unconstitutionally excluded and denied the privileges and emoluments of his office.[11]

Powell's attorneys did not amend their original complaint of March 1967. They reasoned that there was no need to file an amended complaint regarding the constitutionality of the resolution of the 91st Congress which fined Powell and divested him of his seniority. As they had in the hearings before Judge Hart, they maintained that the issues of seniority and fine were already before the court in the original complaint because the resolution of the 91st Congress amounted to a continuation of the unconstitutional exclusion. A tactical reason for not amending was that they did not want to set forth an additional claim to which the government could raise all of the procedural and jurisdictional barriers raised in the litigation which had been carried to the Supreme Court. Converging with the legal reasons was a third reason. Powell was less interested in challenging the action of the 91st Congress on fine and seniority than he was receiving back salary due him because of his exclusion.

236

Thus it remained for the government to answer the original complaint, which it did on April 3, 1970, almost three years after the filing of the original Powell complaint. In its answer, the Justice Department set forth five defenses: the court lacked jurisdiction over the subject matter; the complaint failed to state a claim upon which relief could be granted; the plaintiffs named the wrong party to the action (the complaint should have named the U. S. government as party; the plaintiffs could not sue the 90th Congress' agents, who no longer existed); the action thus was an uncontested suit; and any claims set forth in the complaint (except the declaratory judgment Hart had indicated he would eventually grant) were now moot and failed to present a justiciable controversy. Thus, the answer urged that Judge Hart enter the declaratory judgment and dismiss the action regarding the remaining three defendants. The government did not file counterclaims to recover funds allegedly misappropriated. However, if Judge Hart were to dismiss the action and if Powell were to bring action in the court of claims, the government could set off counterclaims at that time.

There matters stood by the end of the summer. Even the attorneys involved seemed unsure of the status of the case. One of Powell's attorneys quipped that he and some of his comrades were suffering from "benign neglect."

Absent a political compromise, the possibility of which appeared increasingly unlikely, what were the options open to Judge Hart? He still had to contend with the obdurate questions of seniority, back salary, and fine.

The first matter could be disposed of easily. He could simply decide that the issue had not been raised in Powell's complaint. Alternatively, he could hold that it was generally agreed that the right of seniority in Congress was an internal matter, solely the prerogative of the House. It was not a right that could be obtained in a court of law, although it could be an item in any compromise fashioned between Powell and the House. Kinoy had argued, on the other hand, that the matter of seniority could be adjudicated because the voters

237

considered seniority in electing Powell, as was the case with many other congressmen, and therefore the voters had a legitimate interest in seeing the seniority system operate. However, even if his seniority were restored, his coveted chairmanship surely would elude him. Hart would have little difficulty in dismissing the claim and Powell's lawyers were not really pressing the issue.

More complicated was the question of back salary. Judge Hart could issue an order directing the sergeant-at-arms to reimburse Powell the $55,000 salary to which he would have been entitled had he not been excluded from the House; or he could order the payment of $5,000 for the two months between the time Powell was excluded and the time he was reelected and held a valid election certificate from the State of New York. A ruling for the latter amount could be issued on the grounds that Powell did not pursue the remedies available to him at the time: that he did not present himself to the House to be seated after his reelection in April 1967. It could be argued on Powell's behalf that because H. Res. 278 had barred Powell from the entire 90th Congress, he was under no obligation to present himself, despite the fact that Speaker McCormack had said that the matter would be reconsidered in the event of Powell's reelection. For Powell to have presented himself would have been a vain act. It could be argued also that if the exclusion was unconstitutional, then the special election was superfluous, and Powell did not need to present himself. However, he had allowed his name to be entered as a candidate.

An order for salary, whatever the amount, raised certain difficulties. The 90th Congress, from which Powell was excluded, had expired, and the funds for that Congress were no longer in existence. More importantly, any such order was likely to provoke the confrontation with Congress that all of the courts were anxious to avoid.

A distinct possibility was that Judge Hart, taking a cue from Justice Stewart, would rule that the claims of Powell should be litigated in the court of claims, where the parties would be Powell and the United States government. A claim for back salary should be brought against the government, rather than the agents of the 90th Congress no longer in existence, at which time the counterclaim for $46,000 could be raised because the real party of interest was not Congress but the government, since the funds allegedly misappropriated belonged to the government.

In actions before the court of claims, one of the specialized federal courts, the government waives its sovereign immunity and allows itself to be sued by private citizens. An obvious advantage of this course of action would be the reduction of potential conflict between the courts and Congress by the replacement of Congress as one of the parties of interest. Yet the mere transfer of the action to the court of claims would not entirely remove Congress from the dispute. Should the court of claims award Powell back salary, the Congress had the power to refuse to pay the court of claims judgment.

The question of the fine levied by the 91st Congress upon Powell's taking the oath of office on January 3, 1969, would be more easily resolved. Powell's attorneys had argued in the hearings before Judge Hart that the fine, levied on a member-elect as a condition for his being sworn in, in effect added to the three standing qualifications for membership and amounted to a continuation of the unconstitutional action of the previous Congress. Hart, however, rejected their contention during the hearings when he stated that the issue was not before the court. He would probably dismiss this claim.

Thus Powell probably would emerge from the district court litigation with only a declaratory judgment that his exclusion was unconstitutional and an order for costs, Judge Hart having dismissed the other claims. The unsettled issues did not admit to easy resolution, and potentially the litigation could drag on for several years.

In the event that a political compromise was not forthcoming, Powell's attorneys probably would not file in the court of claims for salary and fine, because of the possibility of a government counterclaim and because of their contention that Judge Hart was not carrying out the mandate of the Supreme Court. Instead, they would probably appeal Judge Hart's decision. Should the dispute be appealed ultimately to the Supreme Court, Powell would encounter a different forum. Chief Justice Burger would not participate in the deliberations because of his role in the case as court of appeals judge. Justices Harlan, White, Stewart, and Blackmun[12] might be chary of a confrontation with Congress. If Powell also lost his case in the court of appeals, an even split on the Supreme Court would mean that the decision of the appellate court would stand.

14 Conclusions

The victory was not Adam Powell's. He had said this himself on hearing of the decision, perhaps without realizing the prophetic nature of his words. It was apparent that he would never regain what had once been his, despite persistent and competent efforts on his behalf. Never again would he regain the chairmanship, the source of his power and influence, that he had used brilliantly when he so chose and that had allowed him the opportunity for abuse. His misuse of that power at a time of acute sensitivity on the Hill to ethical standards had brought about his downfall. Ironically, he had first been shorn of his chairmanship by his own party caucus, in an effort to hold at bay those who were threatening exclusion. Equally elusive would be his claims to back salary and fine, claims that were but minor compared with the claim to seniority.

Tired, and in declining health, the "old man of the sea," as he had referred to himself, had lost what was important to him as a representative of Harlem. And in the years following his exclusion, including those after he was readmitted to the House, Harlem was in fact without congressional representation through Powell's inactivity, illness, and loss of power, which must have made congressional politics less interesting to him. At the very time when his Harlem constituents were most in need of effective representation in Congress, they were without it.

Although Powell would never receive the personal benefits from the court's decision, that decision was an important legacy for those who would come after him. By litigating the case, Powell had confounded his adversaries and had made an important contribution to representative government. Paradoxically, at the very time when he was least effective as elected representative of his Harlem constituency, he was catalytic in establishing the principle that the people shall choose whom they wish to govern them. Perhaps unintentionally, Powell had given the Warren court the opportunity to state this principle emphatically and to state again in a new context the principle that the Supreme Court was the ultimate interpreter of the Constitution. In *Powell*, the court reaffirmed the principle enunciated by Justice Brennan in *Baker*:

> Deciding whether a matter has in any measure been committed by the Constitution to another branch of government, or whether the action of that branch exceeds whatever authority has been committed, is itself a delicate exercise in constitutional interpretation and is the responsibility of this Court as ultimate interpreter of the Constitution.

And, said the court, the possibility of a confrontation between the court and the Congress did not impel the court's abdication of this role.

Drawing a distinction between exclusion and expulsion, the court observed that the House's action was a denial in the first instance of the right of a representative, duly elected and possessing the three requisite qualifications of age, citizenship, and inhabitancy, to be seated. The three qualifications were exclusive. There could be no middle ground which would allow the House to exclude for some additional reasons, such as misconduct, but not for others where there was a specific denial of a constitutional right, such as exclusion because of race, religion, or political philosophy. The difficulty in drawing a line between which additional grounds for exclusion were constitutionally permissible and which were not was exposed during the oral argument. The electorate was to be the judge of qualifications. Congress' ability to preserve its institutional integrity was maintained by its authority to expel a member, after he had been seated, by a two-thirds majority. What limits, if any, there might be to the expulsion power was not resolved. In reaching its decision, the court noted that it would not give weight to precedents of exclusion which had occurred during periods of national hysteria, for past unconstitutional action did not render subsequent action any less unconstitutional.

It all had happened because of an action the House should not have taken in the first place. By rejecting the recommendations of its own committee, and over the strong objections of Chairman Celler, the House had provoked the confrontation with Powell and the court which many congressmen had hoped to avoid. In pressing for exclusion, the House unwittingly had prepared the ground for the decision which limited the power of the House to judge the qualifications of its members—surely a result that Congress had not wanted.

At a critical juncture in history, the court as political institution had played a decisive role. A great deal more than the fortunes of one representative and one district had been at stake. It was not unforeseeable that Congress might look somewhat critically at its own membership as new groups with specific ideological orientations organized to send their own candidates to Congress. In the wake of the decline in the influence of the traditional parties, the House particularly might see the entrance of some unorthodox congressmen. The new members clearly would have to be seated if they met the constitutional requirements of age, citizenship, and inhabitancy. Any tampering with the constituents' selection could be done only by a two-thirds vote under expulsion proceedings. At the very least, expulsion could not be accomplished at the whim of a bare majority.

Despite adversity, Powell never abandoned his style. But the times had passed him by. The mantle of leadership was passing to others, in Congress and in the black community. He had taught them much, and they had heeded his admonition, "Keep the faith baby, spread it gently and walk together, children." But to do it, to walk together, the black community needed leadership that was more aggressive and effective than that which Powell was able or willing to provide. There was no answer to the Biblical question Powell was fond of citing, "If a man falls, shall he not rise again?" His legacy as congressman from Harlem was incidental to his really important contribution to representative democracy.

244

Appendices

A   Significant Dates in the Powell Narrative

1966

Sept. 22: Education and Labor Committee by a 27-1 vote changes its rules, restricting Powell's power as chairman.

Sept. 26: House Administration Special Subcommittee on Contracts (Hays committee) begins investigation.

1967

Jan. 3:   Hays committee issues report (H. Rept. 2349) charging that Powell and some of his committee staff members misused travel funds and that Powell's wife does no work in his district or in Washington, D. C.

Jan. 9:   House Democratic caucus by voice vote strips Powell of his chairmanship.

Jan. 10: Congress convenes; House by a 363-65 roll-call vote adopts resolution (H. Res. 1) to refuse to seat Powell and ordering investigation.

Jan. 19: Select committee appointed to investigate Powell, under chairmanship of Emanuel Celler (D–N. Y.).

Feb. 8:   Celler committee opens public hearings; Powell testifies.

Feb. 23: Celler committee reports (H. Rept. 27), recom-

	mending that Powell be seated but censured and fined.
Mar. 1:	House by a 307-116 roll-call vote adopts resolution (H. Res. 278) excluding Powell from 90th Congress.
Mar. 8:	Powell files lawsuit to win back his seat.
Apr. 7:	Lawsuit dismissed by federal district judge.
Apr. 11:	Powell reelected in special election in Harlem.
Apr. 27:	Circuit court of appeals hears arguments on Powell's lawsuit to regain his seat.
May 29:	Supreme Court refuses to expedite Powell's case.
Sept. 11:	Powell appears before grand jury investigating him in District of Columbia.
Oct. 9:	Special grand jury sworn in in District of Columbia to investigate Powell.

1968

Feb. 28:	Court of appeals unanimously rules against Powell on his suit to regain his seat.
Nov. 5:	Powell overwhelmingly reelected to Congress.
Nov. 18:	Supreme Court agrees to review Powell's suit to regain his seat.
Dec. 9:	Grand jury investigating Powell expires; Justice Department does not recommend indictment and none is returned.

1969

Jan. 3:	House seats Powell after voting to fine him $25,000 and stripping him of seniority.
Apr. 21:	Supreme Court hears arguments on Powell's suit.
June 16:	The Supreme Court, reversing ruling of lower court, by a 7-1 vote rules that the House did not have the authority to exclude from membership a duly elected representative who met the constitutional qualifications of age, inhabitancy, and citizenship.

July 25:   Proceedings before Judge Hart to implement the Supreme Court opinion are commenced.

Aug. 29:   Judge Hart issues an order dismissing the defendant members of the House as parties to the litigation and indicates that when the proceedings are completed, he will issue a declaratory judgment to the effect that Powell met the constitutional qualifications for House membership and was entitled to be seated in the 90th Congress and entitled to the court costs of the Supreme Court litigation.

Nov. 1:   Powell's attorneys file mandamus action, *Powell* v. *Hart*, in the Supreme Court seeking enforcement of the court's opinion.

1970

Feb. 2:   Supreme Court denies hearing on mandamus action.

June 24: Powell defeated by Charles Rangel, by 150 votes, in the New York Democratic congressional primary.

Parts of this narrative were produced from *CQ Guide to Current American Government*, Fall, 1969 (Washington: Congressional Quarterly Service, 1969), p. 56. Reproduction permission granted.

B Relevant Constitutional Provisions

Art. I, § 2, clause 2: "No Person shall be a Representative who shall not have attained to the age of twenty five Years, and been seven Years a Citizen of the United States, and who shall not, when elected, be an Inhabitant of the State in which he shall be chosen."

* * *

Art. I, § 5, clause 1: "Each House shall be the Judge of the Elections, Returns and Qualifications of its own Members, and a Majority of each shall constitute a Quorum to do Business; but a smaller Number may adjourn from day to day, and may be authorized to compel the Attendance of absent Members, in such Manner, and under such Penalties as each House may provide."

Art. I, § 5, clause 2: "Each House may determine the Rules of its Proceedings, punish its Members for disorderly Behavior, and, with the Concurrence of two thirds, expel a Member."

* * *

Art. I, § 6, clause 1: "The Senators and Representatives shall receive a Compensation for their Services, to be ascertained by Law, and paid out of the Treasury of the United States. They shall in all Cases, except Treason, Felony, and Breach of the Peace, be privileged from Arrest during their Attendance at the Session of their respective Houses, and in going to and returning from the same; and for any Speech or Debate in either House, they shall not be questioned in any other Place."

* * *

Art. III, § 2, clause 1: "The judicial Power shall extend to all Cases, in Law and Equity, arising under this Constitution, the Laws of the United States, and Treaties made, or which shall be made, under their Authority;. . . ."

C   Supreme Court Opinions, Powell vs. McCormack, 395 U.S. 486 (1969)

Opinion of the Court, Delivered by Chief Justice Warren

. . . .The District Court dismissed petitioners' complaint "for want of jurisdiction of the subject matter." The Court of Appeals affirmed the dismissal, although on somewhat different grounds, each judge filing a separate opinion. We have determined that it was error to dismiss the complaint and that Petitioner Powell is entitled to a declaratory judgment that he was unlawfully excluded from the 90th Congress.

* * *

II
Mootness

After certiorari was granted, respondents filed a memorandum suggesting that two events which occurred subsequent to our grant of certiorari require that the case be dismissed as moot. On January 3, 1969, the House of Representatives of the 90th Congress officially terminated, and Petitioner Powell was seated as a member of the 91st Congress. 115 Cong. Rec. 22 (daily ed., January 3, 1969). Respondents insist that the gravamen of petitioners' complaint was the failure of the 90th Congress to seat Petitioner Powell and that, since the House of Representatives is not a continuing body and Powell has now been seated, his claims are moot. Petitioners counter that three issues remain unresolved and thus this litigation presents a "case or controversy" within the meaning of Art. III. (1) whether Powell was unconstitutionally deprived of his seniority by his exclusion from the 90th Congress; (2) whether the resolution of the 91st Congress imposing as "punishment" a $25,000 fine is a continuation of respondents' allegedly unconstitutional exclusion, see H. R. Res. No. 2, 91st Cong., 1st Sess., 115 Cong. Rec. 21 (daily ed., January 3, 1969); and (3) whether Powell is entitled to salary withheld after his exclusion from the 90th Congress. We conclude that Powell's claim for back salary remains viable even though he has been seated in the 91st Congress and thus find it unnecessary to determine whether the other issues have become moot.

* * *

Finally, respondents seem to argue that Powell's proper action to recover salary is a suit in the Court of Claims, so that, having brought the wrong action, a dismissal for mootness is appropriate. The short answer to this argument is that it confuses mootness with whether Powell has established a right to recover against the Sergeant-at-Arms, a question which is inappropriate to treat at this stage of the litigation.

* * *

III
Speech or Debate Clause
Respondents assert that the Speech or Debate Clause of the Constitution, Art. I, Sect. 6, is an absolute bar to petitioners' action. This Court has on four prior occasions—Dombrowski

v. Eastland, 387 U. S. 82 (1967); United States v. Johnson, 383 U. S. 169 (1966); Tenney v. Brandhove, 341 U. S. 367 (1951); and Kilbourn v. Thompson, 103 U. S. 168 (1880)—been called upon to determine if allegedly unconstitutional action taken by legislators or legislative employees is insulated from judicial review by the Speech or Debate Clause. Both parties insist that their respective positions find support in these cases and tender for decision three distinct issues: (1) whether respondents in participating in the exclusion of Petitioner Powell were "acting in the sphere of legitimate legislative activity," Tenney v. Brandhove, supra, at 376; (2) assuming that respondents were so acting, does the fact that petitioners seek neither damages from any of the respondents nor a criminal prosecution lift the bar of the clause; and (3) even if this action may not be maintained against a Congressman, may those respondents who are merely employees of the House plead the bar of the clause. We find it necessary to treat only the last of these issues.

The Speech or Debate Clause, adopted by the Constitutional Convention without debate or opposition, finds its roots in the conflict between Parliament and the Crown culminating in the Glorious Revolution of 1688 and the English Bill of Rights of 1689. Drawing upon this history, we concluded in United States v. Johnson, supra, at 181, that the purpose of this clause was "to prevent intimidation [of legislators] by the executive and accountability before a possibly hostile judiciary." Although the clause sprung from a fear of seditious libel actions instituted by the Crown to punish unfavorable speeches made in Parliament, we have held that it would be a "narrow view" to confine the protection of the Speech or Debate Clause to words spoken in debate. Committee reports, resolutions, and the act of voting are equally covered, as are "things generally done in a session of the House by one of its members in relation to the business before it." Kilbourn v. Thompson, supra, at 204. Furthermore, the clause provides not only a defense on the

255

merits but also protects a legislator from the burden of defending himself. Dombrowski v. Eastland, supra, at 85; see Tenney v. Brandhove, supra, at 377.

Our cases make it clear that the legislative immunity created by the Speech or Debate Clause performs an important function in representative government. It insures that legislators are free to represent the interests of their constituents without fear that they will be later called to task in the courts for that representation. Thus, in Tenney v. Brandhove, supra, at 373, the Court quoted the writings of James Wilson as illuminating the reason for legislative immunity: "In order to enable and encourage a representative of the publick to discharge his publick trust with firmness and success, it is indispensably necessary, that he should enjoy the fullest liberty of speech, and that he should be protected from the resentment of every one, however powerful, to whom the exercise of that liberty may occasion offence."

Legislative immunity does not, of course, bar all judicial review of legislative acts. That issue was settled by implication as early as 1803, see Marbury v. Madison, 1 Cranch 137, and expressly in Kilbourn v. Thompson, the first of this Court's cases interpreting the reach of the Speech or Debate Clause. Challenged in Kilbourn was the constitutionality of a House resolution ordering the arrest and imprisonment of a recalcitrant witness who had refused to respond to a subpoena issued by a House investigating committee. While holding that the Speech or Debate Clause barred Kilbourn's action for false imprisonment brought against several members of the House, the Court nevertheless reached the merits of Kilbourn's attack and decided that, since the House had no power to punish for contempt, Kilbourn's imprisonment pursuant to the resolution was unconstitutional. It therefore allowed Kilbourn to bring his false imprisonment action against Thompson, the House's Sergeant-at-Arms, who had executed the warrant for Kilbourn's arrest.

* * *

That House employees are acting pursuant to express orders of the House does not bar judicial review of the constitutionality of the underlying legislative decision.

. . . .The purpose of the protection afforded legislators is not to forestall judicial review of legislative action but to insure that legislators are not distracted from or hindered in the performance of their legislative tasks by being called into court to defend their actions. . . . Freedom of legislative activity and the purposes of the Speech or Debate Clause are fully protected if legislators are relieved of the burden of defending themselves.

* * *

IV
Exclusion or Expulsion

The resolution excluding Petitioner Powell was adopted by a vote in excess of two-thirds of the 434 Members of Congress—307 to 116. . . .* Respondents assert that the House may expel a member for any reason whatsoever and that, since a two-thirds vote was obtained, the procedure by which Powell was denied his seat in the 90th Congress should be regarded as an expulsion not an exclusion.

* * *

Although respondents repeatedly urge this Court not to speculate as to the reasons for Powell's exclusion, their attempt to equate exclusion with expulsion would require a

---

*Powell was "excluded" from the 90th Congress, i.e., he was not administered the oath of office and was prevented from taking his seat. If he had been allowed to take the oath and subsequently had been required to surrender his seat, the House's action would have constituted an "expulsion." Since we conclude that Powell was excluded from the 90th Congress, we express no view on what limitations may exist on Congress' power to expel or otherwise punish a member once he has been seated.

257

similar speculation that the House would have voted to expel Powell had it been faced with that question. Powell had not been seated at the time House Resolution 278 was debated and passed. After a motion to bring the Select Committee's proposed resolution to an immediate vote had been defeated, an amendment was offered which mandated Powell's exclusion. Mr. Celler, chairman of the Select Committee, then posed a parliamentary inquiry to determine whether a two-thirds vote was necessary to pass the resolution if so amended "in the sense that it might amount to an expulsion." 113 Cong. Rec. 1942 (daily ed., March 1, 1967). The Speaker replied that "action by a majority vote would be accordance with the rules." Ibid. Had the amendment been regarded as an attempt to expel Powell, a two-thirds vote would have been constitutionally required. The Speaker ruled that the House was voting to exclude Powell, and we will not speculate what the result might have been if Powell had been seated and expulsion proceedings subsequently instituted.

Nor is the distinction between exclusion and expulsion merely one of form. The misconduct for which Powell was charged occurred prior to the convening of the 90th Congress. On several occasions the House has debated whether a member can be expelled for actions taken during a prior Congress and the House's own manual of procedure applicable in the 90th Congress states that "both Houses have distrusted their power to punish in such cases."

* * *

. . . .Members of the House having expressed a belief that such strictures apply to its own power to expel, we will not assume that two-thirds of its members would have expelled Powell for his prior conduct had the Speaker announced that House Resolution 278 was for expulsion rather than exclusion.*

* * *

....We must decline respondents' suggestion that we overrule the Speaker and hold that, although the House manifested an intent to exclude Powell, its action should be tested by whatever standards may govern an expulsion.

V
Subject Matter Jurisdiction

As we pointed out in Baker v. Carr, 369 U. S. 186, 198 (1962), there is a significant difference between determining whether a federal court has "jurisdiction over the subject matter" and determining whether a cause over which a court has subject matter jurisdiction is "justiciable." The District Court determined that "to decide this case on the merits . . . would constitute a clear violation of the doctrine of separation of powers" and then dismissed the complaint "for want of jurisdiction of the subject matter." Powell v. McCormack, 266 F. Supp. 354, 359, 360 (D. C. D. C. 1967). However, as the Court of Appeals correctly recognized, the doctrine of separation of powers is more properly considered in determining whether the case is "justiciable." We agree with the unanimous conclusion of the Court of Appeals that the District Court had jurisdiction over the subject matter of this case. However, for reasons set forth in Part VI, infra, we disagree with the Court of Appeals' conclusion that this case is not justiciable.

VI
Justiciability

Having concluded that the Court of Appeals correctly ruled

---

*We express no view as to whether such a ruling would have been proper. A further distinction between expulsion and exclusion inheres in the fact that a member whose expulsion is contemplated may as a matter of right address the House and participate fully in debate while a member-elect apparently does not have a similar right. In prior cases the member whose expulsion was under debate has been allowed to make a long and often impassioned defense.

that the District Court had jurisdiction over the subject matter, we turn to the question whether the case is justiciable. Two determinations must be made in this regard. First, we must decide whether the claim presented and the relief sought are of the type which admit of judicial resolution. Second, we must determine whether the structure of the Federal Government renders the issue presented a "political question"—that is, a question which is not justiciable in federal court because of the separation of powers provided by the Constitution.

A. General Considerations

In deciding generally whether a claim is justiciable, a court must determine whether "the duty asserted can be judicially identified and its breach judicially determined, and whether protection for the right asserted can be judicially molded." Baker v. Carr, supra, at 198. Respondents do not seriously contend that the duty asserted and its alleged breach cannot be judicially determined. If petitioners are correct, the House had a duty to seat Powell once it determined he met the standing requirements set forth in the Constitution. It is undisputed that he met those requirements and that he was nevertheless excluded.

* * *

B. Political Question Doctrine

1. Textually Demonstrable Constitutional Commitment

Respondents maintain that even if this case is otherwise justiciable, it presents only a political question. It is well-established that the federal courts will not adjudicate political questions. See, e.g., Coleman v. Miller, 307 U. S. 433 (1939); Oetjen v. Central Leather Co., 246 U. S. 297 (1918). In Baker v. Carr, supra, we noted that political questions are not justiciable primarily because of the separation of powers within the Federal Government. After reviewing our decisions in this area, we concluded that on the surface of any case held to involve a political question was at least one of the following formulations:

"a textually demonstrable constitutional commitment of the issue to a co-ordinate political department; or a lack of judicially discoverable and manageable standards for resolving it; or the impossibility of deciding without an initial policy determination of a kind clearly for nonjudicial discretion; or the impossibility of a court's undertaking independent resolution without expressing lack of the respect due coordinate branches of government; or an unusual need for unquestioning adherence to a political decision already made; or the potentiality of embarrassment from multifarious pronouncements by various departments on one question." Id., at 217.

Respondents' first contention is that this case presents a political question because under Art. I, Sect. 5, there has been a "textually demonstrable constitutional commitment" to the House of the "adjudicatory power" to determine Powell's qualifications. Thus it is argued that the House, and the House alone, has power to determine who is qualified to be a member.

In order to determine whether there has been a textual commitment to a co-ordinate department of the Government, we must interpret the Constitution. In other words, we must first determine what power the Constitution confers upon the House through Art. I, Sect. 5, before we can determine to what extent, if any, the exercise of that power is subject to judicial review. Respondents maintain that the House has broad power under Section 5, and, they argue, the House may determine which are the qualifications necessary for membership. On the other hand, petitioners allege that the Constitution provides that an elected representative may be denied his seat only if the House finds he does not meet one of the standing qualifications expressly prescribed by the Constitution.

If examination of Sect. 5 disclosed that the Constitution gives the House judicially unreviewable power to set qualifications for membership and to judge whether prospective members meet those qualifications, further review of the House determination might well be barred by the political question doctrine. On the other hand, if the Constitution gives the House power to judge only whether elected members possess the three standing qualifications set forth in the Constitution, further consideration would be necessary to determine whether any of the other formulations of the political question doctrine are "inextricable from the case at bar."* Baker v. Carr, supra, at 217.

In other words, whether there is a "textually demonstrable constitutional commitment of the issue to a coordinate political department of government" and what is the scope of such commitment are questions we must resolve for the first time in this case. For, as we pointed out in Baker v. Carr, supra, "[d]eciding whether a matter has in any measure been committed by the Constitution to another branch of government, or whether the action of that branch exceeds whatever authority has been committed, is itself a delicate exercise in constitutional interpretation and is the responsibility of this Court as ultimate interpreter of the Constitution." Id., at 211.

In order to determine the scope of any "textual commitment" under Art. I, Sect. 5, we necessarily must determine the meaning of the phrase to "judge the qualifications of its members." . . . Our examination of the relevant historical materials leads us to the conclusion that

---

*Consistent with this interpretation, federal courts might still be barred by the political question doctrine from reviewing the House's factual determination that a member did not meet one of the standing qualifications. This is an issue not presented in this case and we express no view as to its resolution.

petitioners are correct and that the Constitution leaves the House without authority to exclude any person, duly elected by his constituents, who meets all the requirements for membership expressly prescribed in the Constitution.

a. The Pre-Convention Precedents

Since our rejection of respondents' interpretation of Sect. 5 results in significant measure from a disagreement with their historical analysis, we must consider the relevant historical antecedents in considerable detail. As do respondents, we begin with the English and colonial precedents.

The earliest English exclusion precedent appears to be a declaration by the House of Commons in 1553 " 'that Alex. Nowell, being Prebendary [i.e., a clergyman] in Westminster, and thereby having voice in the Convocation House, cannot be a member of this house. . . .' " . . . This decision, however, was consistent with a long-established tradition that clergy who participated in their own representative assemblies or convocations were ineligible for membership in the House of Commons. . . . Nowell's exclusion, therefore, is irrelevant to the present case, for petitioners concede—and we agree—that if Powell had not met one of the standing qualifications set forth in the Constitution, he could have been excluded under Art. I, Sect. 5. The earliest colonial exclusions also fail to support respondents' theory.

* * *

Apparently the re-election of an expelled member first occurred in 1712. The House of Commons had expelled Robert Walpole for receiving kickbacks for contracts relating to "foraging the Troops," 17 H. C. Jour. 28, and committed him to the Tower. Nevertheless, two months later he was re-elected. The House thereupon resolved "[t]hat Robert Walpole, Esquire, having been, this Session of Parliament, committed a Prisoner to the *Tower* of *London*, and expelled

[from] this House, . . . is incapable of being elected a Member to serve *in this present Parliament*. . . ." Id., at 128. (Emphasis added in part.) A new election was ordered, and Walpole was not re-elected. At least two similar exclusions after an initial expulsion were effected in the American colonies during the first half of the 18th century.

. . . .Clearly, however, none of these cases supports respondents' contention that by the 18th century the English Parliament and colonial assemblies had assumed absolute discretion to exclude any member-elect they deemed unfit to serve. Rather, they seem to demonstrate that a member could be excluded only if he had first been expelled.

Even if these cases could be construed to support respondents' contention, their precedential value was nullified prior to the Constitutional Convention. By 1782, after a long struggle, the arbitrary exercise of the power to exclude was unequivocally repudiated by a House of Commons resolution which ended the most notorious English election dispute of the 18th century—the John Wilkes case. While serving as a member of Parliament in 1763, Wilkes published an attack on a recent peace treaty with France, calling it a product of bribery and condemning the Crown's ministers as " 'the tools of despotism and corruption.' " R. Postgate, That Devil Wilkes 53 (1929). Wilkes and others who were involved with the publication in which the attack appeared were arrested. Prior to Wilkes' trial, the House of Commons expelled him for publishing "a false, scandalous, and seditious libel." 15 Parl. Hist. Eng. 1393 (1764). Wilkes then fled to France and was subsequently sentenced to exile. 9 L. Gipson, The British Empire Before the American Revolution 37 (1956).

Wilkes returned to England in 1768, the same year in which the Parliament from which he had been expelled was dissolved. He was elected to the next Parliament, and he then surrendered himself to the Court of King's Bench. Wilkes was convicted of seditious libel and sentenced to 22 months' imprisonment. The new Parliament declared him ineligible for membership and ordered that he be "expelled this House." 16 Parl. Hist. Eng. 545 (1769). Although Wilkes was re-elected to fill the vacant seat three times, each time the same Parliament declared him ineligible and refused to seat him. See 11 L. Gipson, supra, at 207-215.

Wilkes was released from prison in 1770 and was again elected to Parliament in 1774. For the next several years, he unsuccessfully campaigned to have the resolutions expelling him and declaring him incapable of re-election expunged from the record. Finally, in 1782, the House of Commons voted to expunge them, resolving that the prior House actions were "subversive of the Rights of the Whole Body of Electors of this Kingdom." 22 Parl. Hist. Eng. 1411 (1782).

With the successful resolution of Wilkes' long and bitter struggle for the right of the British electorate to be represented by men of their own choice, it is evident that, on the eve of the Constitutional Convention, English precedent stood for the proposition that "the law of the land had regulated the qualifications of members to serve in parliament" and those qualifications were "not occasional but fixed." 16 Parl. Hist. Eng. 589, 590 (1769). Certainly English practice did not support, nor had it ever supported, respondents' assertion that the power to judge qualifications was generally understood to encompass the right to exclude members-elect for general misconduct not within standing qualifications. With the repudiation in 1782 of the only two precedents for excluding a member-elect who had been previously expelled, it appears that the House of Commons also repudiated any "control over the eligibility of candidates, except in the administration of the laws which define their [standing] qualifications." May's Parliamentary Practice 66 (13th ed. Webster 1924). See Taswell-Langmead's, supra, at 585.

The resolution of the Wilkes case similarly undermined the precedential value of the earlier colonial exclusions, for the principles upon which they had been based were repudiated by the very body the colonial assemblies sought to imitate and whose precedents they generally followed. See M. Clarke, supra, at 54, 59-60, 196. Thus, in 1784 the Council of Censors of the Pennsylvania Assembly denounced the prior expulsion of an unnamed assemblyman, ruling that his expulsion had not been effected in conformity with the recently enacted Pennsylvania Constitution. In the course of its report, the Council denounced by name the Parliamentary exclusions of both Walpole and Wilkes, stating that they "reflected dishonor on none but the authors of these violences." Pennsylvania Convention Proceedings: 1776-1790, at 89 (1825).

Wilkes' struggle and his ultimate victory had a significant impact in the American colonies. His advocacy of libertarian causes and his pursuit of the right to be seated in Parliament became a cause celebre for the colonists. . . . It is within this historical context that we must examine the Convention debates in 1787, just five years after Wilkes' final victory.

b. Convention Debates

Relying heavily on Professor Charles Warren's analysis of the Convention debates, petitioners argue that the proceedings manifest the Framers' unequivocal intention to deny either branch of Congress the authority to add to or otherwise vary the membership qualifications expressly set forth in the Constitution. We do not completely agree, for the debates are subject to other interpretations. However, we have concluded that the records of the debates, viewed in the context of the bitter struggle for the right to freely choose representatives which had recently concluded in England and in light of the distinction the Framers made between the power to expel and the power to exclude, indicate that petitioners' ultimate conclusion is correct.

* * *

On August 10, the Convention considered the Committee of Detail's proposal that the "Legislature of the United States shall have the authority to establish such uniform qualifications of the members of each House, with regard to property, as to the said Legislature shall seem expedient." Id., at 179. The debate on this proposal discloses much about the view of the Framers on the issue of qualifications. For example, James Madison urged its rejection, stating that the proposal would vest

"an improper & dangerous power in the Legislature. The qualifications of electors and elected were fundamental articles in a Republican Govt. and ought to be fixed by the Constitution. If the Legislature could regulate those of either, it can by degrees subvert the Constitution. A Republic may be converted into an aristocracy or oligarchy as well by limiting the number capable of being elected, as the number authorized to elect. . . . It was a power also, which might be made subservient to the views of one faction agst. another. Qualifications founded on artificial distinctions may be devised, by the stronger in order to keep out partisans of a [weaker] faction." Id., at 249-250.

Significantly, Madison's argument was not aimed at the imposition of a property qualification as such, but rather at the delegation to the Congress of the discretionary power to establish any qualifications. The parallel between Madison's arguments and those made in Wilkes behalf is striking.

In view of what followed Madison's speech, it appears that on this critical day the Framers were facing and then rejecting the possibility that the legislature would have power to usurp the "indisputable right of the people to return whom they thought proper" to the legislature. Oliver Ellsworth, of Connecticut, noted that a legislative power to establish property qualifications was exceptional and "dangerous because it would be much more liable to abuse."

Id., at 250. Gouverneur Morris then moved to strike "with regard to property" from the Committee's proposal. His intention was "to leave the Legislature entirely at large." Ibid. Hugh Williamson, of North Carolina, expressed concern that if a majority of the legislature should happen to be "composed of any particular description of men, of lawyers for example,.... the future elections might be secured to their own body."̈ Mr. Madison then referred to the British Parliament's assumption of the power to regulate the qualifications of both electors and the elected and noted that "the abuse they had made of it was a lesson worthy of our attention. They had made the changes in both cases subservient to their own views, or to the views of political or Religious parties." Shortly thereafter, the Convention rejected both Gouverneur Morris' motion and the Committee's proposal. Later the same day, the Convention adopted without debate the provision authorizing each House "to be the judge of the ... qualifications of its own members."

One other decision made the same day is very important to determining the meaning of Art. I, Sect. 5. When the delegates reached the Committee of Detail's proposal to empower each House to expel its members, Madison "observed that the right of expulsion . . . was too important to be exercised by a bare majority of a quorum: and in emergencies one faction might be dangerously abused." He therefore moved that "with the concurrence of two-thirds" be inserted. With the exception of one State, whose delegation was divided, the motion was unanimously approved without debate, although Gouverneur Morris noted his opposition. The importance of this decision cannot be over-emphasized. None of the parties to this suit disputes that prior to 1787 the legislative powers to judge qualifications and to expel were exercised by a majority vote. Indeed, without exception, the English and colonial antecedents to Art. I, Sect. 5, cl. 1 and 2, support this conclusion. Thus, the Convention's decision to increase the vote required to expel, because that power was "too important to be exercised by a bare majority," while at the same time not similarly restricting the power to judge qualifications, is compelling evidence that they considered the latter already limited by the standing qualifications previously adopted.

Respondents urge, however, that these events must be considered in light of what they regard as a very significant change made in Art. I, Sect. 2, cl. 2, by the Committee of Style. When the Committee of Detail reported the provision to the Convention, it read:

"Every member of the House of Representatives shall be of the age of twenty-five years; shall have been a citizen of [in] the United States for at least three years before his election; and shall be, at the time of his election, a resident of the State in which he shall be chosen." Id., at 178.

However, as finally drafted by the Committee of Style, these qualifications were stated in their present negative form. Respondents note that there are no records of the "deliberations" of the Committee of Style. Nevertheless, they speculate that this particular change was designed to make the provision correspond to the form used by Blackstone in listing the "standing incapacities" for membership in the House of Commons. See 1 Blackstone's Commentaries* 175-176. Blackstone, who was an apologist for the anti-Wilkes forces in Parliament, had added to his Commentaries after Wilkes' exclusion the assertion that individuals who were not ineligible for the Commons under the standing incapacities could still be denied their seat if the

---

*Although Professor Chafee argued that congressional precedents do not support this construction, he nevertheless stated that forbidding any additions to the qualifications expressed in the Constitution was "the soundest policy." Z. Chafee, Free Speech in the United States 256 (1941).

Commons deemed them unfit for other reasons. Since Blackstone's Commentaries were widely circulated in the Colonies, respondents further speculate that the Committee of Style rephrased the qualifications provision in the negative to clarify the delegates' intention "only to prescribe the standing incapacities without imposing any other limit on the historic power of each house to judge qualifications on a case by case basis."

Respondents' argument is inherently weak, however, because it assumes that legislative bodies historically possessed the power to judge qualifications on a case-by-case basis. As noted above, the basis for that conclusion was the Walpole and Wilkes cases, which, by the time of the Convention, had been denounced by the House of Commons and repudiated by at least one State government. Moreover, respondents' argument misrepresents the function of the Committee of Style. It was appointed only "to revise the style of and arrange the articles which had been agreed to. . . ." 2 Farrand 553.

"The Committee . . . had no authority from the Convention to make alterations of substance in the Constitutions voted by the Convention, nor did it purport to do so; and certainly the Convention had no belief . . . that any important change was, in fact, made in the provisions as to qualifications adopted by it on August 10."

Petitioners also argue that the post-Convention debates over the Constitution's ratification support their interpretation of Sect. 5. For example, they emphasize Hamilton's reply to the antifederalist charge that the new Constitution favored the wealthy and well-born:

"The trust is that there is no method of securing to the rich the preference apprehended but by prescribing qualifications of property either for those who may elect or be elected. But this forms no part of the power to be conferred upon the national government. Its authority would be expressly

270

restricted to the regulation of the *times,* the *places,* the *manner* of elections. *The qualifications of the persons who may choose or be chosen, as has been remarked upon other occasions, are defined and fixed in the Constitution, and are unalterable by the legislature.*" The Federalist 371 (Mentor ed.). (Emphasis added in part.)

Madison had expressed similar views in an earlier essay, and his arguments at the Convention leave no doubt about his agreement with Hamilton on this issue.

* * *

c. Post-Ratification

As clear as these statements appear, respondents dismiss them as "general statements . . . directed to other issues." They suggest that far more relevant is Congress' own understanding of its power to judge qualifications as manifested in post-ratification exclusion cases. Unquestionably, both the House and the Senate have excluded member-elect for reasons other than their failure to meet the Constitution's standing qualifications. For almost the first 100 years of its existence, however, Congress strictly limited its power to judge the qualifications of its members to those enumerated in the Constitution.

Congress was first confronted with the issue in 1807, when the eligibility of William McCreery was challenged because he did not meet additional residency requirements imposed by the State of Maryland. In recommending that he be seated, the House Election Committee reasoned:

"The Committee proceeded to examine the Constitution with relation to the case submitted to them, and find that qualifications of members are therein determined, without reserving any authority to the State Legislatures to change, add to, or diminish those qualifications; and that, by that instrument, Congress is constituted the sole judge of the qualifications prescribed by it, and are obliged to decide agreeably to the Constitutional rules. . . ."

* * *

There was no significant challenge to these principles for the next several decades. They came under heavy attack, however, "during the stress of civil war [but initially] the House of Representatives declined to exercise the power [to exclude], even under circumstances of great provocation." Rules of the House of Representatives, H. R. Doc. No. 529, 89th Cong., 2d Sess., Sect. 12, at 7 (1967). The abandonment of such restraint, however, was among the casualties of the general upheaval produced in war's wake. In 1868, the House voted for the first time in its history to exclude a member-elect. It refused to seat two duly elected representatives for giving aid and comfort to the Confederacy. See 1 Hinds Sects. 449-451. "This change was produced by the North's bitter enmity toward those who failed to support the Union cause during the war, and was effected by the Radical Republican domination of Congress. It was a shift brought by the naked urgency of power and was given little doctrinal support." Comment, Legislative Exclusion: Julian Bond and Adam Clayton Powell, 35 U. Chi. L. Rev. 151, 157 (1967). From that time until the present, congressional practice has been erratic; and on the few occasions when a member-elect was excluded although he met all the qualifications set forth in the Constitution, there were frequently vigorous dissents.* Even the annotations to the official manual of procedure for the 90th Congress

---

*During the debates over H. R. Res. No. 278, Congressman Celler, chairman of both the Select Committee and the Judiciary Committee, forcefully insisted that the Constitution "unalterably fixed and defined" the qualifications for membership in the House and that any other construction of Art. I, Sect. 5, would be "improper and dangerous." 113 Cong. Rec. 1920 (daily ed. March 1, 1967).

manifests doubt as to the House's power to exclude a member-elect who has met the constitutionally prescribed qualifications. See Rules of the House of Representatives, H. R. Doc. No. 529, 89th Cong., 2d Sess., Sect. 12, at 7-8 (1967).

Had these congressional exclusion precedents been more consistent, their precedential value still would be quite limited. See Note, the Power of a House of Congress to Judge the Qualifications of its Members, 81 Harv. L. Rev. 673, 679 (1968). That an unconstitutional action has been taken before surely does not render that same action any less unconstitutional at a later date. Particularly in view of the Congress' own doubts in those few cases where it did exclude members-elect, we are not inclined to give its precedents controlling weight. The relevancy of prior exclusion cases is limited largely to the insight they afford in correctly ascertaining the draftsmen's intent. Obviously, therefore, the precedential value of these cases tends to increase in proportion to their proximity to the Convention in 1787. See Myers v. United States, 272 U. S. 52, 175 (1926). And, what evidence we have of Congress' early understanding confirms our conclusion that the House is without power to exclude any member-elect who meets the Constitution's requirements for membership.

d. Conclusion

Had the intent of the Framers emerged from these materials with less clarity, we would nevertheless have been compelled to resolve any ambiguity in favor of a narrow construction of the scope of Congress' power to exclude members-elect. A fundamental principle of our representative democracy is, in Hamilton's words, "that the people should choose whom they please to govern them." 2 Elliot's Debates 257. As Madison pointed out at the Convention, this principle is undermined as much by limiting whom the people can select or by limiting the franchise itself. In apparent agreement with this basic philosophy, the Convention adopted his suggestion limiting the power to expel. To allow essentially that same power to be exercised under the guise of judging qualifications, would be to ignore Madison's warning, borne out in the Wilkes case and some of Congress' own post-Civil War exclusion cases, against "vesting an improper & dangerous power in the Legislature." 2 Farrand 249. Moreover, it would effectively nullify the Convention's decision to require a two-third vote for expulsion. Unquestionably, Congress has an interest in preserving its institutional integrity, but in most cases that interest can be sufficiently safeguarded by the exercise of its power to punish its members for disorderly behavior and, in extreme cases, to expel a member with the concurrence of two-thirds. In short, both the intention of the Framers, to the extent it can be determined, and an examination of the basic principles of our democratic system persuade us that the Constitution does not vest in the Congress a discretionary power to deny membership by a majority vote.

For these reasons, we have concluded that Art. I, Sect. 5, is at most a "textually demonstrable commitment" to Congress to judge only the qualifications expressly set forth in the Constitution. Therefore, the "textual commitment" formulation of the political question doctrine does not bar federal courts from adjudicating petitioners' claims.

2. Other Considerations

Respondents' alternate contention is that the case presents a political question because judicial resolution of petitioners' claim would produce a "potentially embarrassing confrontation between coordinate branches" of the Federal Government. But, as our interpretation of Art. I, Sect. 5, discloses, a determination of Petitioner Powell's right to sit would require no more than an interpretation of the Constitution. Such a determination falls within the traditional role accorded courts to interpret the law, and does not involve a "lack of respect due (a) coordinate branch of government," nor does it involve an "initial policy determination of a kind clearly for nonjudicial discretion." Baker v. Carr, supra, at 217. Our system of government requires that federal courts on occasion interpret the Constitution in a manner at variance with the construction given the document by another branch. The alleged conflict* that such an adjudication may cause cannot justify the courts' avoiding their constitutional responsibility.

Nor are any of the other formulations of a political question "inextricable from the case at bar." Baker v. Carr, supra, at 217. Petitioners seek a determination that the House was without power to exclude Powell from the 90th Congress, which, we have seen, requires an interpretation of the Constitution—a determination for which clearly there are "judically manageable standards." Finally, a judicial resolution of petitioners' claim will not result in "multifarious pronouncements by various departments on one question." For, as we noted in Baker v. Carr, supra, at 211, it is the responsibility of this Court to act as the ultimate interpreter of the Constitution. Marbury v. Madison, 1 Cranch 137 (1803). Thus, we conclude that petitioners' claim is not barred by the political question doctrine, and having determined that the claim is otherwise generally justiciable, we hold that the case is justiciable.

VII
Conclusion

To summarize, we have determined the following: (1) This case has not been mooted by Powell's seating in the 91st Congress. (2) Although this action should be dismissed against respondent Congressmen, it may be sustained against their agents. (3) The 90th Congress' denial of membership to

---

*In fact, the Court has noted that it is an "inadmissible suggestion" that action might be taken in disregard of a judicial determination. McPherson v. Blacker, 146 U. S. 1, 24 (1892).

Powell cannot be treated as an expulsion. (4) We have jurisdiction over the subject matter of this controversy. (5) The case is justiciable.

Further, analysis of the "textual commitment" Art. I, Sect. 5 (see Part VI, Section B (1)), has demonstrated that in judging the qualifications of its members Congress is limited to the standing qualifications prescribed in the Constitution. Respondents concede that Powell met these. Thus, there is no need to remand this case to determine whether he was entitled to be seated in the 90th Congress. Therefore, we hold that that, since Adam Clayton Powell, Jr., was duly elected by the voters of the 18th Congressional District of New York and was not ineligible to serve under any provision of the Constitution, the House was without power to exclude him from its membership.

Petitioners seek additional forms of equitable relief, including mandamus for the release of Petitioner Powell's back pay. The propriety of such remedies, however, is more appropriately considered in the first instance by the courts below. Therefore, as to Respondents McCormack, Albert, Ford, Coller, and Moore, the judgment of the Court of Appeals for the District of Columbia Circuit is affirmed. As to Respondents Jennings, Johnson, and Miller, the judgment of the Court of Appeals for the District of Columbia Circuit is reversed and the case is remanded to the United States District Court for the District of Columbia with instructions to enter a declaratory judgment and for further proceedings consistent with this opinion.

IT IS SO ORDERED

[Justice Douglas wrote a separate concurring opinion.]

Dissenting Opinion of Justice Stewart

I believe that events which have taken place since certiorari was granted in this case on November 18, 1968, have rendered it moot, and that the Court should therefore refrain from deciding the novel, difficult, and delicate constitutional questions which the case presented at its inception.

I

The essential purpose of this lawsuit by Congressman Powell and members of his constituency was to regain the seat from which he was barred by the 90th Congress. That purpose, however, became impossible of attainment on January 3, 1969, when the 90th Congress passed into history and the 91st Congress came into being. On that date, the petitioner's prayer for a judicial decree restraining enforcement of House Resolution No. 278 and commanding the respondents to admit Congressman Powell to membership in the 90th Congress became incontestably moot.

The petitioners assert that actions of the House of Representatives of the 91st Congress have prolonged the controversy raised by Powell's exclusion and preserved the need for a judicial declaration in this case. I believe, to the contrary, that the conduct of the present House of Representatives confirms the mootness of the petitioners' suit against the 90th Congress. Had Powell been excluded from the 91st Congress, he might argue that there was a "continuing controversy" concerning the exclusion attacked in this case. And such an argument might be sound even though the present House of Representatives is a distinct legislative body rather than a continuation of its predecessor, and though any grievance caused by conduct of the 91st Congress is not redressable in this action. But on January 3, 1969, the House of Representatives of the 91st Congress admitted Congressman Powell to membership, and he now sits as the Representative of the 18th Congressional District of New York. With the 90th Congress terminated and Powell now a member of the 91st, it cannot seriously be contended that there remains a judicial controversy between these parties over the power of the House of Representatives to exclude Powell and the power of a court to order him reseated.

* * *

II

The passage of time and intervening events have, therefore, made it impossible to afford the petitioners the principal relief they sought in this case. If any aspect of the case remains alive, it is only Congressman Powell's individual claim for the salary of which he was deprived by his absence from the 90th Congress. But even if that claim can be said to prevent this controversy from being moot, which I doubt, there is no need to reach the fundamental constitutional issues that the Court today undertakes to decide.

* * *

There are, then, substantial questions as to whether, on his salary claim, Powell could obtain relief against any or all of these respondents. On the other hand, if he was entitled to salary as a member of the 90th Congress, he has a certain and completely satisfactory remedy in an action for a money judgment against the United States in the Court of Claims. While that court could not have ordered Powell reseated or entered a declaratory judgment on the constitutionality of his exclusion, it is not disputed that the Court of Claims could grant him a money judgment for lost salary on the ground that his discharge from the House violated the Constitution. I would remit Congressman Powell to that remedy, and not simply because of the serious doubts about the availability of the one he now pursues. Even if the mandatory relief sought by Powell is appropriate and could

278

be effective, the Court should insist that the salary claim be litigated in a context that would clearly obviate the need to decide some of the constitutional questions with which the Court grapples today, and might avoid them altogether. In an action in the Court of Claims for a money judgment against the United States, there would be no question concerning the impact of the Speech and Debate Clause on a suit against members of the House of Representatives and their agents, and questions of jurisdiction and justiciability would, if raised at all, be in vastly different and more conventional form.

In short, dismissal of Powell's action against the legislative branch would not in the slightest prejudice his money claim, and it would avoid the necessity of deciding constitutional issues which, in the petitioners' words, "touch the bedrock of our political system and [strike] at the very heart of representative government." If the fundamental principles restraining courts from unnecessarily or prematurely reaching out to decide grave and perhaps unsettling constitutional questions retain any vitality, see Ashwander v. TVA, 297 U. S. 288, 346-348 (Brandeis, J., concurring), surely there have been few cases more demanding of their application than this one. And those principles are entitled to special respect in suits, like this suit, for declaratory and injunctive relief, which it is within a court's broad discretion to withhold. "We have cautioned against declaratory judgments on issues of public moment, even falling short of constitutionality, in speculative situations." Public Affairs Press v. Rickover, 369 U. S. 111, 112. "Especially where governmental action is involved, courts should not intervene unless the need for equitable relief is clear, not remote or speculative." Eccles v. Peoples Bank of Lakewood Village, 333 U. S. 426, 431.

If this lawsuit is to be prolonged, I would at the very least not reach the merits without ascertaining that a decision can lead to some effective relief. The Court's remand for determination of that question implicitly recognizes that there may be no remaining controversy between the Petitioner Powell and any of these respondents redressable by a court, and that its opinion today may be wholly advisory. But I see no good reason for any court even to pass on the question of the availability of relief against any of these respondents. Because the essential purpose of the action against them is no longer attainable and Powell has a fully adequate and far more appropriate remedy for his incidental back pay claim, I would withhold the discretionary relief prayed for and terminate this lawsuit now. Powell's *claim* for salary may not be dead, but this *case* against all these respondents is truly moot. Accordingly, I would vacate the judgment below and remand the case with directions to dismiss the complaint.

Notes

Chapter 1

1. Richard Harwood, "Harlem's Rep. Adam Clayton Powell: There Is Nothing Ordinary About Him," *Washington Post*, January 9, 1967, p. A18, col. 2.

2. "House Committee Votes to Reduce Powell's Authority," *Congressional Quarterly*, XXIV (1966), 2213-14.

3. "Controversy Marks Career of Harlem Representative," ibid., 2223.

4. Edward Bennett Williams, *One Man's Freedom* (New York: Atheneum, 1962), p. 214. For a discussion of the case, see pp. 207-14.

5. See Robert S. Tomasson, "Powell Case, in 6½ Years, Has Involved 80 Judges, 10 Courts, 4 Juries, 15 Lawyers and Congress," *New York Times*, January 15, 1967, p. 69, cols. 1, 2.

6. Powell v. James, 379 U.S. 966 (1965).

7. For material on Mrs. James's action and Powell's appeal, see U.S. Congress, House, Select Committee Pursuant to H. Res. 1, *In Re Adam Clayton Powell: Hearings*, 90th Cong., 1st sess., 1967, pp. 114-17, hereafter cited as *Hearings*. Material on cases discussed subsequently in this chapter can also be found in *Hearings*, pp. 114-72.

8. James v. Powell, 43 Misc. 2d 314 (1964).

9. James v. Powell, *New York Law Journal*, August 1, 1966.

10. James v. Powell, ibid., October 6, 1966.

11. Ibid.

12. Ibid., November 14, 1966.

13. One other lawsuit deserves mention. In April 1965, Mrs. James sought to have a federal district court order the U.S. attorney-general to bring suit to determine Powell's right to his seat, hoping thereby to end his congressional immunity claims. District Judge Tenney dismissed the application on several grounds, among them the assertion that federal courts have no jurisdiction to pass on qualifications and legality of election of any member of the House of Representatives. Application of Esther James, 241 F. Supp. 858 (S.D.N.Y. 1965).

Chapter 2

1. See the listing in P. Allan Dionisopoulos, "A Commentary on the Constitutional Issues in the Powell and Related Cases," *Journal of Public Law*, XVII (1968), 108, n 16. This article was invaluable in developing the historical material relating to expulsion and exclusion.

2. Baker v. Carr, 369 U.S. 217 (1962).

3. John P. Frank, "Political Questions," in *Supreme Court and Supreme Law*, Edmond Cahn, ed. (Bloomington: Indiana University Press, 1954), p. 37. An example is the Supreme Court's refusal to hear cases challenging the constitutionality of the war in Vietnam, apparently on the basis that to do so might violate some of the political question criteria set forth in *Baker.*

4. Baker v. Carr, 369 U.S. 211 (1962).

5. "Warren Press Conference," *Congressional Quarterly*, XXVI (1968), 1837.

Chapter 3

1. "Powell Disdains Fight in House," *New York Times*, December 10, 1966, p. 28, col. 4.

2. "Celler Proposes Powell Inquiry," ibid., December 12, 1966, p. 1, col. 5.

3. "Few Precedents Guide House in Powell Affair," *Congressional Quarterly*, XXV (1967), 26.

4. The two letters below are found in U.S. Congress, House, Committee on House Administration, *Report of Special Investigation into Expenditures During the 89th Congress by the House Committee on Education and Labor and the Clerk-Hire Status of Y. Marjorie Flores (Mrs. Adam C. Powell)*, H. Rept. 2349, by a Special Subcommittee on Contracts, 89th Cong., 2nd sess., pp. 82-84. Hereafter cited as *Hays Report.*

5. U.S. Congress, House, Committee on House Administration, *Hearings, Relating to the Investigation into Expenditures During the 89th Congress by the House Committee on Education and Labor, and the*

Clerk-Hire Payroll Status of Y. Marjorie Flores, before the Special Subcommittee on Contracts, 89th Cong., 2nd sess., pp. 25-34, 367. Hereafter cited as *Hays Hearings.*

6. *Hays Report,* p. 93. Mrs. Powell subsequently told the Celler committee that this was done in the hopes that it would make her husband take her off the payroll or bring her back to Washington. See U.S. Congress, House, Select Committee Pursuant to H. Res. 1, *In Re Adam Clayton Powell: Hearings,* 90th Cong., 1st sess., 1967, p. 225.

7. These and following facts and correspondence on efforts of the subcommittee to obtain Mrs. Powell's testimony are taken from *Hays Hearings,* pp. 344-62.

8. *Hays Report,* pp. 6-7.

9. Ibid., pp. 7-8.

10. Joseph A. Loftus, "House Unit Drops Wife of Powell from U.S. Payroll," *New York Times,* January 4, 1967, p. 27, cols. 2-3.

11. "Few Precedents Guide . . .," loc. cit.

12. Ibid., p. 27.

13. David Halberstam, "Powell Supported by Negro Leaders," *New York Times,* December 30, 1966, p. 30, col. 1.

14. Joseph A. Loftus, "3rd Bid Ignored by Powell's Wife," ibid., December 31, 1966, p. 8, col. 5.

15. Copies of the January letter and the documentation were kindly supplied by Congressman Van Deerlin.

16. This statement may be found in *New York Times,* January 6, p. 38, cols. 1-4; and *Congressional Quarterly,* XXV (1967), 50, 82.

17. "Powell Loses Chairmanship; Seat in Doubt," ibid., 49.

18. Ibid.

19. Thomas A. Johnson, "Powell Shaken by House Action," *New York Times,* January 10, 1967, p. 30, col. 7.

Chapter 4

1. The following account of the debates is condensed from the *Congressional Record,* 90th Cong., 1st sess., 1967, pp. H14-H27.

2. Thomas A. Johnson, "Powell Backers Besiege Capitol," *New York Times,* January 11, 1967, p. 20, col. 6.

Chapter 5

1. Civil Rights Lobby Fails to Support Powell," *Congressional Quarterly,* XXV (1967), 99.

2. The resolution in final form read: "That the question of the right of Adam Clayton Powell to be sworn in as a Representative from the State of New York in the Ninetieth Congress, as well as his final right to a seat therein as such Representative, be referred to a special committee. . . ." See Chapter 4.

3. U.S. Congress, House, Select Committee Pursuant to H. Res. 1, *In Re Adam Clayton Powell,* H. Rept. 27, 90th Cong., 1st sess., 1967, pp. 5-6. Hereafter cited as *Report.*

4. That portion of Rule XI, para. 26, relating to investigative hearings reads: (f) Each committee shall, so far as practicable, require all witnesses appearing before it to file in advance written statements of their proposed testimony, and to limit their oral presentation to brief summaries of their argument. The staff of each committee shall prepare digests of such statements for the use of committee members. (g) All hearings conducted by standing committees or their subcommittees shall be open to the public, except executive sessions for marking up bills or for voting or where the committee by majority vote orders an executive session. (h) Each committee may fix the number of its members for taking testimony and receiving evidence, which shall be not less than two. (i) The chairman of an investigative hearing shall announce in an opening statement the subject of the investigation. (j) A copy of the committee rules, if any, and paragraph 26 of rule XI of the House of Representatives shall be made available to the witness. (k) Witnesses at investigative hearings may be accompanied by their own counsel for the purpose of advising them concerning their constitutional rights. (l) The chairman may punish breaches of order and decorum, and of professional ethics on the part of counsel, by censure and exclusion from the hearings; and the committee may cite the defender to the House for contempt. (m) If the committee determines

that evidence or testimony at an investigative hearing may tend to defame, degrade, or incriminate any person, it shall—(1) receive such evidence or testimony in executive session; (2) afford such person an opportunity voluntarily to appear as a witness; and (3) receive and dispose of requests from such person to subpoena additional witnesses. (n) Except as provided in paragraph (m), the chairman shall receive and the committee shall dispose of requests to subpoena additional witnesses. (o) No evidence or testimony taken in executive session may be released or used in public sessions without the consent of the committee. (p) In the discretion of the committee, witnesses may submit brief and pertinent sworn statements in writing for inclusion in the record. The committee is the sole judge of the pertinency of testimony and evidence adduced at its hearings. (q) Upon payment of the cost thereof, a witness may obtain a transcript copy of his testimony given at a public session or, if given at an executive session, when authorized by the committee.

5. The Powell brief below is reproduced from U.S. Congress, House Select Committee pursuant to H. Res. 1, *In Re Adam Clayton Powell: Hearings,* 90th Cong., 1st sess., 1967, pp. 7-14. Hereafter cited as *Hearings.*

6. The following account of committee proceedings is condensed from *Hearings.* The complete transcript is found on pp. 1-107.

7. The right to cross-examine, a right constitutionally protected in criminal proceedings, is not guaranteed in proceedings before a congressional committee. It is certainly arguable that the right is required for "due process of law" where denial of the right to be seated in Congress is at stake. Powell's attorneys argue, in a memorandum submitted subsequently to the committee, that when the House or its committee investigates the right of a member to sit in Congress, the House is performing a quasi-judicial function; the proceedings are adversary in nature and must be conducted in accord with constitutional due process safeguards. The memorandum notes that the right to cross-examine has been honored in certain precedents, notably the case of Brigham Roberts (1900). See *Hearings,* pp. 263-66.

8. The following account of the hearings is condensed from *Hearings,* pp. 109-202.

9. See *Hearings,* pp. 255-66.

10. See the speech of John Conyers, Jr. during the debate in the House, Chapter 6.

11. Joseph A. Loftus, "Powell Is Linked to Corporation in the Bahamas by House Panel," *New York Times,* February 15, 1967, p. 26, col. 6.

12. The following account is condensed from *Hearings,* pp. 203-54.

13. Quoted in Robert E. Tomasson, "Justice Rejects New Charge of Contempt Against Powell," *New York Times,* February 10, 1967, p. 16, col.6.

14. George Dugan, "Church Council Official Scores Demotion of Powell in Congress," ibid., February 23, 1967, p. 27, col. 2; Thomas P. Ronan, "Presbytery Here Supports Powell," ibid., February 19, 1967, p. 1, col. 4.

15. Paul Duke, "The Powell Case: Bungling All Around," *The Reporter,* April 20, 1967, p. 34.

16. The following is a summary of the 35-page *Report.*

17. Sec. 2 of H. Res. 294, 88th Cong., provides: "No person shall be paid from any clerk-hire allowance if such person does not perform the services for which he receives such compensation in the offices of such Member . . . in Washington, District of Columbia, or in the State or the District which such Member . . . represents." This provision was readopted in the 89th Congress by H. Res. 7, and then by statute, Public Law 89-90, sec. 103, 79 Stat. 281 (1965).

18. This resolution subsequently was assigned number 278.

Chapter 6

1. The following account of the debates has been condensed from U.S. Congress, House, *Congressional Record,* 90th Cong., 1st sess., 1967, pp. 4997-5039.

2. "Ethical Problems," *Congress and the Nation,* Vol. II, *1965-1968* (Washington, D.C.: Congressional Quarterly, Inc., 1969), p. 897.

3. "House Refuses to Seat Powell," *Congressional Quarterly*, XXV (1967), 291.

Chapter 7

1. Sylvan Fox, "Vote Stirs Anger of Negro Leaders," *New York Times*, March 2, 1967, p. 1, col. 7, p. 28, col. 7.

2. Robert E. Tommasson, "Suit To Bar Race by Powell Lost," ibid., March 30, 1967, p. 28, col. 5.

3. Filed in Powell v. McCormack, 266 F. Supp. 354 (1967).

4. Article I, Sec. 9 of the Constitution says that Congress may not enact a bill of attainder or an ex post facto law. A bill of attainder is a legislative enactment determining that a particular person is guilty of a crime and inflicting punishment on him without a judicial trial. An ex post facto law is one that retroactively makes conduct punishable, even though the conduct had been legal when committed.

5. A writ of mandamus (literally, "we command") is a court order directing a public officer to perform an official duty that is ministerial (nondiscretionary).

6. Declaratory judgment proceedings, in cases of "actual controversy," enable a plaintiff to get a binding judicial determination of his legal rights; no coercive order is normally issued, for the assumption is that once the law has been declared, the parties will act according to it. However, the judgment may be made the basis of further relief, if necessary, and frequently a petition for a writ of injunction is joined with a declaratory judgment action.

7. U.S. Congress, House, *Congressional Record* (daily ed.), 90th Cong., 1st sess., March 9, 1967, p. H2398.

8. Ibid., p. H2400.

9. Filed in Powell v. McCormack, 266 F. Supp. 354 (1967).

10. The opinion is found in Powell v. McCormack 266 F. Supp. 354 (1967).

11. Hearing in district court, August 27, 1969. See Petitioners Petition

for a Writ of Mandamus, Powell v. Hart, No. 1197 Misc. (October Term, 1969), pp. 35-36.

Chapter 8

1. A per curiam is an unsigned opinion in which the authorship is not attributed to any particular justice. Such an opinion is often handed down when the court resolves a controversy summarily, without waiting for oral arguments or even briefs on the merits.

2. U.S. Congress, House, *Congressional Record* (daily ed.), 90th Cong., 1st sess., March 1, 1967, p. H1942.

3. Ibid., May 1, 1967, p. H4869.

4. Revised Rules of Supreme Court, Rule 20. See 98 L. Ed. Appendix, p. 17.

5. Amicus curiae ("friend of the court") briefs are filed by parties who believe they have an interest in the litigation but who are not parties to the litigation. Such briefs may shed light on facts or questions of law that the counsel for the actual parties cannot adequately present; in addition, amicus briefs provide an informal tally of public pressures.

6. Powell v. McCormack, 387 U.S. 933 (1967).

7. "Concessions Discounted," *New York Times,* June 28, 1967, p. 9, col. 1.

8. "Powell Censure Bid Rejected in Capitol," ibid., June 29, 1967, p. 11, col. 1.

9. Filed in Powell v. McCormack, 395 F. 2d 577 (1968). The following discussion treats only those parts of the appellants' and respondents' briefs presenting new and compelling material.

10. The following is a summary of the supplement.

11. Powell v. McCormack, 395 F. 2d 577 (1968).

12. The district court had dismissed the complaint "for want of jurisdiction of the subject matter," so as not to violate the separation of powers doctrine. The Court of Appeals recognized, however, that

separation of powers should be considered in determining whether the case is "justiciable." The court of appeals concluded that the district court did have jurisdiction over the subject matter but that the case was not justiciable. See the second part of Justice Burger's opinion.

13. Congressman Curtis, sponsor of H. Res. 278, stated that in his opinion the power to expel included the power to exclude and that both required a two-thirds vote. See the debates in the House, March 1, 1967, Chapter 6.

14. The factors that are relevant to this kind of determination obviously include the nature of the relief sought—in this case, injunction, mandamus, and declaratory judgment. All have traditionally been regarded as reposing peculiarly in the discretion of the court and as subject to denial, even after hearing on the merits, for reasons unrelated to the merits. The potential embarrassments and confusions, both within the House and between it and the judicial and executive branches, inevitable upon their grant in this case, are worthy of sober remark. These and like matters are legitimately the setting in which are to be considered the urgencies, in terms of simple justice, of the bringing to bear of judicial power.

Chapter 9

1. Clayton Knowles, "Powell Back, Granted Parole Pending Appeal in Contempt," *New York Times,* March 23, 1968, p. 14, cols. 6-8; "Powell," *Congressional Quarterly,* XXVI (1968), 742.

2. "Powell," *Congressional Quarterly,* XXVI (1968), 742.

3. Ibid.

4. "Powell To Open Campaign in May," *New York Times,* April 20, 1968, p. 20, col. 5.

5. Thomas P. Ronan, "Powell's Power Is Seen Waning," ibid., June 20, 1968, p. 38, col. 4.

6. Ibid.

7. "Powell Tells Student Group That He Respects Wallace," ibid., October 4, 1968, p. 42. col. 6.

8. Powell v. McCormack, 393 U.S. 949 (1968).

9. "Powell Is Cleared in Misuse of Funds," *New York Times,* December 10, 1968, p. 36, col. 4.

10. The statement is reprinted in U.S. Congress, House, *Congressional Record* (daily ed.), 91st Cong., 1st sess., January 3, 1969, pp. H8-H9.

11. Richard L. Madden, "Friends of Powell Optimistic That the House Will Seat Him," *New York Times,* January 1, 1969, p. 12, col. 1.

12. The House proceedings are based on U.S. Congress, House, *Congressional Record* (daily ed.), 91st Cong., 1st sess., January 3, 1969, pp. H4-H22.

13. U.S. Congress, House, *Congressional Record* (daily ed.), 91st Cong., 1st sess., January 7, 1969, p. H155.

14. Ibid., February 25, 1969, pp. H1181-82, and April 15, 1969, p. H2681.

Chapter 10

1. "Memorial for Stanley M. Silverberg," in Philip Elman, ed., *Of Law and Men* (New York: Harcourt, Brace & Co., 1956), pp. 320-21.

2. The following condensation of oral argument is taken from Powell v. McCormack, 395 U.S. 486 (1969). Transcript of the oral argument before the Supreme Court, April 21, 1969.

3. Immediately after the seating of Powell in the 91st Congress, the House's attorneys filed a memorandum on January 11, 1969, with the court arguing that two events had mooted the issues, meaning that there was no longer any real controversy between the parties. The two issues on which the mootness argument was based were (1) that the 90th Congress was no longer in existence, and accordingly Powell could not be seated in that body; and (2) that Powell had been seated in the 91st Congress. The Supreme Court postponed further consideration of this suggestion pending the oral argument, 393 U.S. 1060 (1969).

Chapter 11

1. Powell v. McCormack, 395 U.S. 486 (1969). See Appendix C for the Supreme Court opinion.

292

2. On June 17, 1970, the justices refused to agree to accept the code, maintaining that the Judicial Conference lacked the power to require justices of the Supreme Court to report. However, almost all of them have submitted reports voluntarily.

3. The legislation purported to overturn three decisions: Mallory v. United States, 354 U.S. 449 (1957); Miranda v. Arizona, 384 U.S. 436 (1966); and U.S. v. Wade, 388 U.S. 218 (1967).

4. Powell v. McCormack, 395 F. 2d 577, 604-05, (1968).

5. For further discussion on the second point, see Morton Gitelman's essay in a symposium entitled "Comments on *Powell v. McCormack,*" *UCLA Law Review,* XVII (November 1969), 160-64. The entire issue is devoted to comments on the Powell case.

6. D. S. Hobbs, ibid., 131.

7. Ralph F. Bischoff, ibid., 160. Most Congressmen saw the opinion as an unwarranted intervention by the court into an area that was solely within the goverance of the House. For additional discussion, see Chapter 12.

8. The comments were made at a press conference in the Supreme Court building on July 5, 1968, the first general press conference ever held by a sitting chief justice. Although the court provided no text of the questions and answers, most of the text was taken down by a stenographer for *U.S. News & World Report.* The text was reprinted in "Warren Press Conference," *Congressional Quarterly,* XXVI (1968), 1836.

9. Editorial, *New York Times,* June 17, 1969, p. 46, cols. 1-2.

10. James Reston, "Justice Warren Goes out with a Bang," ibid., June 18, 1969, p. 46, cols. 2-6.

11. The following remarks, made on June 23, 1969, are found at 23 L. Ed. 2d xli-xlv (1969).

Chapter 12

1. "House Leaders Urge Delay on Powell," *New York Times,* June 18, 1969, p. 54, col. 3, 5.

2. Warren Weaver, Jr., "Congress Defiant on Powell Ruling," ibid., June 17, 1969, p. 1, col. 7.

3. William Greider, "High Court Finds House Wrong in Powell Exclusion," *Washington Post,* June 17, 1969, p. A8, col. 3.

4. Ibid.; "Powell Case Brings Varied Reaction," *Congressional Quarterly,* XXVII (1969), 1059.

5. "Powell Case Brings Varied Reaction," loc. cit.

6. Ibid.

7. "Harlem Leaders Hail Ruling," *New York Times,* June 17, 1969, p. 36, col. 5.

8. "The Powell Case," *CQ Guide to Current American Government,* Fall 1969 (Washington, D.C.: Congressional Quarterly, Inc., 1969), p. 58.

9. "House Bill Seeks Return to Powell of Seniority and Back Pay," *New York Times,* June 20, 1969, p. 18, col. 5.

10. "The Powell Case: More Legislative Battles in Store?" *Congressional Quarterly,* XXVII (1969), 1125.

Chapter 13

1. The following correspondence between Judge Hart and the parties may be found as exhibits A, B, C, D, pp. 9-20, in the Petition for a Writ of Mandamus submitted by Powell's attorneys, in Powell v. Hart, No. 1197 Misc. (October Term, 1969).

2. Richard L. Madden, "Powell Would Waive Back-Pay if House Would Drop Fine," *New York Times,* August 28, 1969, p. 30, cols. 5-8.

3. The following summary of the hearing before Judge George L. Hart, August 27, 1969, appears as exhibit E, pp. 21-54, in Powell v. Hart, No. 1197 Misc. (October Term, 1969). Also appearing at the hearing on behalf of the defendants were John R. Hupper, Lloyd N. Cutler, and John H. Pickering. They made no comments during the proceedings, however.

4. The August 29, 1969, hearing appears as exhibits F and G, pp. 55-60, in Powell v. Hart, No. 1197 Misc. (October Term, 1969).

5. Marjorie Hunter, "Powell To Ask Top Court To Order Return of Back Pay and Seniority," *New York Times,* September 30, 1969, p. 29, cols. 1-2.

6. The following petition and memorandum were filed in Powell v. Hart, No. 1197 Misc. (October Term, 1969).

7. Statements at the news conference were reported by Andrew H. Malcolm, "Powell Ill, Says He'll Have Tests," *New York Times,* December 1, 1969, p. 31, col. 1.

8. Thomas A. Johnson, "Anti-Powell Forces Are Gaining in Harlem," ibid., December 5, 1969, p. 47, col. 4.

9. Emmanuel Perlmutter, "Sutton Calls on Powell To Resign from Congress or Be Challenged," ibid., December 21, 1969, p. 51, cols. 2-3.

10. Thomas A. Johnson, "Powell Backing Protest of a Possible Fare Increase," ibid., December 23, 1969, p. 63, col. 4.

11. See Chapter 7 for complaint filed in district court.

12. Harry A. Blackmun, 61, of Minnesota, was nominated by President Nixon in April, 1970, after the ill-fated appointments of Clement Haynsworth, Jr., and G. Harrold Carswell failed to receive Senate confirmation. He was confirmed by the Senate on May 12, 1970. Phi Beta Kappa at Harvard, former law school professor, and court of appeals judge since 1959, Blackmun was assessed by Nixon as a "strict constructionist."

Sources

Chapter 1

Biographical Dictionary of the American Congress.

Congressional Directory, 89th Congress.

Congressional Quarterly, XXIV (1966), 2213-14, 2222; XXV (1967), 27.

James v. Powell, *New York Law Journal*, August 1, October 6, November 14, 1966.

New York Times, January 15, 1967.

Powell v. James, 379 U.S. 966 (1965).

U.S. Congress, House, Select Committee Pursuant to H. Res. 1. *In Re Adam Clayton Powell. Hearings.* 90th Cong., 1st sess., 1967.

Washington Post, January 9, 1967.

Williams, Edward Bennett. *One Man's Freedom.* New York: Atheneum, 1962.

Wilson, James Q. "Two Negro Politicians: An Interpretation," *Midwest Journal of Political Science,* IV (1960), 346-69.

Chapter 2

Baker v. Carr, 369 U.S. 186, 211, 217 (1962).

Biographical Directory of the American Congress, 1774-1961.

Congressional Quarterly, XXV (1967), 25; XXVI (1968), 1837.

Congressional Quarterly Almanac, 1968.

Dionisopoulos, P. Allan. "A Commentary on the Constitutional Issues in the Powell and Related Cases," *Journal of Public Law,* XVII (1968), 103-50.

Frank, John P. "Political Questions," *Supreme Court and Supreme Law.* Edited by Edmond Cahn. Bloomington: Indiana University Press, 1954.

Getz, Robert S. *Congressional Ethics: The Conflict of Interest Issue.* Princeton, New Jersey: D. Van Nostrand Company, Inc., 1966.

Chapter 3

Congressional Quarterly, XXIV (1966), 2308; XXV (1967), 26, 27, 47, 50, 82, 90.

New York Times, December 1, 10, 12, 16, 20, 21, 29, 30, 31, 1966; January 3, 4, 5, 6, 7, 8, 9, 10, 1967.

U.S. Congress, House, Committee on House Administration. *Hearings. Relating to the Investigation into Expenditures During the 89th Congress by the House Committee on Education and Labor, and the Clerk-Hire Payroll Status of Y. Marjorie Flores.* Special Subcommittee on Contracts, 89th Cong., 2nd sess., 1966.

U.S. Congress, House, Committee on House Administration. *Report of Special Investigation into Expenditures During the 89th Congress by the House Committee on Education and Labor and the Clerk-Hire Status of Y. Marjorie Flores (Mrs. Adam C. Powell).* H. Rept. 2349. Special Subcommittee on Contracts, 89th Cong., 2nd sess., 1967.

Chapter 4

Congressional Quarterly, XXV (1967), 38, 47, 99.

New York Times, January 11, 1967.

U.S. Congress, House. *Congressional Record.* 90th Cong., 1st sess., 1967, pp. H14-H27.

Washington Post, January 9, 1967.

Chapter 5

Congressional Quarterly, XXV (1967), 47, 99, 196, 246-47, 626.

Duke, Paul. "The Powell Case: Bungling All Around," *Reporter* (April 20, 1967), pp. 32-35.

New York Times, January 13, 14, 16, 17, 19, 20, 21, 23; February 1, 10, 12, 13, 15, 19, 23, 24, 25, 26, 27; April 6, 1967.

U.S. Congress, House. *Congressional Record* (daily ed.). 90th Cong., 1st sess., 1967, pp. H1091-92.

U.S. Congress, House, Select Committee Pursuant to H. Res. 1. *In Re Adam Clayton Powell. Hearings.* 90th Cong., 1st sess., 1967.

U.S. Congress, House, Select Committee Pursuant to H. Res. 1. *In Re Adam Clayton Powell.* H. Rept. 27. 90th Cong., 1st sess., 1967.

Chapter 6

Congressional Quarterly, XXV (1967), 291, 334-35, 2651.

"Ethical Problems," *Congress and the Nation.* Vol. II, *1965-1968.* Washington, D.C.: Congressional Quarterly, Inc., 1969.

New York Times, March 1, 2, 1967.

U.S. Congress, House. *Congressional Record.* 90th Cong., 1st sess., 1967, pp. 4997-5039.

Chapter 7

Congressional Quarterly, XXV (1967), 344-45, 379, 444, 499, 533, 536.

New York Times, March 1, 2, 3, 8, 9, 12, 13, 14, 15, 16, 17, 19, 20, 22, 23, 26, 30; April 2, 5, 7, 8, 1967.

Powell v. McCormack, 266 F. Supp. 354 (1967).

U.S. Congress, House. *Congressional Record.* 90th Cong., 1st sess., 1967, pp. H2392-H2406.

Chapter 8

Congressional Quarterly, XXV (1967), 600, 626, 1106, 1864, XXVI (1968), 71, 9A.

New York Times, April 8, 13, 15, 20, 22; June 2, 28, 29; July 22, 24, 27; August 13; September 12, 13; October 10, 30; November 3, 6, 9; December 22, 1967; January 14, 15; February 16, 1968.

Powell v. McCormack, 387 U.S. 933 (1967).

Powell v. McCormack, 395 F. 2d 577 (1968).

U.S. Congress, House. *Congressional Record* (daily ed.). 90th Cong., 1st sess., 1967, pp. H1942, H4869.

Chapter 9

Congressional Quarterly, XXVI (1968), 742, 962, 3165, 3184, 3267; XXVII (1969), 58, 1125.

New York Times, April 15; October 10, 1967; March 23, 24, 25, 26, 28; April 20; May 6, 20; June 5, 20, 21; July 12, 17, 19, 21, 22, 28; August 21; September 23; October 4, 30; November 10, 19, 21, 23; December 3, 10, 11, 1968; January 1, 3, 4, 5, 6; February 10, 21, 22; March 16, 23, 26; April 4, 11, 1969.

Powell v. McCormack, 393 U.S. 949 (1968).

Washington Post, November 10, 1968.

U.S. Congress, House. *Congressional Record* (daily ed.). 91st Cong., 1st sess., 1969, pp. H4-H22, H155, H551, H1181-82, H2681, H3185-86, H3192-93.

Chapter 10

Elman, Philip, ed. **Of Law and Men.** New York: Harcourt, Brace & Co., 1956.

Powell v. McCormack, 395 U.S. 486 (1969). Transcript of the oral argument before the Supreme Court, April 21, 1969.

Chapter 11

"Comments on Powell v. McCormack," *UCLA Law Review,* XVII (November, 1969). (Symposium.)

Congressional Quarterly, XXVI (1968), 1836.

New York Times, June 17, 18, 1969.

Powell v. McCormack, 395 F. 2d 577 (1968).

Powell v. McCormack, 395 U.S. 486 (1969).

Chapter 12

Congressional Quarterly, XXVII (1969), 1059, 1125.

New York Times, June 17, 18, 20, 1969.

"The Powell Case," *CQ Guide to Current American Government,* Fall 1969. Washington, D.C.: Congressional Quarterly, Inc. 1969, 58.

Washington Post, June 17, 1969.

Chapter 13

New York Times, August 28; September 30; December 1, 5, 21, 23, 1969.

Powell v. Hart, No. 1197 Misc. (October Term, 1969).

SELECTED READINGS

Books

Elman, Philip, ed. *Of Law and Men.* New York: Harcourt, Brace & Co.,1956.

Frank, John P. "Political Questions," *Supreme Court and Supreme Law,* Edited by Edmond Cahn. Bloomington: Indiana University Press, 1954.

Getz, Robert S. *Congressional Ethics: The Conflict of Interest Issue.* Princeton, N.J.: D. Van Nostrand Company, Inc., 1966.

Hapgood, David. *The Purge That Failed: Tammany v. Powell.* Eagleton Foundation Case Studies in Practical Politics. (Pamphlet). Henry Holt and Company, Inc., 1959.

Pearson, Drew and Anderson, Jack. *The Case Against Congress: A Compelling Indictment of Corruption on Capitol Hill.* New York: Simon and Schuster, 1968.

Williams, Edward Bennett. *One Man's Freedom.* New York: Atheneum, 1962.

Articles

"Comments on Powell v. McCormack." Symposium. *UCLA Law Review,* XVII (November, 1969), entire issue.

Curtis, Thomas B. "The Power of the House of Representatives to Judge the Qualifications of Its Members." *Texas Law Review,* XLV(1967), 1199-1204.

Dionisopoulos, P. Allan. "A Commentary on the Constitutional Issues in the Powell and Related Cases." *Journal of Public Law,* XVII (1968), 103-150.

Eckhardt, Robert C. "The Adam Clayton Powell Case." *Texas Law Review,* XLV (1967), 1205-1211.

"Exclusion and Expulsion from the House of Representatives." Note. *Howard Law Journal,* XIV (1968), 162-172.

"Exclusion of a Member-Elect by a House of Congress." Note. *New York University Law Review,* XLII (1967), 716-732.

"The Powell Case," *CQ Guide to Current American Government,* Fall, 1969. Washington, D.C.: Congressional Quarterly, Inc., 1969, 54-58.

"The Power of a House of Congress to Judge the Qualifications of its Members." Note. *Harvard Law Review,* LXXXI (1968), 673-684.

Wilson, James Q. "Two Negro Politicians: An Interpretation." *Midwest Journal of Political Science,* IV (1960), 346-69.

Public Documents

U.S. Congress. House. Committee on House Administration. *Hearings. Relating to the investigation into expenditures during the 89th Congress by the House Committee on Education and Labor, and the clerk-hire payroll status of Y. Marjorie Flores.* Special Subcommittee on Contracts. 89th Cong. 2nd sess., 1966. (Hays Hearings).

U.S. Congress. House. Committee on House Administration. *Report of the Special Investigation into expenditures during the 89th Congress by the House Committee on Education and Labor and the clerk-hire status of Y. Marjorie Flores (Mrs. Adam C. Powell).* H. Rept. 2349. Special Subcommittee on Contracts. 89th Cong. 2nd sess., 1967. (Hays Report).

U.S. Congress. House. Select Committee Pursuant to H. Res. 1. *In Re Adam Clayton Powell. Hearings.* 90th Cong. 1st sess., 1967. (Celler Hearings).

U.S. Congress. House. Select Committee Pursuant to H. Res. 1. *In Re Adam Clayton Powell.* H. Rept. 27. 90th Cong. 1st sess., 1967. (Celler Report).

Epilogue

Adam Clayton Powell was not returned to the 92nd Congress by his constituents, and his departure from the Hill was virtually unnoticed. In his place was sworn in former State Assemblyman Charles Rangel, who in June 1970 had wrested the Democratic nomination from Powell by a 150-vote margin.

Powell's vulnerability had been exposed in the 1968 Democratic primary, when a political unknown had garnered 40 percent of the votes. Ironically, Powell himself had opened the way for a successor late in 1969 by his frank and public discussion of his poor health. People had begun to talk about possible successors to Powell, but the talk was always couched in the context of the possibility that Powell might choose not to run. His illness gave a legitimate basis for discussion of successors, without the appearance of a direct challenge to the incumbent Congressman. In late December 1969 the quiet movement to replace Powell became public, when Manhattan Borough President Percy Sutton called on Powell to resign. Sutton's statements, which praised Powell's past accomplishments, were directed to the question of effective representation for Harlem. That question provided the legitimizing issue. Harlem's needs were too great for her Congressman to give them less than full attention.

The surprise came in early January, when Powell announced that he would seek re-election and that he was in "perfect health." John Young, his opponent in the 1968 primary, had already announced his candidacy. Others had waited to determine Powell's intentions. But the surge for fresh leadership had gained momentum. There was no turning back.

The field of challengers grew as Young was joined by Jesse Gray, Ramon Martinez, and Rangel. Gray had built up a constituency of his own as leader for rent strikes in 1963 and 1964 and had run for public office on several occasions. Martinez, a lawyer, spoke for Harlem's Puerto Rican community. The candidates were reluctant to take on Powell directly. No one mentioned his alleged misappropriation of Congressional funds. Harlem's needs for full-time and active representation was the single issue of the campaign. Of Powell, Gray said with feeling, "We love Adam—I do. He's been a beautiful Congressman in years past. But he's tired."[1] Young was more direct: "Mr. Powell is physically and psychologically unable now to contribute the hard work, the understanding, the responsibility and the dedication necessary to grapple with the great problems of the troubled 18th District."[2] Powell had been a great Congressman, his opponents were quick to recognize, but he didn't offer Harlem much any more.

Rangel, whose candidacy had been nurtured by Sutton, Basil Patterson, and a number of other black leaders, emerged as the strongest challenger. Under court order, the entire state had been redistricted in February 1970, resulting in the addition to the 18th Congressional District of a 16-block area of west-side Manhattan, racially mixed and predominantly middle class. After the redistricting, Rangel's Assembly District fell almost entirely within the boundaries of the 18th. Rangel and Sutton had been building a grass-roots service-oriented political machine in central Harlem, through the Martin Luther King Democratic Club, offering free help on legal problems, housing, jobs, and education. From the political club—similar to Powell's own Alfred E. Isaacs Democratic Club—Rangel ran an effective campaign. Rangel's theme was simply that Harlem needed a full-time Congressman, and he cited Powell's high absentee record in the 91st Congress. The young Assemblyman received a number of endorsements. When he was endorsed by Mayor John Lindsay, Howard J. Samuels, candidate for the Democratic nomination for Governor, and Shirley Chisholm, Brooklyn Congresswoman, Powell dismissed the three as "ungrateful Little Boy Blue, Whitey and Aunt Jemima."[3] Powell, Gray and Young

1. David K. Shipler, "Powell, in Race, Has Faith in Himself," *New York Times,* June 16, 1970, p. 50, col. 2.

2. "'68 Rival of Powell to Try Once More to Obtain Seat," *New York Times,* Jan. 27, 1970, p. 26, col. 2.

3. Clayton Knowles, "Powell Predicts A 3-To-1 Victory," *New York Times,* June 17, 1970, p. 36, col. 4.

levied charges of party bossism and downtown interference in Harlem affairs. Rangel was the plantation candidate, they said. Scoffed Powell, "They want to elect a nice little black boy who's going to say yussuh."[4] Rangel also picked up endorsements of several Democratic Clubs and the *New York Times*.

Gray's campaign began picking up steam, and for a time Rangel was very concerned that Gray would draw off enough votes to allow Powell to win with a plurality of the total vote. Powell remained confident to the end that he would be overwhelmingly re-elected and predicted that Gray would come in second.

Powell campaigned in his usual style, a non-campaign. He continued to preach in his own Abyssinian Baptist Church and in other Harlem parishes, and he greeted people on the street. But he avoided personal debates with his opponents. "Adam is Adam," said Odell Clark, Powell's Administrative Assistant. "What else is he going to tell them but that he's Adam?"[5] There was no need to debate, said Powell: "If you want to know what I have done ask any of the sales girls on 7th Avenue, ask the bus drivers, ask the blacks and the Puerto Ricans at the telephone company."[6] Powell did try to mend some fences. Never a Democratic regular, he did try to move closer to the party by endorsing Arthur Goldberg's candidacy for Governor, although he had supported Rockfeller in the past. He even opened a campaign headquarters three weeks before the primary.

The jolt came on the day of the primary, June 23, when the unofficial tally gave Rangel a plurality of 203 votes out of 23,919 cast. Rangel and Powell each received roughly one-third of the votes—7,599 and 7,802—Martinez ran third, and Gray and Young a poor fourth and fifth. Immediately, Powell charged that some voting machines had been stolen and that registered Republicans and Liberals had illegally voted in the Democratic primary. Powell had not sent poll watchers into the new area in his district, for he had figured that there were simply not enough Democratic votes there to matter. He claimed later that it was in this area that voters had switched party, a practice not permitted under New York law. Said Powell, a few days after the primary, "Here in New York City we have been confronted with a major scandal—a Black

4. *Ibid.*

5. David K. Shipler, "Powell, in Race, Has Faith in Himself,"*New York Times,* June 16, 1970, p. 50, col. 1.

6. Jesse H. Walker, "The Candidates on the Attack," *Amsterdam News,* June 20, 1970, p. 37, col. 6.

Teapot Dome."[7] The official recount reduced Rangel's margin from 203 to 150 votes.

A twofold rescue operation was begun. First, Powell challenged the validity of the election in the New York courts, claiming that after painstaking analysis of the precinct voter lists, Republican and a few Liberal voters could be identified who had illegally voted in the Democratic primary. Also cited were the NBC and CBS networks precinct analyses that had, on election night, projected him a winner by 2,000 votes. Powell's suit—he has never been involved in a simple lawsuit—was dismissed for technical reasons by the New York courts. On September 22, Powell filed suit in the Federal District Court, where he received an unfavorable ruling. His appeal is still pending. However, there is little likelihood that his challenge to the validity of the June primary will be sustained.

Second, he attempted to have his name placed on the ballot in November as an Independent candidate. Working around the clock, Odell Clark and volunteers combed the lists of voters to identify those who would meet New York's stringent requirements for eligibility to sign a petition for Powell; signatures could be obtained only from persons who had not signed a petition of any candidate in the primary and who had not voted in the primary. Thus, obvious Powell supporters were excluded by the regulation. Hoping to obtain 6,000 signatures, or twice the required number, Powell's people obtained only 3,222 signatures, allowing only a small margin for error. The petitions were filed on the deadline, August 21, and their validity was challenged by Rangel. Powell was fighting for his political life, yet strangely, all of this activity received little attention in the press. The Board of Elections found that Powell had failed to file by a substantial quantity the required number of valid signatures. This decision was not challenged in the courts.

What had gone wrong? Two-thirds of the voters had cast their ballots in the primary for candidates other than the "Old Man of the Sea." There was no single explanation. Powell's lack of accountability, his failure to campaign as effectively as his opponents, and the presentation of credible alternatives were all contributory.

Powell's constituency had changed. The addition of an entirely new area, where residents had no ties to Powell, was only part of the story. In Harlem new leaders had emerged, for whom the memory of Powell

---

7. "Powell Complains as Recount Begins," *New York Times,* June 27, 1970, p. 26, col. 1.

as fighting committee chairman was not enough. They were demanding leadership in Congress and the deliverance of service to the people of Harlem now. His absenteeism provided a legitimate reason for seeking an alternative. Having lost the power and influence that his chairmanship had once given him, Powell was no longer able to offer his constituents any more than could any freshman Congressman.

Had Powell accurately gauged the growing disenchantment in the district and the strength of his opponents, he might have campaigned more actively. His traditional campaign style was inadequate in the face of strong challenges. He did not campaign at all in the new area of the district. His real efforts, in contesting the results of the primary and in mounting a drive for Independent candidacy, were too late.

Finally, Rangel's candidacy provided the voters a viable option. A young, articulate, and capable lawmaker, he had provided service to his constituents and promised to offer the leadership which Harlem needed. No doubt the support he received from a number of prominent people was significant in helping him to dislodge the incumbent.

Powell was embittered by his defeat and believed that the nomination should have been his. Retired by the very people who had been his source of strength for 24 years, Powell's long and eventful political career had come to an end. [8] But Adam had left his mark. Harlem would not forget Adam. And the decision reached in *Powell vs. McCormack* would long serve coming generations of aspiring Congressmen.

---

8. Still pending, however, was Powell's claim for back salary and fine. With Powell's defeat and the passage of time, the prospects for a political settlement with Congress appeared somewhat improved.